Say Everything

Say Everything

A MEMOIR

Ione Skye

GALLERY BOOKS

New York   Amsterdam/Antwerp   London   Toronto   Sydney   New Delhi

Gallery Books
An Imprint of Simon & Schuster, LLC
1230 Avenue of the Americas
New York, NY 10020

Copyright © 2025 by Ione Skye

First Gallery Books hardcover edition March 2025

GALLERY BOOKS and colophon are registered trademarks of Simon & Schuster, LLC

For information about special discounts for bulk purchases, please contact Simon & Schuster Special Sales at 1-866-506-1949 or business@simonandschuster.com.

The Simon & Schuster Speakers Bureau can bring authors to your live event. For more information or to book an event, contact the Simon & Schuster Speakers Bureau at 1-866-248-3049 or visit our website at www.simonspeakers.com.

Interior design by Karla Schweer

Manufactured in the United States of America

1 3 5 7 9 10 8 6 4 2

Library of Congress Cataloging-in-Publication Data is available.

ISBN 978-1-6680-4826-9
ISBN 978-1-6680-4828-3 (ebook)

To the Isle of Skye.
I'll visit you one day.

Contents

PART TWO

Womanhood

Prologue

I still keep the picture in my grandma Tillie's black lacquer box in my closet, though it's not as meaningful to me as it once was. It was taken in 1969, on the Isle of Skye in Scotland. The coast is gray and wind whips my father, Donovan's, dark curls. He wears wellies and the softest-looking fur jacket, trimmed with brocade ribbon. My mom, Enid, wears a tweed skirt and tall leather boots and holds my scowling brother Dono (short for Donovan Jr.) on her hip. He was just a baby, and I wasn't born yet.

When I was a kid, I thought Mom was pregnant in the picture—with me. She was a former model (in Paris, for Oscar de la Renta!) and willowy thin, but under her wool turtleneck, inside her still-flat belly, was supposed to be me. That was the story I told myself, the reason I cherished the photo. I'd never met my father, and this had always been the closest thing I had to a family portrait. All of us together in one frame, just this once.

"Oh, sorry, no, pussycat," Mom corrected me one day. "We conceived you on the Isle of Skye, but I wasn't pregnant yet in that one." So, no family portrait for me. But I did get a great namesake.

The photo ran in a magazine article about Donovan, who was a famous Scottish folk singer, known for the hits "Catch the Wind," "Mellow Yellow," "Sunshine Superman," "Season of the Witch," and "Hurdy Gurdy Man," among others. Was he still in love with Mom when they posed on the cliffs that day? I like to think so.

They'd met in 1966, at the Whisky a Go Go in LA. She was twenty-one and Donovan was twenty. Mom had dated famous men before—Jim Morrison, Keith Richards, Denny Doherty from the Mamas and the Papas, and (most exciting to me) Dudley Moore. But the night she spotted Donovan across the crowded Whisky, that was it for her. The Sunshine Superman, as they called him, swept her off her feet and away to Greece, then London. When she got pregnant with Dono, they moved into a fairy-tale house in the English countryside. Mom was born in Brooklyn and raised in Queens, but England was her happy place. As she once told me, sounding uncharacteristically New Agey: "It was as if I'd lived there in another life." Donovan was happy too, for a spell, chopping firewood and writing poems and songs about their budding family. His album *A Gift from a Flower to a Garden* is pretty much all about that time. In "Song of the Naturalist's Wife" you can even hear my brother's first cries.

Donovan ticked all the boxes for Mom: creative, exciting, handsome, and a good provider. She wanted more than anything to be his wife, but he never proposed. By the time I was conceived in Donovan's gypsy caravan on the Isle of Skye, he was already drifting back to his ex-girlfriend Linda Lawrence. Then my father left Mom for good, having won Linda back from Brian Jones of the Rolling Stones.

For a short time after my birth in London, Donovan put Mom, Dono, and me up in a flat, but according to Mom, he was uninterested in helping further—except to fly us back to the States. After that, Mom hated to ask him for more help, but she had no job, degree, or childcare, so she swallowed her pride and hired a lawyer to get child support, using her first check to move us into a small apartment in Los Angeles, my first real home.

In the end, it was Linda who married Donovan, claiming the rock-wife fantasy life Mom had thought was her destiny.

The way I always saw it, my father's love had been like the best dream ever, until he waved his hand like a magician and woke Mom up. It was hard to believe something so great could be an illusion. Why trust love if it could vanish into thin air, just like that?

PART ONE

Girlhood

1

The Bastard

1973–1979

I was three years old and my brother six when Carl, our first step-dad, blasted into our lives. Within weeks of their first date, Mom had accepted his marriage proposal, and the three of us left sunny LA for the East Coast and a man we hardly knew. Carl was really from Florida but moved around a lot—we didn't yet know why. He was rich and had recently purchased a brand-new modern house in lush, green Ridgefield, Connecticut. It was ten times the size of our snug West Hollywood apartment, with sky-high ceilings and wall-to-wall windows. Like living in a big glass box set down next to a forest.

Mom had let her friends talk her into marrying Carl: "Let someone look after you, for a change," they'd said. A nice Jewish girl at heart, Mom *did* want looking after. And Ridgefield was only an hour-and-a-half train ride from my grandpa Benny and grandma Tillie in Queens. The comfort of having her parents nearby was the deciding factor for Mom. This partnership wasn't about love; it was, she hoped and believed, about security.

I was too young to remember the wedding in our new backyard but old enough that moments from the day—brought back to life by photos and long talks with Mom and Dono—are clear enough to touch. Like following my big brother away from the noisy party and down the sloping lawn and into the quiet woods. Smoke, the white German shepherd puppy Carl had given us, bounded ahead as we disappeared into the pines, leaving the wedding and all that it meant for us behind.

It was Carl who finally came looking for us. We heard his big, booming laugh when we appeared from the trees—Dono in his mini suit, me picking pine needles from my hair. Carl still had his dark Florida tan, which was set off by his bright white three-piece suit and matching bright white teeth. His hair was long and blond, and gold rings shaped like suns and moons flashed on his fingers.

"Look at your mother," he said, leading us back to the party. "Isn't she the most beautiful woman in the world?"

In pictures of the reception, Enid stands, unsmiling, under a yellow-and-white-striped tent, surrounded by the guests in their embroidered prairie dresses and velvet suits and over-the-knee suede boots and capes and fedoras. She is undeniably beautiful, and wispy as a daffodil in her white silk wedding suit. Before we left Los Angeles, she'd had her long strawberry waves cropped into a pixie cut that made her a dead ringer for the actress Mia Farrow. With almost no makeup, her skin glows, but her eyes are dull and faraway.

I already understood at that young age that beauty mattered. When Mom read to me from *Grimm's Fairy Tales*, the word jumped from practically every page. In "The Pink," the maiden was more beautiful than any artist could portray with paint; in "Snow White," the evil queen's sole desire was to be the most beautiful in the land; in "Sleeping Beauty," beauty was one of the gifts the fairies gave Princess Aurora.

From the way Carl spoke, it seemed that beauty might be the most valuable gift of all. Because beautiful girls would always be taken care of.

———

For a time, we coasted on the adventure side of the wave. Carl bounded around the house like a jittery giant who'd consumed too much sugar, but our stoic nanny, Cosette, kept the peace and made us feel safe. She was from Haiti and spoke to us in English and French as she carried us around, one on each hip.

"Cosette, put them down!" Mom would say. "They're too heavy!"

Fortunately for us, Cosette didn't seem to mind. We needed her warmth and attention. Mom's once-powerful maternal instincts weren't what they'd been before Carl. Her thoughts seemed a million miles away; she stopped cooking and got paper-thin.

I thought Carl was exciting, in a dangerous kind of way. I loved discovering the random treasures he brought from his mysterious travels to South America, tucked into drawers and bookshelves, like Easter eggs. When I admired a heavy pewter seal that materialized one day, Carl said proudly, "You like that? I stole that for your mother."

I'd nod along when he explained that stealing wasn't wrong, getting caught was.

Back then I still had my father's last name, Leitch. Skye was my middle name, which Carl liked best.

"One day, Skye," he liked to say, "I'm gonna buy you a purple jet. Because 'Ione' means 'purple jewel,' did you know that?"

I didn't believe everything he said but pretended to. With each of my fathers, I would try to be easy and sweet, wanting them to love me more than anyone else, even more than my mom, as I always wanted to be somebody's favorite.

Sometimes Carl's promises did come true. "I'll bring you back an emerald," he said as he and Mom headed off on a business trip to

Bogotá, Colombia. And sure enough, they returned with a bag of sparkling emeralds. I got to pick one to have made into a ring.

On my fourth birthday, Carl presented me with my emerald, set in gold prongs on a delicate band. It was very fancy and too grown-up for a little girl, which made it even better.

He told me I was special because I was deep and beautiful, like Mom, and an older soul than my big brother. (Carl was fond of Dono, but I got all the compliments.) He also told me, often, that I was the reincarnated soul of a baby Mom almost had once but didn't (which I would later learn was an abortion). I had really wanted to be here, so I came back. "And *that* is why *you* are so special," he'd explain.

I had no understanding of what exactly he was talking about but often fantasized about a ghost baby, flying around a fairy-tale English cottage, waiting to be born as me. It was a funny image but also strange and unsettling.

Carl did not share his reincarnation theory with Mom, only me. There was something melancholy about it, and Mom didn't like to talk about sad things. She was sad enough already. Anyone could see Mom wasn't thriving in her role as Carl's Beautiful Wife. She'd grown distant and closed off, retreating more every day into a shell that looked like our mom but wasn't her. She was surely suffering from worry, stress, and depression, but as kids, we didn't know that term. The best word we had for Mom in Ridgefield was "frozen."

Mom wasn't just isolated and missing her old friends; she'd been tricked. We all had. It turned out the excitable, big-kid version of Carl we'd all liked at first was just one side of him. The other side had a terrible temper, possibly fueled by cocaine, in retrospect. Before Ridgefield, Carl had hidden his bad side from us, but now that he had us, he didn't need to do that anymore.

The scariest thing about Carl's temper was how unpredictable it was. All of us were bracing for a big explosion the time Mom accidentally threw away $10,000 in cash he'd hidden in a wastebasket. As the two of them vainly scoured the local dump for the money, Mom remembers thinking, *If he hits me, I'll have a reason to leave.* But Carl just laughed and delivered a philosophical speech about how his "material stuff"—the BMWs, the boat, the gold watches and custom suits—didn't matter to him. Only love mattered. Carl gave this speech often and genuinely seemed to mean it every time. But then, maybe the next day, he'd find a half-eaten bowl of chicken soup Dono had left under his bed (Carl was a health nut, so we were supposed to be vegetarians) or a wet bathing suit on the Eames chair in the living room, and the windows would vibrate from his rage.

We'd all grown to fear Carl, but Dono did the most. My brother especially hated being picked up from school by our speed-demon stepdad. "*Ask Carl to slow down,*" he'd whisper, gripping my wrist in the backseat. I liked going fast and wanted to impress Carl by being tough and unafraid, but I knew the rules. If Dono asked Carl to slow down, he might swerve the car to scare him even more. It was shameful for a boy to be afraid but charming for a girl. So, I learned to play Damsel in Distress. "Please slow down, Carl," I'd plead. "I'm *scared.*"

I think we were always waiting for Carl to hurt Dono with more than his words—for the moment he'd finally raise his hand to my brother. The day it happened, Carl was supposed to be on a business trip, so Dono and I were in the living room, wrestling with the leather Sacco beanbag chair that was *not a toy.* I was pinned underneath, screaming and laughing, when I felt Dono's weight jerk away. There was a *whack* and a thud. The beanbag lifted from me and I saw Carl press it down on my fallen brother. Dono's screams grew muffled and he thrashed his skinny legs like a bug under a rock.

"How do you like it!?" Carl yelled, veins bulging.

My brother stopped kicking, stopped screaming. Why couldn't *I* scream? Why couldn't *I* kick? I wanted to kick Carl, right in the shins. I didn't ask to be saved like this! But I couldn't make myself move. Slowly, my brother sat up, and Carl walked away. Dono wasn't crying, just staring ahead with a blankness that reminded me of Mom. He'd gone to the frozen place, where it was easier to be.

It would be years before we told Mom about what happened that day. Worrying her would only make her worse, we thought.

The longer we stayed in Ridgefield, the less she spoke or laughed or came out of their bedroom. In Los Angeles, Mom's door had always been open to us. Every morning, I'd climb out of my toddler bed, run to her room, and throw myself onto her sleeping body. Mom would open her arms and pull me close. But I was more cautious now. I rarely knocked on the double bedroom doors when she was in there. Sometimes I'd stand outside, my cheek pressed to the heavy wood, until I heard her breathe or cough or rustle the covers. In wintertime, if it was too quiet, I'd pull on my coat and snow boots and run outside to check that her window was closed.

I was worried Mom might literally freeze, like our pet parakeets had our first winter in Ridgefield. Ice Storm Felix had been a hell of a storm. The power lines came down in the middle of the night, and without heat the house got so cold that Carl carried us from our beds to sleep by the fire in the sunken living room. In the morning, our glass-walled box looked out on a glistening white wonderland, so beautiful that we gasped and saw our breath. "*Choo-choo!*" went Dono, puffing clouds of white vapor. "*Choo-choo!*" I mimicked, running after him to the kitchen. We both screamed at once. The little yellow birds we'd brought home from the pet store just a week earlier lay stiff and frozen on the bottom of their cage. I wouldn't have expected Carl to remember them, but Mom loved the birds as much as we did. She'd loved them and still had forgotten about them.

Mom wasn't strong enough to protect us, but the woods were. If the weather allowed, that's where we'd be. Dono would take off on Carl's ATV (he could barely see over the wheel) and I'd wander, running my stick through the soft earth beside me and stopping every few steps to crouch in the roots and leaves, communing with the gleaming, crawling beetles. I loved to build fairy houses. A mushroom cap for a table, soft moss for a carpet, a fir-branch roof . . . In my fairy houses, there were no sharp corners, no closed doors, and no fathers.

When I was five, Carl announced that we were moving back to the West Coast. He said he was craving a "more happening scene" and Topanga Canyon, in the Santa Monica Mountains, was where it was at. Really, I think he was trying to hold on to Mom, hoping Los Angeles would warm her up and bring her back to him. Dono and I wanted Mom to come back too, but not back to Carl.

Topanga was most definitely a scene—a fringy hippie enclave where babies were bathed outdoors in tin buckets and pot plants grew in window boxes. Artists, musicians, and off-the-grid types had flocked there since the sixties. Some of the most famous townsfolk were members of the Eagles, the Beach Boys, and the Doors. Neil Young recorded *After the Gold Rush* in his house at the top of the canyon.

Though Carl's new biker friends seemed to feed his bad side, he was around less, and life was good again. Dono and I went a little feral, running barefoot all year long, riding the neighbors' ponies bareback and drinking fresh milk from their goats. In summertime, we went to a local day camp. Every morning, a counselor in a beige Ford Pinto would come to pick us up, blasting our theme song, Glen Campbell's "Rhinestone Cowboy," through the open windows. I'd always have to sit on a teenage boy camper's lap, which I came to realize I didn't mind one bit.

Mom's eyes got their shine back in Topanga. She was cooking again, something she'd always loved to do before Ridgefield, and she'd even started a freewheeling annual party by the local creek.

But the three of us knew, without even talking about it, that the restless canyon wasn't our forever home. More like a stepping stone to a new life.

In the bicentennial summer of 1976, Mom took her first step toward independence from Carl. She didn't have the courage or money to just walk away but somehow convinced him that they should try living apart, for the sake of convenience. He would stay in Topanga, where it was easier to run his "business"—exactly what that was, Mom would never tell us—and the three of us would move back to Hollywood, closer to good schools and Mom's old friends.

I would miss Topanga's creeks and tadpoles, the goats and owls and wildflowers, the twisty, wind-whipped drive to the beach. But I wouldn't miss Carl, as much as I'd liked being his favorite. The story of how Mom quietly, passively shook him for good—by encouraging one of her easily persuadable girlfriends to "steal" him away—is for another time, but know that she did. She divorced him and we were free!

For a spell, it was us against the world. Mom found a cheap rental house, a 1917 Craftsman on Wilton Place in the Hollywood foothills—safely above Franklin Avenue, the gateway to Hollywood's gritty side. Dono and I adored our new home. It was so warm and cozy, we didn't mind the occasional raccoon in the attic, the skunks in the basement, or even the possible ghost of old Mrs. Plato, the previous tenant, who'd died in Mom's room. The neighborhood was great too. Instead of bikers watching over us, we now had a friendly community of working-class families. Kids played ball in the street and we all knew the mailman, just like on TV.

How fun newly single Enid was—back to her old, magnetically maternal self. Everyone wanted to be near her, and the porch door slammed nonstop with friends coming and going. If Topanga was "Rhinestone Cowboy," Wilton Place was "Let 'Em In" by Paul McCartney.

To support us, Mom found part-time work catering and waitressing at Oscar's Wine Bar on Sunset. On the side, she started selling pot, which involved lots of hanging out at home and of course lots of smoking. Mom didn't like the feeling of alcohol or hard drugs, but she did like pot.

Aside from "Be kind" and her bedtime mantra, "Wash your face and hands and brush your teeth," there were no rules anymore. No one to shame or inhibit us. Dono and I were free to be him and me, raiding Mom's closet and running wild in her groovy sixties relics. Happiness was a messy house, steaming bowls of chicken soup, and dozing off in Mom's bed to the *Taxi* theme song on TV.

I can't say I missed my dad. He'd never been there to miss. I don't remember questioning why he wasn't a flesh-and-blood person who could hug me and teach me to ride a bike, but just a soothing voice flowing from the speakers. Only in my teens would Donovan's songs of love and togetherness start to really sting.

In second grade, I discovered that I was something called a "bastard." I learned it from a TV miniseries we were all talking about at school called . . . *The Bastard*. Like all my classmates who were allowed to watch it, I loved the show, a period piece about the illegitimate son of an English duke. During one post-episode recap in the schoolyard, I proudly announced to my circle of friends: "*I'm* a bastard!" This did not make me more popular, surprisingly. Apparently, some kids (squares) had to ask their parents if they were allowed to play with bastards. While this hurt my feelings, I knew plenty of kids outside of school who could relate to my nontraditional family.

I was beginning to develop what would be a lifelong intrigue with other kids of famous dads. I felt an easy familiarity with them, and they weren't hard to find. A few of Mom's very best friends were: Jenny Boyd, whose daughter with Mick Fleetwood was Amelia Fleetwood; Nurit Wilde, who had Jason Nesmith with the Monkees' Michael Nesmith; and Marsha Hunt, mother to Mick Jagger's daughter Karis.

I'll never forget the first time I saw Karis. I came flying down the stairs from my bedroom in a disco tube top and terry cloth shorts, excited to meet the new girl in town, fresh from London. Mom was at the door, hugging a chic Black woman with red lips and full, glamorous hair. I'd heard all about Marsha Hunt, the singer and actress who'd starred in the London musical *Hair* and likely inspired the Rolling Stones' song "Brown Sugar." But it was Karis I wanted to see. She had a shy smile and shiny brown curls and looked uncomfortably hot in her prim wool skirt and knee socks.

"Hi!" I said, already turning back up the stairs. "Come on!"

Karis and I were inseparable from that day on. We made up dance routines to Michael Jackson's *Off the Wall*, sang along to the *Wiz* soundtrack, watched every episode of *The Love Boat* and *Fantasy Island*, and endlessly painted our nails, or preferably our mothers'. Marsha was always game to let us mess her fingers up. Laughing her lovely, throaty laugh, she'd complain that the polish contained "bits of carpet and fluff," then let us do it all over again the next week.

Karis was a private person by nature. She rarely talked about her dad, but I knew from Mom that Mick had been absent for much of Karis's life. I also knew that thanks to some nudging from Mick's new fiancé, Jerry Hall, he'd been seeing more of Karis. I wanted to know what it was like to meet your famous dad. How were you supposed to act? Did Karis call him Dad or Mick? Did she like him? Love him? Did he say he loved her? What I ended up asking, when I finally got the nerve, wasn't any of those things.

We were having a sleepover, lying on Enid's rattan chaise longue and reading comics. I touched my friend's foot with mine. "Karis?" I said, trying to sound off-the-cuff.

She didn't look up from her *Archie* comic. "Yes?" she said in her proper English accent.

"Are you ever mad at your dad?"

Now she looked up. By the way she pursed her lips, I could tell she didn't want to go there, but she did, for me.

"Oh, I don't know," she said. "Once, I showed him a picture of me from when I was little, and he said, 'I remember that sweater.'" She crossed her arms, looking out the window.

"And?" I said.

"And I thought, *No you don't, you weren't there.*"

"Did you say that?" I asked.

"No." She shook her head.

That was all I got. It wasn't the big emotional conversation I'd been hoping for, but it was something.

Watching Karis grow closer to her dad, I thought more and more about mine. Sometimes I imagined him doing normal dad things like driving me to school or hugging me good night. Sometimes, I pictured us taking a trip to India, where Donovan had gone with the Beatles to visit the Maharishi. I would wear purple tie-dye and flowers in my hair, like Cynthia Lennon in a magazine picture I'd seen of the group. My father would wear a canary-yellow tunic and make up funny songs about me, strumming his guitar. Although I couldn't imagine what he'd write about, not knowing me.

When I was seven I had my first opportunity to meet Donovan. He was opening for Yes at the Forum, and Nurit offered to take us and her son, Jason, who was Dono's age. My brother was so excited to see our dad after seven years. "I can't believe he's at the Forum!" he kept saying. "The Who just played there!"

I was too proud to go. If our father had wanted us there, he would have invited us. He would have sent tickets.

The morning after the concert, my brother came bounding down to the breakfast table, manic with stories about Yes's light show and our dad's freestyle rendition of "Cosmic Wheels" and Chris Squire's triple-neck bass and his epic solo riff on "Round-about" and—

"Did you talk to Don?" Mom finally interrupted.

"Yeah," said my brother, through a mouthful of cereal, "he was *really* nice."

"Hmmm," Mom replied opaquely.

"Did he ask about me?" I had to know.

"Uh, no, but he sort of patted Jason's hair and said, 'You must be the girl.'"

"The girl?" I said, confused. I didn't yet know that in his few and far-between letters to Mom (sent through lawyers, with his monthly child support checks), Donovan had never once referred to me by my name. To my father I was always, only, "the girl," lowercase.

"I think he thought Jason was you," Dono clarified.

I was horrified. Jason had long hair and big pretty eyes, but still . . . my father thought a boy was me!

"Did you tell him it wasn't me?!" I demanded.

"I, um . . . ," said Dono, scratching his head.

"Did you tell him?!" I screeched.

"I think Jason was about to," said Dono, "but then . . . Donovan just . . ."

Mom set her mug down a little too hard, splashing coffee. "He just what?"

"Well, he was busy, and there were people everywhere, and he just sort of . . ."—my brother looked down at his lap, as if realizing he didn't have the answer we were looking for—". . . walked away."

It was hard to pinpoint what hurt most: that my father had thought a boy was me, or that he'd called me "the girl," or that, moments after meeting me for the very first time in my life (so he thought), Donovan had done it again: just walked away.

2

Birth of a Social Climber

1980–1983

When I was ten, Mom threw herself into a big entrepreneurial venture, borrowing money from friends to open her own restaurant, Enid's, in the front room of the legendary Improv comedy club on Sunset. I loved visiting the place, sneaking around behind the potted palms and playing hopscotch on the black-and-white checkered floors. Most of all, I loved seeing my mom out in the world, boldly single and making her own way. Sadly, the restaurant never made money, and Mom was forced to shutter her dream after only a year. She took it hard, parenting from bed for several months and rarely changing out of her favorite old kimono.

My brother and I responded to the return of Mom's depression in our typical ways. My way was to be sweet and helpful and perfect. Each night, after bringing Mom her Red Zinger tea and soaking up as much of her pain as I could, I'd retire to my room, put on my *Little House on the Prairie* nightgown, brush my hair with a hundred strokes, and fall asleep with my hands folded on my chest like a little vampire angel. Dono's way was to act out. The more Mom disappeared into her frozen shell, the worse my brother behaved. By the end of seventh grade, he'd mutated into a shoplifting, fire-starting, day-drinking vandal. "Our own punk rock Eddie Haskell," said Mom, who'd all but resigned as disciplinarian.

Enter Billy, soon to be Stepdad Number Two.

Mom's new boyfriend and savior was an aspiring screenwriter, gaffer on film sets, and bartender at the Improv—where they'd met. He was only twenty-three to Mom's thirty-five but had no problem taking charge. When Dono chopped a hole in our garage door with an ax, Billy promptly grounded him for the rest of summer break. Naturally, at first, my brother despised our new father figure. "You can't tell me what to do! You're not my dad!" he'd yell from the top of the stairs, like every *Afterschool Specials* troubled teen ever.

But the tough love must have worked: In eighth grade, my quick-change-artist brother transformed yet again. Dono turned his grades around, received the "Most Improved Student at Le Conte Jr. High" award, found himself a talent agent, and plunged into the pursuit of stardom. Meanwhile, Enid slowly came out of her funk, hosting poker nights at the kitchen table, taking carpool shifts, and restarting her pot business. By the fall of '82, she'd retired the kimono and adopted a new uniform of army pants, tanks, and combat boots (mine—I tried not to mind). She resumed dying her hair, which turned out fuchsia instead of the old soft auburn, making her even cooler.

Mom didn't love Billy the way he loved her, but she loved having a parenting partner, and it didn't hurt that Billy was gorgeous—tall, dark, and shaggy, like a 1960s Keith Richards. After a dozen or so proposals, she'd agreed to marry him, and I was all for it. Dono was coming around too.

Billy wasn't so hard to like. He owned the first Walkman we'd ever seen and a cool open Jeep that whipped our hair into beach waves. And for now, at least, he made Mom happy. Billy was actually a pretty sweet guy, under his macho front. Once, he'd brought Mom a pair of doves—live props from a job he'd worked on. They'd let us cuddle them like bunnies and I wanted to keep them forever. But the frozen parakeet incident in Ridgefield had left its mark on Mom. So, after letting the doves fly free in our dining room for a few weeks, she took them to live happily ever after in a lush aviary at the director Tony Richardson's house.

Unlike Dono, I didn't fantasize about "making it" in Hollywood. At least not the brash, smoggy Hollywood I could see from my favorite dreaming spot, the wedge of rooftop outside my bedroom window. Bookish, quiet, and obsessed with all things retro, I preferred the Tinseltown Hollywood of the 1940s and '50s—those heady days of Hitchcock, Cukor, Bogie, and Bacall that I saw on channel 5 on weekend afternoons. I loved dressing up in thrift store hats and gloves, and once—pushing through my shyness—invited Dono and his cute friends to the basement to watch me do the "Let Me Entertain You" striptease from *Gypsy*. The routine was G-rated but my appalled brother vetoed the performance regardless.

The spring of my sixth-grade year at Cheremoya Avenue Elementary School (where you went if you lived in Hollywood but your dad didn't run Hollywood), a few of my closest classmates decided to apply to Immaculate Heart, a Catholic prep school for grades six through twelve. Never mind that I was Jewish, I was desperate to go too. I craved structure. Rules. Formality. Everything I didn't have at home.

"Please, please, *please*, let me go!" I begged Enid one Sunday morning, falling to my knees at her bedside. I'd been pleading my case for days, getting nowhere. Private Catholic school was expensive and didn't vibe with Enid's lefty socialist sensibility. Plus, Mom—despite having been a hippie—was still a product of the fifties, when girls were brainwashed to want husbands, not degrees. Knowing how much school stuff intimidated her, I'd barged in when Billy was sure to be around. The guy was already our go-to homework helper

and education czar. Plus, he came from an Italian American family.
A Catholic family.

"Oh, pussycat," Mom sighed. "I just can't afford it."

But the very next day, she agreed to let me apply to Immaculate
Heart. It couldn't have been an easy decision. Billy would be of no help
with the tuition, and Mom was already scrambling to pay our rent. I
knew because she sent Dono and me each month to deliver the late
check to our scowling landlady up the street.

I had to read the acceptance letter several times. Had I really
gotten in? I'd been the last to finish the entrance exam, the room
emptying around me as I took an extra forty minutes erasing and
rewriting my answers. But it was true: I was headed to Immaculate
Heart!

Mom bought me all the clothes on the school uniform list: gray
skirt, white oxford shirt, navy vest, saddle shoes. I even got the optional
yellow cardigan with shiny white buttons. I felt so puffed up leaving
that department store. I'd gotten into a hard school! I'd been chosen,
and I dug the feeling.

Perched on a sunny hill, Immaculate Heart's mission-style campus
covered acres of wide rolling lawns. Fountains trickled in red-tile court-
yards, and birds of paradise lined graceful arched porticos. Surrounded
by so much beauty, I started to feel exceptional too.

Happily, the nuns who ran the place were a far cry from the hu-
morless caricatures I'd expected. They sported sensible slacks instead
of habits and told us we were all unique and worthy just as we were.
For the first time in my school career, I wasn't afraid to be called on in
class. Even if I never raised my hand, my teachers were too attentive
to let me disappear behind my shyness.

Sure, it was a little strange being Jewish amid this great advertise-
ment for Catholicism. My grandpa Benny fought in World War II, and
having grown up with his stories about the Nazis, I'd always sensed

that I should hide my roots. There was safety in hiding—could any Jew argue with that?

That year, my friend Halle had a costume party for her thirteenth birthday. The theme was to dress as your favorite literary character, and Mom and I spent weeks planning and thrift shopping and stitching. On the big night, I entered Halle's softly lit Beachwood Canyon bungalow as Meg from *Little Women*, wearing a Gunne Sax dress with bloomers, lace-up granny boots, mint-green gloves, and a little straw hat from my collection. "Little Red Corvette" came on and the party was just getting fun when in walked a trio of giggling girls in jeans and black leotards, their faces penciled with smeary whiskers: the Aprils.

Individually known as April, April P., and Candace, the Aprils were the school's most fearsome clique. Rich, blue-blooded, and untouchable, they were our version of the Heathers, as in the soon-to-be-made movie. I'd never actually spoken to the Aprils and tried to play it cool as the three of them approached, looking me up and down. April P., the curly redhead, broke the ice. "Who're you?" she demanded, looking straight at me.

I touched my finger to my right front tooth, something I did when I felt judged. (It was dead and gray from a fourth-grade playground accident, and Enid was still saving for the repair.) *Stop touching it, you look gnarly!* Dono yelled in my head, but I couldn't move my hand. "I'm Ione," I mumbled.

April, the queen of the Aprils, gave my shoulder a hard little shove, laughing. "We know who you are, *Ione*." She gestured at my granny boots, my long dress. "But who are you *supposed* to be?"

The room fell silent. The music stopped, or maybe I couldn't hear it through my shock. April knew my name? I'd been watching her from afar since the first day of school. You couldn't *not* watch her. She demanded it. April wasn't technically the prettiest girl but was by far the most stunning: tall and broad shouldered, both feminine and masculine, with freckles, long blond hair, and a killer smile—even through her braces. At lunch, she never sat still but darted around like a bee in search of the plummiest flower. Amplifying her power was her über-popular senior-year sister, Brooke. April was practically born to rule the school.

"She's Meg, from *Little Women*," Halle piped up, saving me.

"Cute," sniffed Candace, the quiet one.

Apparently, the Aprils were the three blind mice. Judging by their lackluster costumes, they thought dressing up as characters from books was stupid and childish, so geeky they'd hardly bothered.

The party soured after that. Watching the Aprils in action, stalking disdainfully around the sweet little house Halle's father had built by hand, I didn't know how to feel. Part of me wanted to punch the girls' smug faces; another part was dumbstruck with embarrassment over my silly, overdone costume; and another part, admittedly the biggest part, burned with excitement. The queen of the Aprils knew my name!

For days after the party, April's teasing voice echoed in my head: *We know who you are,* Ione. God, it was validating. In homeroom, I studied her with a new intensity. April controlled her own narrative. She told us who she was, and we listened. I longed, in a deep, evolutionary way, to know that kind of power. And so—like early man learning to walk upright or a vine reaching toward the sun— a social climber was born.

3

Hungry Like the Wolf
1984

Before I could infiltrate the Aprils' preppy world, I would have to understand it.

The Official Preppy Handbook, which I didn't realize was satirical and studied religiously, was the big book of the moment. Following it to the letter, I lined my locker with pink and green Laura Ashley "Cottage Sprig" wallpaper and made Mom buy me a pink collared polo shirt and matching headband. For historical perspective, I read the society columns in old *Women's Wear Daily* magazines I found at vintage shops.

It didn't occur to me that perhaps *I* was the lucky one, not the Aprils. While I coveted their manicured lives, I got to live at messy, loopy Wilton Place, where you never knew who was about to walk through your front door and dazzle your socks off.

One Saturday, as I was flipping through the new L.L.Bean catalog on the living room floor, Dono burst in with a golden, pert-nosed boy he'd just met outside.

"Ione, meet River Phoenix!" my brother announced with fanfare.

"Ione," the boy said in a raspy voice. "That's a nice name." He looked about my age—thirteen—and had a playful aura, like he wouldn't be above climbing a tree or riding bikes (things I hadn't done since the Aprils and sorely missed).

"Yours too," I said, shoving the catalog under an armchair.

River made himself at home, plopping down on our worn green corduroy sofa as Dono explained that our guest was an actor, making a movie down the block. (Our neighborhood had a leafy, "Anywhere, USA" pleasantness that made it a popular filming location.)

"He's on that show *Seven Brides for Seven Brothers*," Dono told me.

I'd never seen it but happily pictured River singing in tall cowboy boots, twirling a lady in a gingham skirt. I was utterly and completely charmed.

"I've gotta get back to work," River said. "Maybe I'll call you sometime, Ione?"

He would call, at last, a year or so later, inviting me to the movies in Westwood. I'd say yes, of course. But then he'd phone again, just before the date, to say he'd booked a movie called *The Mosquito Coast* with Harrison Ford and was headed to Belize. "I'll call you when I'm back," he'd promise. And he would, to let me know that he'd fallen for his costar, Martha Plimpton. The date would be off for good, but our friendship would remain.

Meanwhile, at school, I was forging something like a friendship with the Aprils. Sometimes we sat together at lunch, and I'd get to hear about their modeling ambitions and all the boys April the queen bee had vanquished, including her current long-distance boyfriend, Rob, with whom she'd done something called 69. Though I'd dated a couple of boys and was doing some sexual exploring on my own time, I didn't know what April was talking about and felt a little sick when I later found out. I would also put it together one day that Rob and his brother Chad, with whom April kept promising to set me up, did not exist. Inspired by the brothers Rob and Chad Lowe, she'd made them up. April made *lots* of things up. Not that I'd ever challenge her lies. That wasn't how it worked. How it worked was I took whatever April offered, gratefully.

I don't remember any of the Aprils asking me about my life, and I didn't volunteer much. I couldn't imagine that having a sixties-legend folk-singer dad would impress my new friends. When I learned they wanted to try pot, I pilfered a baggie from Mom's stash, saying it came from a friend. No *way* could they know the dealer was my mom.

To impress the Aprils, I was learning to be mean. I laughed along when April P. imitated our gay Jazzercise coach's hip-wiggling and asked our religion teacher, "Are priests allowed to masturbate?" When the history teacher was late and someone placed an unused maxi pad on his desk, I stuck a wad of bubblegum on it. Everyone thought that was super, but the teacher wouldn't start class until someone confessed, so I walked up to his desk and quietly took the blame—earning detention, and my first invite to April's house.

I'd driven through the Hancock Park neighborhood lots of times, pining for its mock Tudor and Italianate homes through the passenger window of Mom's faded two-tone station wagon. But even *The Preppy Handbook* couldn't have prepared me for what lay beyond April's arched doorway. Oh, how I swooned for her matching D. Porthault sheet sets and cable-knit cashmere sweaters and wood-handle patchwork Bermuda bags and Popsicles lined up in neat rows in the Sub-Zero . . . There were housekeepers, and sometimes April's big sister breezed through, but I never saw her matching tall blond parents, except in the heart-shaped Tiffany & Co. picture frame on the fireplace mantel.

MTV had just come out and was always blasting from the big TV in April's pool house. In my memory, it's Duran Duran's lushly cinematic "Hungry Like the Wolf" video on the screen—with Simon Le Bon crawling after a painted model in the jungle. It probably says something that I remember my time with the Aprils like a video too: slick and bright and nice to look at, but with not much underneath.

It was different when April and I were alone. It was deeper with her, or at least more intense. I worshipped her, and in exchange, she kept me close—in proximity, at least. April rarely let on what she was feeling. Sometimes I wondered if she could feel at all.

One day in French class, April leaned in, the scent of her Prell shampoo flooring me, as it always did. "My parents are going away this weekend," she whispered. "Can I stay over at your place?"

I forced a nod and a smile, feeling the blood drain from my face. Was it all over? Would she still like me if she saw my weird life? But the excitement eclipsed the dread. The queen of the Aprils wanted to spend the night at my house!

On Judgment Day, I April-proofed the house, hiding my journals and stuffed animals and any signs of Mom's pot business. As I slid a shoebox full of weed under her bed, I found another box, filled with Polaroids. At first, I couldn't make out what they were. Then I saw pubes . . . on pubes! Two bushes together in a close-up. Aghast, I shuffled through the pictures until a smiling shot of Mom, boobs out, made me drop the pile in horror. *These were sex pictures of Mom and Billy!*

Moments later, Billy found me in the garden, attempting to dig up his agave plants with my bare hands. Like Joan Crawford chopping up rosebushes in the middle of the night in *Mommie Dearest*, I was possessed. Those crude, lascivious plants had to go.

"Hey, hey!" Billy said, putting his hand on my back. I shrugged him off and kept clawing away. "Why are you digging up my agaves?"

I wasn't sure, now that he'd broken my trance. I'd convinced myself the succulents were too coarse for April to see, but suddenly they didn't seem worth the effort or dirty nails.

It was Mom I blamed for those nauseating pictures. She and Billy had gotten married the month before, in a no-big-deal ceremony at city hall. But even if Billy was my stepdad now, he was still just a kid him-self, no older than some of the college nerds I'd cosplayed with at last year's Ren Faire. *She* was my real parent. Why couldn't she act like it?

In retrospect, the Polaroids were probably Billy's idea. I didn't know yet that those sweet doves he'd given Mom had come from a photo shoot at the Playboy Mansion, or that Billy sometimes assisted on porn sets, or that the big script he was always trying to finish was called . . . *Pornocchio* (the guy's thing grew when he lied). Mom was even helping write it. That she'd so far kept these embarrassing secrets from me was a rare instance of boundary-setting for Enid, as if she'd sensed my growing disillusionment with our anything-goes lifestyle.

For the twenty-four hours April was at Wilton Place, I experienced a mixed state of disbelief, elation, and terror. It felt surreal to host this mythical creature, as if Princess Diana herself had come for a sleepover. Out of her element, April seemed subdued, even a little lost. She hardly spoke at dinner, probably sensing Mom's quiet disapproval. Enid pre-ferred my old Cheremoya Avenue Elementary friends to the Aprils, who apparently made me "bitchy."

Upstairs, I watched April unpack her Dooney & Bourke week-ender with the keen eye of a detective, noting each of her Clinique facial care products, so I could save up and buy the same. I'd made a soft bed on the floor, but to my surprise, April asked to sleep in my single bed with me.

"Sure!" I said, I hoped not too eagerly. We lay next to each other on our backs, straight as sardines, wrist bones just touching.

"I'm glad we're friends," April mumbled, drifting off.

I could have died happily right then and there. The queen of the Aprils trusted me. She'd peeled off her queenly mask, and—like a good lady-in-waiting—I'd received it with care. Never dreaming she'd offer more.

And then she did. One night that summer, I went with April to her babysitting job at a stately house on June Street. While April read her three-year-old charge a bedtime story, I wandered around the living room, admiring the gingham sofas with elegant brown velvet pillows, the lacquered side tables and Parish-Hadley drapes.

Above, I heard April leaving the child's room. "No coming out or I'll call your mother," she warned. Then, "Fine, but just a crack." That she wasn't a very nice babysitter didn't surprise me. I wanted to go up there and say something reassuring to the kid, but as always, I feared overstepping with April.

In the dazzling white kitchen, we ate strawberries and an entire can of whipped cream, then crept upstairs, past the kid's cracked door to the parents' moonlit bedroom, an ode to damask and chinoiserie. I sat on an ottoman the size of my bed while April dabbed on the mother's L'Air du Temps and rifled through her jewelry box. A diamond stud glinted in her pinched fingers as she pocketed it in her pants. I felt a little sick. I'd seen the Aprils shoplift at Soap Plant on Melrose, but never at someone's house. Why did rich people always want more?

Sitting next to me, April took the earring from her jeans and put it in her ear. "Look good?"

I nodded, though she suddenly looked hard and unattractive, which had never seemed possible before.

April leaned back on her elbows, looking up at me with an unreadable question in her eyes. "Scoot over," she said. I slid to the edge as she flipped onto her stomach, ankles falling across my lap, face buried in her arms. Now she was beautiful again, long and graceful, buttery hair sweeping to the floor. The same snug white polo she'd worn to our sleepover (size small, Lacoste—I'd written it down) rode up to expose her straight, pretty waist. I was afraid to move or breathe, but also overcome with a strange need to touch her. Slowly, warily, my hand lifted. Could I touch her, in a tender way? Should I? Had I *always* wanted to? Did *she* want me to? Such possibilities had never occurred to me before, but the thick summer air wrapping around us felt protective, transformative.

"Give me a massage," she ordered, settling it.

My hands were on her, tracing her spine through the thick cotton shirt, when she abruptly sat up. "Hang on," she said. Turning her back to me, she pulled off her shirt, unhooked her bra, and lay down again. "Now," she said.

April, topless in the moonlight. The sight of her bare, freckled back made me feel funny—at once protective and a little greedy. Powerful. Was this how it felt to be a boy, looking at a half-naked girl? I liked that idea, felt emboldened by it. On my knees, straddling April's back, I started to massage her again, amazed by the softness of her skin under my palms. What was she thinking? *Turn over*, I willed her, surprising myself. *Sit up so I can kiss you.*

April did sit up, but not for a kiss. I sensed she'd felt something too. Something she didn't want to feel, it seemed. Covering herself, she grabbed her shirt, pulled it on, and stalked from the room. Shame crept in then. These feelings weren't me. I wasn't gay, was I? Mom had many gay male friends but lesbians were a mystery, and even a little scary. I'd never met one that I knew of—and surely I'd know if a lesbian were in my presence. Didn't they all have big biceps and leather biker hats?

In Los Angeles, we were waiting for the Big One. The underground plates at the San Andreas Fault were always shifting, building and releasing tension. One day they'd snap apart or together and the entire city would rock to its knees. I thought maybe April and I were like that. To the naked eye, nothing big had happened between us—yet underneath we'd shifted, tensed. I prayed for another massage session, and when April sent me a letter from sleepaway camp signed *Bye, Bi*, my hopes soared.

Bye, Bi, I signed my letter right back. Were we bi? The word was less intimidating than "lesbian," and if April was okay with it, then I was too. Very okay with it.

Then, the night before the first day of eighth grade, April called.

"So," she said sternly, "we need to quit the bi stuff."

"Okay," I said, feeling crushed. The bewitchingly vulnerable girl who'd shared my narrow bed at Wilton Place had never reappeared— not even that time on the ottoman. And now I guessed she never would. But I got it. Whatever feelings we had for each other were taboo. Even I knew the most dangerous place for girls who loved girls was an all-girls school.

4

Losing It
1984

I wasn't sure how to feel about it, but suddenly I was *obsessed* with losing my virginity. After that moonlit night with April, having sex was *all* I could think about. I knew it couldn't be with her—that game was over. And anyway, what I really wanted was to be devirginized. For that, I thought I needed a boy.

It wasn't really about being horny, though I was that. Mostly, I wanted to feel desired, needed. And no one but me (and him, whoever he was) would have to know I'd gone to the other side. My new sexuality would be like secret, invisible armor. It would give me confidence, charisma, a certain je ne sais quoi. "Isn't she beautiful?" people would say, watching me from across every room.

The first person I propositioned was my favorite of all Mom's gay friends, the fashion photographer Johnny Rozsa. It was a Friday evening, and I'd tagged along with him to a chic cocktail party in the Hollywood Hills. We stood on a proper balcony with curved wrought iron railings, surveilling the actress Jacqueline Bisset on the lawn below. I'd loved her as the hot mom in *Class*, and boys everywhere still had that wet T-shirt movie poster from *The Deep* on their walls. At the party, every head turned when she shook her golden-brown curls and laughed. Jacqueline Bisset had surely had lots and lots of sex.

"Will you devirginize me?" I blurted to Johnny.

"*Ew!*" Johnny slapped me on the shoulder, shuddering. I must have looked wounded because he added, kindly, "Maybe when you're fifteen."

Johnny was thirty-five. He sometimes took my picture and we'd recently done a just-for-fun shoot at the Lincoln Heights railroad tracks. His friend, the soon-to-be-big-time makeup artist Paul Starr, gave me smoldering eyes that made Johnny say, "Well, hello, beautiful," and "Darling, you look divine." But Johnny had no intention of sleeping with me, ever, which I must have known. By soliciting a gay man, I'd protected myself from having to follow through with this thing I so wanted and feared.

But I wanted sex slightly more than I feared it and soon set my sights on a more attainable prospect.

It was a warm October evening, and April had dragged me to my first football game.

"See number thirty-seven?" she said, pointing from the bleachers. "That's the most popular guy at Loyola. And the richest. Crew Sinclair." (Not his real name, but it should have been.)

Most popular? I thought, squinting at the fit, slightly stocky player from our brother school. He took off his helmet, revealing Sun In–yellow hair and a square jaw. Not really my type, but definitely cute. If he was the hardest one to get, I wanted him. Or more accurately, I wanted him to want me. "Introduce me?" I said.

After the game, we walked down to the field, and April made the introductions.

"*Hey*," said Crew, zeroing in on me. "Nice to meet you." Then, not a minute later: "Maybe we could go out sometime?"

"Sure," I managed, barely able to look him in the eye. Inside, I was flipping out. It was one of those hyperreal, haloed moments I lived for, when fantasy meshed with reality. Like a scene from *American Graffiti*, with the cheerleaders and the bright lights all around. Yes, number 37 was definitely the one for the job.

We started dating, though it didn't feel like a relationship—more like a rehearsal. Sex would make it real, I was pretty sure. Meanwhile, we met at the movies and made out against walls at parties and even started saying "I love you" at the end of our stilted phone conversations. Thanks to Crew's propriety, I remained extremely inexperienced. I'd almost touched a penis once (not his) in a movie theater but freaked out and quickly pulled my hand back the moment my finger brushed a pube. No one had ever touched my vagina. But sex wasn't baseball. Who said you couldn't skip bases?

I was determined to cross home plate on the night of Crew's winter formal, to which I'd worn my most nonvirginal strapless black dress and silver choker. I'd stolen a condom from Dono's secret drawer and slipped it in my purse, knowing Crew would be too polite to assume. After the dance, we parked behind a church in his mom's chic Mercedes convertible, top up (less *American Graffiti*, more *American Gigolo*, which was fine by me). There was some chaste front-seat kissing, then we clambered into the back and lay down, Crew on top. As his lips covered my neck, I let my hair fan dramatically over the seat's edge, the way April's had that night on the ottoman. *If I were a boy, I would have touched her*, I often thought. But that wasn't right. You didn't need to be a boy to make the first move, you just needed to have some nerve.

"Sleep with me?" It came out high and squeaky, but never mind, I'd said it!

Crew jolted upright. "Nope!" he said, running a hand through his stiff-gelled hair. "You're too young. You're not even in high school."

"*You've* done it," I retorted. One of the few personal things I knew about my sixteen-year-old boyfriend was that he'd lost his virginity (to "an older woman" was all he'd say, leaving me to picture a tawdry but rousing Tom Cruise–Rebecca De Mornay *Risky Business* scenario).

"It's different for girls," said Crew.

I sat up, fixing my dress and turning my choker around the right way. "You don't have to treat me like a kid," I said. As I snatched my purse from the floor to fix my lip gloss, a folded square of paper fell out: an old note from Karis—the *I* in *Ione* childishly dotted with a pink heart. I held it crumpled in my fist the whole ride home. It felt like a sign, delivered from my heart, saying, *Hold on to your girlhood.*

But there was still that other, more ambitious voice, like a pillow placed firmly over my true feelings, saying, *Shhhh. Don't you want to be somebody?* It wasn't the voice of my mother, who did her best to shelter me, but it was probably informed by her example. Mom had made her mark by using her womanhood. I wanted to make mine.

A few weeks later, I saw the inside of Crew's monumental Hancock Park mansion for the very first time. I'd finally worn him down. The plan was to have supper at the house, hit a party on Arden, then head back to his place to devirginize me. Was it weird or good that Crew had invited me to meet his mother tonight, of all nights? I couldn't decide.

Mrs. Sinclair, who probably pegged me for a gold digger, had the beauty and reproachful, divinely chic air of the famous socialite Doris Duke. I tried not to offend her, sitting carefully on my frail antique chair and complimenting her rosebushes instead of asking nosy questions like I wanted to. I held my utensils Continental style and cut tiny bites of steak that I could still barely swallow. Food had taken on a newly antagonistic role in my life since my decision to have sex. If my butt and stomach were flat and small, maybe I'd be more comfortable being naked. Or maybe I'd never feel comfortable with Crew. That was possible too. His slightly younger brother, seated across the lap-pool-sized dining table, was already easier to talk to, funny and warm. *Is it too late to choose the brother instead?* I wondered. It didn't occur to me that I could simply choose myself.

At the party, Crew went off with his friends and I sullenly smoked the better part of a stolen Enid joint. Driving back to his home with the convertible top down, I was grateful for the wind, an excuse not to talk. I didn't want to tell him I'd felt abandoned on the night of my great deflowering. What would be the point? Anyway, he wouldn't ignore me after tonight.

Crew killed the headlights and crawled the Mercedes up the driveway, past the mansion and swimming pool, stopping outside a two-story stone cottage.

"This is it," he said. "Used to be the caretaker's house."

My hands shook as I fished the roach from my pocket and lit up. I wasn't numb yet, and I wanted to be numb. "Want some?" I offered.

"No, I'm good," said Crew, one of those strictly-alcohol jocks.

At least the cottage was pretty, with a gabled roof and roses crawling up the side. *Like Sleeping Beauty's house*, I thought, a little sadly.

Inside, he led us up the creaky wooden stairs and into a dark room. As I felt my way toward a small daybed in the corner, the lights flickered crazily on and off. I whirled around. "What's that?!"

Crew laughed. "Just messing with you, stoner."

"Ha-ha," I said, wondering, *Do we even like each other?* That was a question for later.

He turned on a small lamp and I registered the room's nautical theme—framed signal flags, rope clocks, a vintage life ring with the faded words WELCOME ABOARD, and blue and white stripes running every which way. Was I seasick or way too stoned? *No turning back,* I reminded myself as Crew tossed a box of Trojans onto the bedside table. He stripped to his tighty-whities and I peeled down to my specially purchased peach Calvin Klein bra and panty set, and we perched on the edge of the bed, kissing. I was worried about my stomach and lay back to flatten it. "Should we now?" I said.

Crew laid his tan, hairless Ken-doll body on top of mine—his left hand on my boob, his right reaching for the condoms.

As he wedged himself inside me, I turned my face to the pillow, tears in my eyes. Not because it hurt. I felt no pain, just an awful rush of regret.

"I'm so young," I heard myself saying, "I'm so young." It was finally sinking in.

"*Shhh*," he said. "You'll make me lose my hard-on."

There was a long, awkward stretch where our bodies rocked like buoyed canoes.

"Is the condom on?" I asked.

"*Shhh*, it's fine," he said, looking past me.

I don't know why, but I kept seeing his mother—a bird's-eye view of her, waiting at that long, lacquered table as we came down the grand staircase for supper. How beautiful she'd looked, with her princess posture and ice-blond coif. But also, how alone.

When he was done, Crew went to the bathroom and announced, "I've never come that much!"

First, I was pleased. That meant it was good, right? Then I remembered: There were two of us. Sex was supposed to be about my pleasure too. In *Forever . . .* by Judy Blume, Katherine had (miraculously, I now know) orgasmed her first time. Why hadn't I?

The next day, I stole *The Teenage Body Book* from Dono's bookshelf. Flipping to the Q and A section, my eye stopped on a question from someone who worried they were using masturbation as "a crutch." I had a teenage brother, so that didn't surprise me. What surprised me—no, blew my mind: The letter was signed

"Lucy." I couldn't believe it! Had a girl really written that? *Did girls masturbate too?*

I flipped to the index, where "masturbation, female" pointed me to the chapter that changed the world as I knew it: Yes, it was true! I could give an orgasm *to myself. The Teenage Body Book* even had instructions.

Electrified, I gathered the recommended supplies, then locked my bedroom door and tore off my pants. Flopping onto my bed (under my Maxfield Parrish *Ecstasy* poster), I got to work examining my vagina with a hand mirror. *Whoa.* It was a shock, but not exactly a bad one. I pulled out my diary and scribbled *vagina* on my list of body parts I liked the look of, after *arms, breasts, stomach, face, hair, feet, hands,* and *tops of thighs.* (Not on the list: *hips, butt,* or *backs of thighs.*)

Next, as suggested, I tried gliding the convex side of a spoon over my clitoris. *Meh.* I turned on my side and reopened to the masturbation chapter: "We fantasize about all kinds of things," it said. "Why not sex?"

Fantasize? Oh, I could do *that.*

I closed my eyes and conjured my own imaginary porno—a mash-up of a creepy old black-and-white Disney cartoon I used to watch called *The Mad Doctor* and sadomasochistic scenes from books by my newest favorite authors, Anaïs Nin and Jerzy Kosinski. I wasn't a player in my movie, but more like a cameraman, watching as a naked woman had sexual things done to her (like in Kosinski's *The Painted Bird*) while strapped to the Mad Doctor's conveyor belts. Had I created a sex machine? Was that Anaïs pulling the penis levers? *Oh, wow, oh . . .*

Cut to me, alone, flushed and sweaty, eyes rolling back in my head like the girl from *The Exorcist.*

Holy. Hell.

All this time, everyone had been walking around, keeping *that* feeling under their hats? I wanted to shout it from the rooftops: "I did it! I had a climax!"

Crew and I only slept together one more time before he dumped me. I wasn't too broken up about it. Now that I'd found my go-to masturbation method—on my stomach as I touched myself and, yes, fantasized—I was keeping myself plenty occupied.

5

The Star Hatchery

1985

In ninth grade, I transferred to Hollywood High, the big, anonymous public school where Dono had gone. I was crushed about leaving Immaculate Heart but stoically accepted my fate. Mom couldn't swing paying another four years of tuition.

Like everything in this town, I would have much preferred Hollywood High in the dreamy olden days. They'd once called the school "the Star Hatchery" for all the great movie icons it produced: Carole Lombard, Judy Garland, Mickey Rooney, Lana Turner, Alan Ladd, Sharon Tate, Cher . . . But the school's heyday was now over, which was Ronald Reagan's fault, as Grandpa Benny explained whenever he called from Queens. The president and former California governor had slashed educational funding to bits, and my new school, with its peeling paint, tired teachers, and crowded classrooms, sure showed it.

Dono, of course, had managed just fine at Hollywood High. He'd been his class president, the prom king, an ardent baseball player, the star of school plays, and the leader of a pop-locking crew.

"Dono's your brother?" people would ask me in the hallways. Then: "Oh, I love that guy!" Or "Oh, I hate that guy."

I was proud of but a little embarrassed by my brother, who could rub people the wrong way with his exuberance and chameleon style— by turns mod, punk, preppy, New Romantic, or B-boy. Dono didn't care if they called him a poser; it was funny to answer the door in Mom's bikini top or go to school in a *Sgt. Pepper's* marching-band suit. Me, I hated having to choose an outfit every day and mostly stuck to vintage-y new wave—1940s polka-dot day dresses with my combat boots, a jean jacket, and black eyeliner. If I felt like hiding my butt, I wore my FRANKIE SAY RELAX T-shirt, which went almost to my knees.

It was my brother who encouraged me to embrace where I was and audition for the school's dance magnet program. It was a stretch: I'd dabbled in jazz, ballet, and modern classes and spent countless hours dancing to *West Side Story* in my bedroom, but I didn't enjoy performing if it meant being judged or graded. Thankfully, the dance teacher, Kenny Long, was attentive, not judgy, and I made the cut. It was well-known that Kenny had recently lost his son to the AIDS epidemic, but our teacher had somehow found his joy again and showered it on his students. For the ten hours a week I was in his care, I remembered what it was like to get personalized attention from a loving, ignited mentor. Otherwise, I attached to no one and nothing freshman year. I didn't have the patience or heart to plant friendship roots all over again.

The bus ride home was worse than the quiet, sleepy morning ride. After four p.m., the RTD lugged the weary and the restless, a mix of BO and danger in the air. I'd slouch low behind my hair and blast Kate Bush on Billy's Walkman or read a page or two of *Eve's Hollywood* by Eve Babitz.

Eve was our next-door neighbor and one of Mom's friends. Until recently, I hadn't known she was a famous writer, just that she was messy and twinkly, drove a bummy car, and once fell asleep with a lit cigarette that almost burned her house down. (Billy saw the smoke and flames and pulled Eve to safety!) Then I discovered her books, just when Hollywood High was making me blue and I needed to fall in love with LA again. Eve was one of the great literary protectors of Los Angeles, writing about it as a place full of mystery and unexpectedness. The way that Joan Didion spoke for the naysayers of Los Angeles, Eve spoke for the lovers of the city, which was actually harder to do.

It was always a relief to arrive home in the snug, woodsy foothills. Now that I wasn't friends with the Aprils (we'd parted ways when I left Immaculate Heart), Wilton Place and my overgrown, bohemian neighborhood didn't embarrass me, it comforted me. Our dog, Smoke, was always waiting for me, half-dozing on the front porch. His puppy days were long behind him and his hips ached, but he got himself up to follow me when I pushed open the screen door. Despite the dodgy characters who sometimes wandered up from the flats, we rarely locked our house. Mom had too many friends coming and going, and on our side of Franklin, the neighborhood was safe enough.

"Is that you?" Mom would call.

"It's me," I'd call back, clocking the vibe. If the house resounded with laughter and conversation, I'd stop by the kitchen to visit with whatever fun crowd Mom had drawn to our table. If the house was silent, resonating with an abstract tension, it meant Mom and Billy had been arguing. Those days, I headed straight to my room.

I could see it dawning on Mom that her marriage to Billy had been more of a placeholder than a solution. I'd even heard them talking about divorce. Figuring Billy was on his way out, I definitely didn't want to call him "Dad" like he still wanted me to. The word always froze in my throat, like in a dream where you can't scream.

One afternoon, Dono popped into my room, looking very all-American in blue jeans and a bright white tank under a black bomber—his go-to audition outfit. He was always auditioning and had been getting steady work for a year, popping and locking his way into Lionel Richie's "All Night Long" video, the movie *Breakin' 2: Electric Boogaloo*, and the sitcom *Alice*. A few years before, he'd come painfully close to landing the older brother role in *E.T.* I was never jealous of my brother's success, I was jealous of his clarity. Both of us felt destined to be somebody, but only Dono seemed to know how to go about it.

My brother pulled a script from his messenger bag and tossed it onto my bed. I glanced at the cover page: *River's Edge* by Neal Jimenez.

"I didn't get the part," said Dono, "but they want *you* to read for the female lead. The director is Tim Hunter, who wrote *Over the Edge*!"

"Really?" We *loved* that movie, about teenage rebels who wreck their cookie-cutter community. But I didn't get it. "How do they know about *me*?"

"I showed them your picture in *LA Weekly*," said Dono, the born connector, looking psyched.

One of Mom's many photographer friends had shot the *LA Weekly* Christmas gift guide in our living room, using Dono and me as free models. For the "What to Get Your Clothes Horse" piece, I'd worn a body-hugging silver knit dress with a flamenco ruffle running up the side. In the full-page picture, I was pressed against a Fabio lookalike, our long dark hair tangled together in a gust. I looked older than fifteen, unsmiling and serious, like I thought a model should be.

I loved playing for the camera, that big eye in my face, not looking away. The photographers we knew treated me as an equal who would bring her own story to the table. I often fantasized that one day my dad would stumble across my face on a magazine cover and be overcome with regret for not getting to know such a wonderful girl. So far, the closest I'd come was an album cover I'd done at age ten, for *Young Girls* by the Scooters. I'd worn Chinese-style silk pajamas and posed on a red scooter, surrounded by the brooding, all-male band. The makeup artist had worried out loud that my heavy makeup might be "too *Pretty Baby*," but the art director disagreed and I did too. I adored that movie (and Brooke Shields) and didn't understand why the grown-ups were so scandalized by it. Sure, Brooke played a child prostitute, and it was peculiar that she had to do it with grown-ups, but somehow the movie softened the grimness of that, or I didn't yet see it. What I saw was a young girl whose beauty gave her power over men, which gave her power in the world.

Aside from the thrill of being compared to Brooke, what I remember most about that day was having my first déjà vu experience while looking into the vanity mirror—the kind with light bulbs all around. My hair was crimped into a fantastic mane and my eyelids shimmered like hummingbird wings. I looked nothing like regular Ione, yet I'd never felt more like myself.

But acting was a much scarier beast than modeling. There were so many ways to screw up when you had to open your mouth and talk. I was so insecure, cared *so* much about what people thought. When faced with a challenge at school I'd half-ass it and throw the race rather than risk trying and failing.

I told Dono I'd think about it.

The next day, I took a walk with my godmother, Cynthia, who wasn't just a fun friend of Mom's but someone I felt nurtured by. "I know I should be excited," I told her as we strolled up Foothill Drive. Along the narrow winding road, purple jacarandas tumbled down dirty stone walls, and white magnolia blossoms opened like stars. Their dusky perfume was suddenly overwhelming, and I slumped against a palm tree. "But what if I'm not cut out for it?"

"Well," said Cynthia, "what have you got to lose?"

I considered the question.

"Look at it this way," she added. "If you don't get it, nothing will change, you'll be right where you are now. And if you do get it, you'll have a great adventure."

Cynthia had been looking out for us since even before I was born. Like the time when Mom was all alone and very pregnant with me in England. My father was back together with Linda by then, and they'd offered to help out by taking three-year-old Dono with them to Greece, along with Julian, Linda's kid with Brian Jones. But the day after I was born, they called Mom and said, "He's too difficult. Come and get him." Since that was obviously impossible, Cynthia heroically flew to Greece to fetch little Dono.

So, this was an adventure, *right*? I was trying to see it that way, despite my sickening fear. Having reluctantly decided to audition, I was now sitting in a squeaky plastic chair in an empty casting office lobby, clutching my stomach. I'd made Dono wait in the car, but now I wished he were here with me.

Behind the audition room door, a girl's voice rose and fell. There was laughter, quiet conversation, more laughter. Shaking with dread, I picked a few fuzz balls off my red sweater, brushed some of Smoke's hair off my go-to black cotton miniskirt, fiddled with my bangles. If I'd been braver I would've dressed edgier for the role of Clarissa, a sardonic stoner whose good heart is cloaked beneath layers of defensiveness. Afraid to put anyone off by looking too tough, I had settled for a small new wave touch, the row of black rubber bangles.

Lighting, timing, posture, I silently reminded myself. Mom's friend Bobby Burton, one of my gay "dads," had told me these were an actor's secret weapons. It seemed like good advice now. I'd never studied acting, but I'd been studying actresses for as long as I could remember. Shirley MacLaine in *Terms of Endearment*, Meryl Streep in *Sophie's Choice*, Diane Keaton in *Shoot the Moon* . . . Those performances were proof that acting could be a noble profession, if one I'd never considered for myself.

"Ione Leitch?"

A fresh-faced woman in a navy, double-breasted blazer was standing over me, thrusting out her hand. "Carrie Frazier," she said. The casting director. Dono had told me she cast *Fast Times at Ridgemont High*!

I jumped to my feet, immediately wishing I hadn't worn shoulder pads under my sweater. Were they out of style now? This morning I'd ripped them out, thrown them on the bed, then Velcroed them back in place at the last minute.

"We're happy you're here!" said Carrie.

"Thank you," I mumbled, touching my front tooth. Mom had finally saved enough to get me a porcelain veneer and my smile looked nice again, but I wasn't used to showing it.

"Shaggy, natural . . . ," Carrie mused out loud, studying me. "I'm seeing Meg Tilly, Matt Dillon. Tim directed them in *Tex*, you know."

I nodded. Did I know that? Dono probably did. I let my smile-shaming hand fall to my side. Had she just compared me to Meg Tilly?

Just then, my competition walked out of the audition room, and I scanned her at warp speed: choppy blond hair, button nose, Guess jeans, Chuck Taylors . . . Oh my God, it was Jenny Wright, from *The World According to Garp* and *St. Elmo's Fire*! Of course they'd brought her in; she was perfect for the part. I held my breath, waiting for Carrie to pivot toward the proven talent in the room, but the casting director's attention stayed with me.

"Shall we, then?" said Carrie, waving me in.

Lighting, timing, posture!

I lifted my chin, walked through the open door, and immediately left my body.

"How'd it go?" asked Dono, chauffeuring me home.

"I don't know. I have no idea. I think okay? I don't know." I closed my eyes, tucking my shaking hands between my knees.

"I'm sure it was great."

"Maybe not," I said, fast-forwarding the cassette deck to a mellower song. "The director was nice. It was just so weird. Maybe I was too quiet? Thank God it's over."

Thank God it wasn't over. Days later, I got a callback. They wanted me to come for a chemistry read, to see if I was a good fit with the lead actors—and probably just plain good enough, period. Crispin Glover—George McFly in *Back to the Future*—would be there. He had already been cast as my character's boyfriend. Then there was the guy who'd gotten Dono's would-be part: a twenty-one-year-old Canadian named Keanu Reeves. He'd made a few small movies in Canada, and this was to be his big US debut.

"You *have* to do it," said Dono when I told him the news.

I shook my head. "I don't think I can." To be an actor, you had to want it more than anything—like Dono. I couldn't see *what* I wanted through my fog of fear.

"You're crazy," said Dono. "Every girl in town wants this part."

Something stood up inside me when he said that. This town, obviously, was full of actresses. To be chosen over all of them—what would that feel like? What would it mean? Maybe it was worth the trouble to find out.

"Fine," I said. "I'll try."

For the next two weeks, I diligently practiced my sides (as they call the scenes for an audition) and read the entire script twice. It was a great screenplay, based on the true story of a California kid who strangled his girlfriend to death and then bragged to his friends about it, showing them the body. For several days, they'd been paralyzed, doing nothing. *River's Edge* was about that dilemma: If your friend does something terrible, do you protect them or turn them in? These kids weren't bad, just directionless—going nowhere and doing nothing because nothing they did made a difference anyway. I didn't know anyone who'd murdered their girlfriend, fortunately, but I did know apathy; I felt it every day at Hollywood High.

When the day came for the chemistry read, Mom drove me back to the casting office on the west side. In the audition room, Crispin Glover sat in the driver's seat of a car made from two rows of folding chairs; Keanu Reeves was in the back. Both seemed deep in their heads, preparing for the scene. Tim Hunter introduced us, and the actors said brief, polite hellos and went back into their thoughts. Crispin was like a Dickens character, with his sharp features and sharp-toed shoes. Keanu's jeans were ripped, his sneaker laces artfully untied, and his long, greasy hair fell over his face, so I couldn't see how ridiculously gorgeous he was. The grown women in the room clearly knew. Carrie Frazier sat behind a conference table with the producers, Midge Sanford and Sarah Pillsbury, who made *Desperately Seeking Susan*. All three of them kept their eyes on Keanu, over the moon about their young discovery. I mean, from what I could see of him, I got it, but I was too nervous to let myself dwell on that.

A VHS camera on a tripod faced us, red light glowing expectantly. I gave the big glass eye a shy nod and took a seat next to Crispin. *Please have chemistry with me*, I silently willed him. In the scene we were about to do, my character was conflicted, angry, and disillusioned—like any teenage girl. As I considered this, Tim peered over his wire-rimmed glasses and said, so softly I almost missed it: "Action."

Crispin reached for his invisible steering wheel, slumping low in his seat, and just like that, we were Layne, Matt, and Clarissa, three small-town stoners, driving down a dark road. I crossed my arms, pictured headlights passing, the slick of tires on wet pavement.

"I feel real twisted right now," I said, starting softly. "Twisted, like I should just go to the cops and tell them where John is."

Crispin-as-Layne jerked his gaze toward me. "I wouldn't even joke about that, *Clarissa*."

The way he said "Clarissa," like a threat—that's what did it. I heard myself yelling, fighting back: "What would you do?! Kill me? You'd love that, I bet. You and John could run off and be outlaws together. But first, to show off, strap my dead body on top of this car and drive all over town!"

After two takes, we were through, and the boys, disappointingly, vanished. But I'd done it! If that was acting, it was *fun*. Tim Hunter wore a sly smile, and Sarah Pillsbury rushed over to give me a hug, calling me "a natural." I floated out of that room and all the way home.

The wait to hear back was agonizing. With something real to yearn for, Hollywood High was even harder to bear. I felt like a girl in a horror movie at the moment a crack of light appears at the edge of the door—her last small chance to dive through and escape.

And then, two weeks later . . .

"Hello?"

"Ione?" It was Sarah Pillsbury.

I clutched the phone, feeling a little spinny. "Yes?"

"You got the part."

Was that me, screaming like a Beatles fan? I crumpled to the floor.

Once I'd recovered from the fainting spell, Mom and I called Sarah back to accept. As if there was any question.

Now I had to get emancipated.

As it was explained to me and a visibly uncomfortable Enid, emancipation was a legal process that allowed you to work like an adult when you were still a kid. It was invented for teens who were estranged from their families, so they could support themselves. Then Hollywood got wind of the idea, realizing they could do away with tutoring and rest breaks by requiring their underage actors to get emancipated. Laura Dern, Michelle Williams, Alicia Silverstone, Juliette Lewis—all were emancipated at some point. Because time is money when you're filming.

I thought it sounded fantastic. I was still proud of my cool, beautiful mom but felt a growing need to distance myself from her. Not that I didn't want her around, but some breathing room sounded nice. The "sweet kid" persona I wore around the house to ease her troubles was starting to feel suffocating, on top of my heavy fifteen-year-old emotions. I needed to be my own person, not the caretaker of my mother's heart, trying to fill the void left by my missing dad. Legal emancipation sounded to me like emotional emancipation.

"Don't go moving out," Mom nervously joked as we signed the paperwork in the lawyer's office.

"Of course not!" I said. "I'm still a kid."

Famous last words.

6

River's Edge
1986

Three weeks into production, the *River's Edge* cast and crew traveled to Sacramento to shoot *the* scene, where the kids visit the body on the banks. It had been raining buckets in Northern California and the Sacramento River roared as we tramped, cameras rolling, toward the dead, naked girl. I was nervous to see a corpse, even if it was fake, and hoped this would make up for my not knowing exactly how to *act* nervous. To make our reactions authentic, Tim had directed us not to look at the body until the last possible second. Now, as the others circled and prodded it, I looked.

"Jamie" lay on her back, still and opalescent as a fish on the bright green grass. Her head was turned and she seemed to stare right into me. Those filmy, vacant eyes gave me a shock, as if Jamie were warning me: *Don't let it happen to you.* Fists clenched, I backed off, the dolly zoom swooping after me.

I had so much respect for Danyi Deats, who played Jamie. A real-life goth, she'd lent her own bleachy hair and ragged nude press-on nails to her character, giving the victim a tragic humanity. Once, I'd visited Danyi's trailer and found her lying on the floor, blasting organ music. It was the second movement from Widor's *Symphonie gothique*, she informed me, sitting up; it helped her get in a dead mood. How stoic she was, lying naked and motionless in the cold for days of filming.

Meanwhile, the rest of us were styled cozily in jeans, flannel button-downs, thermals, ratty cardigans, and leather. We were heshers—grungy before grunge was a style, and a far cry from the shiny mall rats of most teen films. Crispin had insisted from the start on wearing head-to-toe motorcycle gear and a slightly lopsided mullet wig that was perfect for his odd-bird character. Keanu was tousled and tie-dyed and denim-vested and hard not to stare at. Dan Roebuck, playing the killer, Samson Toilet, aka "John," liked to put K-Y Jelly in his hair to make it look greasy. We'd all heard the story of his audition, to which he'd arrived with beers stuffed in his coat pockets. He'd popped one open, Tim had reached for his camera, and the rest was history.

As Clarissa, I was the most mainstream of our motley crew. For the riverbank scenes, the costume department had outfitted me in an oversized white fisherman's sweater that I kept tugging down over my bum.

"They got you that big sweater to hide your ass," snarked the actor Josh Richman (Tony) between takes.

I wanted to say, "*Fuck you, motherfucker*," but I said nothing. He must have picked up on my body insecurity. Big butts weren't a thing yet. Elle Macpherson was at the height of her fame, and we were supposed to strive to look like her. I did not look like her. I looked like a normal, healthy teenage girl, and I was hard on myself about that. But still, I was here. I'd captured their attention. *I'm the female lead in a real movie*, I kept reminding myself.

No one seemed too bothered by my lack of experience now that I'd stopped trying to help the crew lug their equipment—a violation of union safety rules, apparently. Tim liked me all the more (in a non-creepy way) for being a novice. A Harvard guy and a literature buff, he gave me copies of Honoré de Balzac's *Lost Illusions* and Gustave Flaubert's *Sentimental Education*, which I wouldn't read until later, when I rediscovered them for myself. I was flattered but have always liked choosing my own mentors, not letting them choose me.

It was a dream, going from high school to this incredible universe where I got to play make-believe all day long. I loved having a costume created for me. I loved gossiping with the makeup artists as their brushes tickled my face. I loved the daily call sheet that told me exactly where to be and when. I loved watching the set decorators create a house, a town, a whole world—and then stepping into that world and almost forgetting it wasn't real. And I loved that I was being paid grown-up money to do all these fun things.

Roxana Zal played my character's friend Maggie with a sweet toughness. She was a year older than me but had been acting since she was eleven and had even won a Primetime Emmy for the TV film *Something About Amelia*. A Santa Monica girl, Roxana had already lived a lot of life, as kids who grew up by the beach in California seemed to. "Slow down when you say your lines," she coached me in our first scene together. "I used to rush when I was nervous too." I loved her gravelly voice and her cute nose that scrunched up when she smiled. Sometimes I caught myself staring at her toned, tomboyish body and quickly looked away, flushed.

All the actors were more experienced than I was and I loved studying them. Crispin, especially. The entire cast was spellbound by his big, bizarre performance as Layne—off-kilter and jittery and always on the edge of too much without tipping over.

Then there was Dennis Hopper, whom we all idolized. Dennis was older and already an acting and directing legend, known for his work on masterpieces like *Giant*, *Rebel Without a Cause*, *Apocalypse Now*, *Easy Rider*, and *Out of the Blue*, to name a few. He'd just come off shooting what would become the cult classic *Blue Velvet*.

Dennis was also an infamous hell-raiser, and all of us actors had expected him to roar up to set on a Harley-Davidson chopper, drunk and drug-addled. "You'll be surprised," Tim had said. "He's cleaned up." Still, it was vaguely shocking when Dennis came to the first table read freshly showered, in a nice suit, carrying a briefcase. After that day, we'd see him as his character, Feck, an old biker guy who sold weed to kids and was suspected of murdering his girlfriend a long time ago. *He* was supposed to be the film's crazy guy. I wondered at first if it would devolve into a competition, a kind of weird-off between Dennis and Crispin. But Dennis played his pain, isolation, and paranoia with a softness that felt achingly true.

One day, Mom, who'd come to Sacramento with me, invited Dennis to get a coffee with us. Unsurprisingly, they had a friend in common, the gorgeous Michelle Phillips from the Mamas and the Papas, who'd been in Hopper's *The Last Movie*. The two had been married, for almost a whole week. (A union their friends described as "the Six-Day War.") After some chitchat about old times, Mom casually asked if Dennis ever knew my father.

"Sure, sure," Dennis answered quietly, "we hung out a few times."

I thought it was strange that Mom brought up Donovan, this person who'd broken her heart and wanted nothing to do with Dono and me. My father wasn't part of our family. Why did she have to bring him up? Later, I'd come to understand: Donovan hadn't given us his time or physical presence, but he'd given us his legacy, which each of us carried in our own way.

After Sacramento, the cast and crew returned to LA for the rest of the shoot. Tim had picked Tujunga, in the foothills, for the major locations. He liked the river rock houses, which gave the place a "land that time forgot" feeling.

I liked anywhere with Keanu.

Strong, gentle, remote Keanu. I'd developed a huge crush on him, surprise, surprise.

Who are you under that hair? I wanted to ask. I studied him the way one studies a horse, in all its quiet magnificence.

One day, passing by Keanu's trailer (for the eighth time since breakfast), I found him sitting in his open doorway, reading a script that was not *River's Edge*.

"What's *that*?" I asked.

"It's for another film," he said. Seeing my confusion, he added, "When this one's done."

Wow. Ambitious. I was impressed but scandalized. Keanu was cheating on *River's Edge* with another film! I was so devoted to this job, I hadn't once imagined another one after it. I didn't even have an agent. This would probably be a one-off for me. A very, very lucky one-off.

Keanu's character and mine, as it turned out, were the heart and soul of the story—the ones who pushed through their teenage misery to do the right thing. Which meant we had lots of scenes together, with Clarissa and Matt growing closer and closer. I'd been anxiously anticipating our first-kiss scene but didn't let myself imagine the sex scene to come after that. All of my attention was focused on trying not to act weird around him.

"Keoni to set, please!" called a PA on the evening of the Kiss. The crew had difficulty pronouncing our unusual names and would merge them when they needed us both. The moniker was a little cringy, but I liked what it made me think of—our bodies, mashing together as one.

The scene was a simple walk to my door at night, with a kiss at the end. As we strolled up the brightly lit sidewalk, blocking the lighting and camera angles, Keanu glanced at me, looking sheepish.

"Um, so, I forgot we, ah, had a kiss in this scene," he bumbled in his charming, stilted way. "And, well, ah, I ate an onion. Sorry."

"That's okay," I said, a little confused. We stopped on Clarissa's front porch and I turned to face him, an assistant holding a light meter to my upturned chin. Keanu bent as if to kiss me without kissing me, and I breathed him in, sharp and a little sweet. "A raw onion?" I asked.

"Uh, yeah," he said through tight lips. "Just had a couple bites."

"Like an apple?"

He nodded.

My heart fell a few inches in my chest. I didn't care about his onion breath. I would've kissed him in almost any case, and the onion thing was interesting, in an eccentric, health-nutty way. But I *did* care that he'd forgotten we were having our kissing scene tonight. Unlike me, Keanu hadn't been anticipating it all day long. Hadn't counted the hours until our lips would meet, let alone the minutes.

Despite the awkward onion kiss, my lust was in full, overpowering bloom by the night of our sex scene a week later. This was in the days before there were intimacy coordinators on set to make sure the actors were comfortable, physically and psychologically. But I had no qualms, just butterflies, as Keanu and I climbed inside a sleeping bag in a dark city park to block the scene. He didn't smell like onions that night; he smelled as good as he looked. Warm and ambery, like pecan pie.

"Got it," interrupted the assistant director. "You two can break while we light."

"That's okay!" I said, thinking quickly. "We can stay in the sleeping bag while you light, it's comfortable."

I could feel the crew smirking. They were onto me, but I didn't care, and Keanu, happily, did not object. I snuggled into the crook of his arm and closed my eyes, in heaven as people moved around us positioning lights and stands.

When Tim called, "Okay, action!" I climbed on top of Keanu,

shivering in my tank top. We began to kiss, awkwardly at first. I was holding back, embarrassed and scared to be exposed in public as the sexed-up person I'd secretly become. It couldn't possibly be smart to show all these grown-ups on set, let alone the whole world, how much my body wanted Keanu's. One of many things I'd learned from watching a million movies was that not *so* much had changed since the black-and-white days. From *A Rage to Live* to *Where the Boys Are* to *Animal House*, the message was consistent: A sexy girl was never really safe.

"A little less serious, Ione?" Tim asked from out there. "You look like you're reading the newspaper."

I heard someone else—Sarah Pillsbury?—whisper, *"How would she know what to do? She's only fifteen!"*

Good, they all thought I was inexperienced—which I technically wasn't but really was. Knowing they saw me as an innocent virgin, I felt a little better. Careful not to let my hair fall over my face, I straddled Keanu and kissed him for real, moving around, parts to parts, missing sometimes and grinding on his leg or stomach.

"Cut!" said Tim. "Nice work, kids. Stand by."

We pulled apart, a little bashful, a little breathless.

"You good?" said Keanu, and I sensed by the husky edge to his voice that it wasn't just me who wanted more.

Tracing my lips to the side of his face, I whispered, "Can I come to your place after wrap?"

On the way there, we stopped at an all-night retro diner, Norms. It was busy and bright inside, but the clatter and voices fell away as we slid into our booth. I couldn't eat, could only marvel at every little thing Keanu did. The way he slung his arm across the back of the booth, tore a sugar packet with his teeth, licked a dot of ketchup from his thumb. Each gesture was sexier than the last. Spacey from lack of sleep and maybe even love, I felt the old diner drifting upward, lifting us into the sky. Just above the city. Just above real life.

Keanu had his own barebones studio apartment to stay in during filming. A brown carpet, a mattress on the living room floor. It wasn't glamorous, but it was. I was a little stiff, at first, still semi-traumatized by my lonely trysts with Crew Sinclair. All the same, I was dying for love, validation, and big experiences, and sensed I was in exactly the right place.

We lay on our sides on his mattress and I ran my hands over Keanu's smooth back as he kissed my face and neck. I felt both shy and proud of my body, my soft skin and full breasts in my pretty peach Calvin Klein bra. I knew I was nice looking but wished I were the most beautiful girl in the world. This might have been the most beautiful boy. He was different from any boy I'd known, self-possessed and calm. I wanted to feel his weight on me, to be crushed under his long body. But when I tried to maneuver him on top of me, he wouldn't budge.

"Let me drive you home," he said abruptly, pulling up my bra strap.

Why had he stopped? Maybe he thought I was too young? Maybe he just wanted to take it slow? Who knew. Sometimes he seemed almost alien—not unfeeling, just tuned in to different cues and frequencies than us humans.

He was all I could think about at work the next day. I had to figure out how to convince him to go all the way! An older actor I'd befriended advised me to let it go till the shoot was over, then see. "Sometimes set crushes aren't real," he said. "It's just the long hours and the creativity." Nodding toward a wardrobe assistant, he added, "I like her, a lot. If I still feel the same after wrap, I'll ask her out."

It was good advice, but I knew I wouldn't follow it. I couldn't wait. I wanted more of Keanu, now.

Soon after that indelible first visit to Keanu's studio, I invited myself back for another try. Wilton Place was just a few miles away, but I felt far, far from home that night. I imagined I was an American woman abroad, about to take my first French lover.

Keanu didn't lead me to the sofa like I'd been hoping. Instead, he went to the sparse kitchen and got us some drinks. As he handed me a Lipton iced tea, I leaned in for a kiss. I was getting more comfortable being the hunter.

Keanu leaned away. "I'm just, ah, going to, ah, shower," he said.

Taking this as a good omen, not a rebuff, I followed him into the bathroom.

Keanu turned on the water and stood with his back to me, hand in the stream, staring up at the showerhead. I maneuvered between him and the open shower curtain, water spraying my back. His beautiful neck was right there, so close I could lick it, so I did. I zeroed in on his beautiful throat, sucking and making out with it. He made a low, growly noise and I felt my stomach turn nicely. "*Oh*," I heard myself say. The room was thick with steam, my wet T-shirt sticking to me, wanting to be peeled off. I ran my hand over his muscular hip jutting from his pants and white briefs, thinking of that line in *Fear of Flying*, where zippers "fell away like rose petals, underwear blew off in one breath like dandelion fluff." I was about to have a zipless fuck!

But when I reached for his belt buckle, Keanu took my wrist, stopping me.

"I, ah, don't think I want to."

I broke out with a quick, shocked laugh. "Sorry!"

"No, don't be," said Keanu, releasing my wrist. We were still stuck together, breathing hard. I pressed my face, red from the kiss and now embarrassment, into his chest. No zipless fuck for me.

Part of me felt a little relieved. Would I have known what to do if my underwear *had* blown off like dandelion fluff? Maybe I wasn't ready to see Keanu naked and go further, though I knew I would have if he hadn't stopped me. I would have kept on steamrolling over that little voice inside that knew what was best for me, like I had with Crew Sinclair and would again and again and again.

"Let me, ah, get you a dry shirt," Keanu said.

Damn. Even the way he'd rejected me was charming.

It was only a little awkward on set the next day. Without saying anything, Keanu let me know he didn't blame me for trying.

Six months later, the two of us sat shoulder to shoulder at the *River's Edge* premiere. Still hopeful, against all odds, I willed Keanu to take my hand as the lights dimmed. No go, but soon I was so swept up in our movie, I forgot what I was missing.

I couldn't believe how good it was: the stunning cinematography by Frederick Elmes; the borderline-comical thrash metal soundtrack and eerie score by Jürgen Knieper; the earthy, timeless locations and sets; the totally committed performances . . . Every one of Tim Hunter's choices, every detail, was masterful. At least to us cast members in the first three rows. Halfway through the film, when I finally returned from outer space and noticed my surroundings, I realized most of the audience seemed shocked, even offended. They weren't laughing at the film's dark humor, and there was no shortage of headshaking during Crispin's most outlandish scenes.

This would be in keeping with the film's wider reception: Audiences either loved it or hated it. But no one could say *River's Edge* didn't make a splash. Tim's indie film, made for $1.7 million, would go on to be nominated for the Grand Jury Prize at Sundance and distributed by Island Pictures. It would win Best Feature at the Independent Spirit Awards and gross $4.6 million at the box office. Roger Ebert would call the movie "an exercise in despair" and "the best analytical film about a crime since *The Onion Field* and *In Cold Blood*."

Meanwhile, if I could have stayed in my red velvet seat and watched *River's Edge* on a loop till sunrise, I would have. Because the minute I left the theater, that would be it: curtains on my magical life in the movies. I'd be a one-hit wonder, back to zero at Hollywood High. The very thought of going back to school was almost too tragic to bear.

So it was bittersweet when the final credits rolled and I saw my name in five-foot letters: IONE SKYE LEITCH.

I'd been thinking of using my middle name and dropping "Leitch" because it sounded prettier, but Tim had talked me out of it. "Ione Skye is lovely," he'd said with his uncomfortable, lopsided smile, "but people know your father, so I think you should keep Leitch." I understood what Tim was saying, though I felt no love for my father's name. "Leitch" was merely a paternal inheritance. But "Skye," the middle name my parents had chosen together, was different. It stood for the brief period of hope when I was conceived—a love child of fantasy and imagination. It was almost a spiritual title.

The house lights, inevitably, rose and I wandered in a daze to the lobby, where Keanu was swarmed by industry people, and the rest of the cast—too young to drink and too overwhelmed to schmooze the grown-ups—stood in a circle, saying sober goodbyes and promising to stay friends forever. As I hugged Roxana, a hand touched my shoulder. I turned to face a man in a suit.

"Do you have representation?" he asked.

I shook my head, and the man gave me his card, which said *something, something,* TALENT AGENT.

"Let's be in touch," said the agent.

From that night forward, I would be Ione Skye.

7

The Breadwinner

1987

"Wake up, pussycat." Mom tickled my nose. "You're missing all this nice food. There's coq au vin!"

I turned over, burrowing under my airplane blanket. The food did smell good, but nothing was better than napping high in the sky. Mom and I were on a (first-class!) flight to Paris, where I was to play Pauline Bonaparte, Napoleon's famously bratty sister, in *Napoleon and Josephine*, an ABC miniseries.

Only nine months had passed since the *River's Edge* premiere—nine magical, heady months in which I'd officially dropped out of high school, hired an agent and a manager, survived a flurry of meetings and auditions, and made two more movies. I'd briefly enrolled in a ho-hum school for delinquents and working actors, but I never had time to go and they kicked me out.

The first movie I'd made after *River's Edge* was *A Night in the Life of Jimmy Reardon*, a teen dramedy filmed in Chicago. I had the time of my life on that one. We shot in beautiful old houses in Evanston, Illinois, and stayed in a Chicago hotel right on the water. My old crush River Phoenix starred as Jimmy, a dreamy Casanova from the wrong side of the tracks. I played a fickle rich girl who falls for Jimmy while dating a nice guy played by a very cute young actor named Matthew Perry.

It was Matthew's first film and my second. He was bouncing off the walls with nervous energy the night before our first shoot, and I assumed the role of seasoned mentor, pulling a pep talk out of my hat: "Once you get the clothes on and get on that set, you'll feel the part and know what to do," I said, thinking of the comfort my oversized fisherman's sweater had brought me on *River's Edge*.

Matthew came to my hotel room after his first scene. "You were right!" he said. "Once I put on my clothes, I knew what to do!"

River was the real pro. I sensed he felt uncomfortable playing a heartthrob, but he couldn't help being one. He definitely kissed like one. We got so swept up in our kissing scene we didn't hear the director's "Cut!" the first five times he yelled it. River was still dating Martha Plimpton, so we never kissed off camera, as much as I'd have liked to.

Though River was just sixteen like me, he seemed older and wiser. He had a suite at the hotel where he could cook his vegan food and record his music while the rest of us teen actors ran in and out of one another's rooms, spent our per diems on clothes we didn't need, and gorged ourselves at grown-up Italian restaurants. We'd often see River sitting alone in the cold on the hotel fire escape, smoking and reading. Sometimes I'd ask if I could join him, and we'd sit and talk, our words pluming in the freezing air. He was mostly self-educated and always reading books. River was especially passionate about animal rights and the environment. This made a real impression on me. I left Chicago with a copy of *Diet for a New America* and became a vegan, if only for a year.

Right after *Jimmy Reardon*, I'd filmed *Stranded*, a sci-fi thriller. Spaceships and aliens weren't really my thing, but the money was good, and someone had to pay Mom's shoebox full of bills. Dono was acting, too, but he hadn't had a big payday yet, and I was making enough that it seemed right to help Mom out. I was kind of proud of my new status as the family breadwinner, but also confused. Did all teenage actors pay their family's rent?

Stranded had also been an opportunity to work with the great Maureen O'Sullivan, a Hollywood star from the Golden Age whom I remembered from and especially adored in *The Thin Man, Anna Karenina, Pride and Prejudice,* and the old black-and-white Tarzan movies. One day, as we sat side by side in the makeup trailer, Maureen saw me frowning at a spot of rosacea on my cheek. "You know, dear," she said, "physical beauty can only be spoiled by lines of discontent. If you live generously without concentrating on yourself, you'll always be lovely." Sensing this was more than just beauty advice, I made a point to remember it.

Maureen played my grandmother. We lived alone on a dusty farm that was supposedly somewhere in the Midwest but was really northeast of LA, in Altadena. In the story, some aliens crash-landed in our field and took us prisoner. One of them was played by this short, wiry, sexy guy named Flea, whose funny name perfectly suited his jumpy energy and bebopping intonation. He was a musician-slash-actor, the bassist in a band called the Red Hot Chili Peppers. (Hardly anyone, myself included, had heard of them yet.) For the movie, he wore cavernous cauliflower ears and a ripply bald cap fringed with stringy hair. Remarkably, his charisma penetrated all of that. This guy's magnetic field was as strong as Jupiter's.

Most of *Stranded* took place at night, so we shot from five p.m. to five a.m., then went home to bed. I loved the upside-down schedule. Mom covered my bedroom windows with black fabric to help me sleep and woke me at two or three p.m. with tea and toast. One early dawn after wrap, I decided not to head straight home. I quickly changed and washed my face, then walked up and down the dirt road

outside Flea's trailer, my old Keanu-stalking trick. Eventually, Flea
came outside, wearing Lakers sweatpants, a Butthole Surfers T-shirt,
and his alien face.

"Hey, hot tomato," he said.

"Hey," I said, kicking the orange dirt with my orange-stained Converse. *He just called me hot!* "Is your makeup hard to get off?"

"It takes a thousand hours!" he said.

"Can I watch?"

Hovering near his makeup chair, I got to see the special effects
makeup artist reveal the real Flea bit by bit: short punk hair, periwinkle
eyes, gap-toothed grin . . . The lady was still swiping his face with toner
when he sprang to his feet. "Ready, tomato?"

"Ready!" I said. Ready for what? I didn't care.

And that was the beginning of our friendship situation.

The first time we kissed, we were parked in Flea's Plymouth Valiant
at the Hollywood Forever Cemetery, Sly and the Family Stone's "If You
Want Me to Stay"—how had I never heard *that* before?—throbbing
from his shitty speakers and all through our connected bodies. Kissing Flea was like kissing pure energy. Now it was all I wanted to do.

But Flea was still hung up on Loesha, his on-again-off-again girlfriend in British Columbia. "We're on a break," he explained forlornly.
I'd seen pictures of Loesha, then wished I hadn't. She wasn't just tall,
blond, and beautiful but a model, and totally punk. Perfect for him.
They weren't *technically* together, I told myself, rationalizing my pursuit. I loved riding home from set with Flea, our craft services bagels on
our laps and the sun rising over the freeway. On a good day, he'd take
me to his charmingly dingy Los Feliz apartment, where we'd analyze
our mutual favorite books (*Jane Eyre* and John Fantes's *Ask the Dust*)
or play records and fool around (if I got my way). He became my musical mentor, introducing me to Wynton Marsalis, Bootsy Collins, the
Germs, Defunkt—stuff they never played on KROQ.

"Listen up, tomato," he'd say, dropping Gang of Four's jittery *Entertainment!* on the turntable, "this one's incredibly fucking important." Next, he'd be headbanging to a "dynamite" Jimi Hendrix guitar riff. Once, he played me the Chili Peppers' second and newest album, *Freaky Styley*. It was rough and funky and kind of a mess in a great way, as if the band was searching for itself in the chaos. There seemed to be plenty of chaos. Two of the Chili Peppers, Hillel Slovak and Anthony Kiedis, were heroin addicts. Flea was always worried about them, afraid they'd OD. I thought it must be awful, loving a drug addict.

Flea was twenty-four to my sixteen, and I think our age difference bothered him. I couldn't figure out why guys made such a big deal about my age. To my mind, it was perfectly normal for the man to be older, sometimes by a lot. At least according to the movies.

One of my absolute favorite movies was Woody Allen's *Manhattan*. I was eight when it came out in theaters and twelve the first time I saw it, on VHS, enraptured by the crisp black-and-white skylines and romantic banter between forty-two-year-old Woody, playing a version of himself, and sixteen-year-old Mariel Hemingway, playing his girlfriend, Tracy. *Manhattan* was on regular rotation at Wilton Place, but I don't remember any grown-up pointing out how fucked-up its love story was. Like Woody's friends in the movie, I accepted the May-September relationship because Tracy was so gung-ho about being with him—and also worldly beyond her years, like I thought I was.

I dreamed of starring in a Woody Allen movie. This was, admittedly, the single biggest reason why I took the part in *Stranded* over some potentially better offers. The social climber in me was hoping Maureen O'Sullivan would introduce me to Woody, who was married to her daughter, Mia Farrow.

To be Woody's next Mariel, I'd probably have to kiss him, but I glossed over that. I suppose through his art, he'd already groomed me for the part.

Stranded wrapped in just thirty days—not enough time to meet Woody, though I wasn't throwing in the towel on that dream. I'd get my audience with him one day.

At Charles de Gaulle Airport in Paris, Mom and I were met by an elegant man who showed us to his black Mercedes. It was almost comical how French he was. "*Mesdemoiselles,*" he said with a wink to Mom, "my name is Bernard. I am at your service for your stay." I widened my eyes at Mom. This was some step up from *Stranded*. Bernard drove us into the city, once around the Arc de Triomphe for fun, then to La Trémoille hotel. Our double room had Juliet balconies and flowers in crystal vases and walls of an icy violet blue. Paris truly was the dreamiest city. I was already pining for Flea, hoping the miles between us would make his heart grow fonder.

In the morning, I rose before Mom and quietly slipped from the room, leaving a note on the bedside table: *Went to my costume fitting. Thought you'd want to sleep in. X, Ione.* If it were up to me, I'd have come to Paris on my own, but sadly the network wouldn't allow it.

Bernard drove me to the outskirts of the city, turning down a wide gravel drive lined with statues and tall linden trees. At the end, ensconcing a grand gravel courtyard, was a breathtaking castle, the Château de Nandy.

In the makeup and costume department, I'd stand for the next five hours being fitted for curly wigs and Empire-waist dresses. The French costume designer and her assistants were all business, turning my body this way and that as they cinched and tucked and pinned me into creamy silk and Dhaka muslin. By the time they were finished, I was starving and dizzy and cold as marble. My Empire dress, with its straight lines and short puffed sleeves, was lovely, but not the voluptuous hourglass shape I'd imagined. Sadly, *Napoleon and Josephine* took place after the fall of Versailles: Glamour was out; modesty was in.

Three weeks into filming I still hadn't spoken to Jacqueline Bisset, who played Josephine, Napoleon's wife. It felt like a lifetime ago that Johnny Rozsa and I had gawked at Jacqueline from the balcony at that party in the Hills. She was even more gorgeous than I remembered and in almost every scene, or else in passionate conversation with Armand Assante (Napoleon) or Anthony Perkins (the French statesman Talleyrand). Twice, to my annoyance, I'd seen Jacqueline chatting and laughing with Mom, who'd already charmed the entire cast and crew with her beauty and nonchalance. Jacqueline was Mom's age, but I had a feeling our similarities would transcend our age gap. I was sure that once we spoke, Jacqueline would sense a kindred spirit and want to get to know me better.

At last, the day came for our first scene together. As the crew prepared the ballroom set, and actors and extras milled about in ball gowns and breeches with silk stockings, I spotted Jacqueline in the wings, looking over the script. Swiping my teeth for errant lipstick, I went to break the ice.

"*Bonjour*, Jacqueline," I said, using the French pronunciation of her name—not *Jac-uh-lynn*, but *Juc-clean*, as Bernard had told me.

Jacqueline looked up from the script, her gray-blue eyes set off by pearl drop earrings, a sparkling tiara, and ruched blue satin. "Hello," she said, glancing at my chest. After weeks of eating brioche, croque monsieurs, and everything smothered in béarnaise and velouté sauce, I was splitting my bustier stitches and spilling out of my once-modest neckline.

"Hi, I'm Ione. I play Pauline. We have this scene together," I said, tucking in a boob.

"Yes, I know," she said, looking down at the pages again.

"Since we're waiting, would you want to run lines?"

I instantly regretted the question. Jacqueline said nothing, but her expressionless expression spoke volumes. She had no interest in running lines with me. That would be like Martina Navratilova warming up with the ball girl. What had I been thinking? Sometimes I worried that quitting school at sixteen had stunted my brain.

Half the job of being an actor is waiting around, and I mostly passed the hours wandering the grounds of the château or looking for an ideal reading spot. Flea had given me a copy of *Siddhartha*, which he said would blow my mind. I was hungry for wisdom of any kind, but the story of young Buddha's path to enlightenment was taking a while to get into.

With Flea an ocean away and Jacqueline off the table, I longed for someone else to learn from. Jane Lapotaire, who played my mother on the show, was the perfect candidate for my worship. Jane was an acclaimed British actress who'd starred in dozens of classic films, playing everyone from Cleopatra to Lady Macbeth to Marie Curie to Edith Piaf. She was in her early forties and had a regal air about her, as if centuries of female wisdom had settled into her bones. I knew I could learn a lot from Jane but was afraid to draw attention to my inexperience, so I'd never asked for her help.

The truth was, I needed help. I'd had some strong moments in *Napoleon and Josephine*, but I was inconsistent. I'd never been able to channel Pauline's anger the way I had in my single audition for the part, when I'd ranted and raved and paced up and down a corporate conference room full of bigwig TV executives. *That* was the feeling I needed to get back to fully capture the depth of my character.

One evening, after delivering a somewhat milquetoasty performance, I swallowed my pride and asked Jane: "Do you ever come home from work and think you could have done better?"

While Jane did not answer the question directly, she seemed to know what I was getting at. "Good acting is about truth," she said, "and empathy. Think about Pauline's love for her son. Can you connect with that?"

"Pauline had a *son*?" I was dumbfounded.

"Why, yes," said Jane. "The real Pauline did. I assumed you knew."

It had never occurred to me to research the *real* Pauline's backstory. Had I done my homework, I would have known about the frail, vulnerable son who didn't exist in our script. It had fallen on Pauline to shield the boy from her ruthless husband, like it had fallen on me to shield Dono from Carl in the Connecticut years.

From then on, I wouldn't play Pauline as a volatile brat. Instead, I'd play her as a protector. It made all the difference.

One night, while Mom was out to dinner with some of the actors from the show, I called Flea from the hotel room.

It took a few tries, but around midnight, Flea finally picked up, sounding breathless.

"Yo!"

"Hi," I said, melting into my pillows. "It's me." Closing my eyes, I pictured us on two sides of a split screen, à la Doris Day and Rock Hudson in *Pillow Talk*. I had the Eiffel Tower in my window, Flea had the Hollywood sign in his.

"Hey . . . you, what's up?" Flea said with the hollow cheeriness of someone trying to place a name or a voice.

"It's Ione," I said.

"Oh, *hey*," he said, this time with real warmth. I heard someone humming in the background, cupboards slamming. "I'm making spaghetti with garlic and olive oil with Hillel. Wanna come by?"

"I'm in Paris." *He doesn't remember. How could he not remember?*

"Oh, snap, right! I thought you were back. How is it? *Hey, Hillel, it's Ione, the one I told you about!*"

A kaleidoscope opened inside me. Hillel was in the band. If a boy told his bandmate about a girl, it had to mean something, didn't it? For about five seconds, I enjoyed the illusion that Flea really did like me the way I liked him. I might have enjoyed it a little longer if I'd played it cool, but of course I had to ask . . .

"What did you tell Hillel about me?"

"Oh, I said you're the girl Anthony's been asking about. *Didn't I say that, Slim?*"

"Yup," said Hillel in the background.

"Anthony from the band?" I said.

"Yeah," said Flea. "He wants to meet you when he's out of rehab."

I wrapped the phone line around my fingers, pulling it painfully tight.

"Sure," I said. "Why not."

Mom had been wanting to visit Jim Morrison's grave since we got to Paris. A million years ago, she and Jim had a summer romance, full of sixties activities like poetry readings and riding bumper cars on acid. Once, they had a big fight and she kicked him out of the little apartment they were sharing, only to find him curled up on the doormat in the morning. Soon after that, she met my dad and left Jim, who wrote "Summer's Almost Gone" about their breakup.

I wasn't in the mood to go sightseeing at a graveyard the morning after Flea unknowingly trampled my heart. But it was our last weekend, and I'd promised Mom I'd go, so I dragged myself out of bed just three hours after falling asleep.

We rode the metro to the twentieth arrondissement, then trudged up boulevard de Ménilmontant, through massive iron gates, and into the shaded grounds of the largest cemetery in Paris, Père Lachaise. I trailed behind, hardly noticing the Gothic skulls and naked nymphs that on any other day would've captivated me.

After a few wrong turns, we came to Jim's graffiti-covered bust, atop a simple slab engraved with the words JIM MORRISON 1943–1971. Someone had painted his hair green and his nose had been lopped off. The ground around the grave was littered with cigarette butts, rotting bouquets, and chewing gum, but Mom didn't seem to notice. Gripping the neck of her blouse, she slowly (melodramatically, I thought, rolling my eyes) crumpled to the edge of Jim's grave. She put her head in her hands, her shoulders shaking.

Was Mom crying? Dono was not going to believe this. Enid never got emotional. The only time we'd seen her shed a single tear was the summer before when our dog Smoke died. And now she was losing it over someone she'd dumped twenty years ago? I didn't buy it.

"I really loved him, you know," Mom said, looking up at me. There was something different in her eyes. Not just tears, but the flash of a wild, unguarded woman I'd never met. The one she might have been, before Donovan, Dono, and me.

I sat down beside her and took her hand. Was young, carefree Enid still alive in Mom somewhere? Maybe so, and Mom kept her hidden, like I hid my feral Topanga girl, so she wouldn't get hurt. I pictured our innocent former selves locked up inside us and felt sad, but closer to Mom than I had in a long while.

8

Famous Fathers
1987

Mama, I'm jealous
you had my father,
the phantom, the bottle lost at sea.
—From my journal

What serendipity that Karis and her mom, Marsha, had moved to St. John's Wood, the North West London district where I was born. I'd come straight from Paris to visit Karis on her break from Bedales boarding school in Hampshire. The neighborhood was even prettier than it looked on the cover of the Beatles' *Abbey Road*, with redbrick row houses and canopies of ash trees dripping rain.

I wondered if my father still had a flat nearby. If I passed him on the sidewalk, he probably wouldn't know who I was. Maybe I'd just keep walking. *River's Edge* was the only film of mine released so far, and it hadn't come to England yet. If I was going to meet my dad on a sidewalk, I'd rather be famous first. I wanted to see admiration in his eyes, or at the very least recognition.

London felt damp and chilly to my California bones, but Marsha and Karis's little flat was cozy, with overstuffed armchairs, book-lined walls, and cups of steaming tea. Marsha was a writer now. Recently, at forty, she'd published her first book, a memoir called *Real Life*. The cover image was a black-and-white glamour shot of Marsha—her long, natural hair filling the frame, lips parted, and gold earrings throwing the light. MARSHA HUNT ran across the image in bold red *Flashdance*-y letters, even bigger than the title.

Whenever Karis wasn't looking, I snuck *Real Life* from the bookshelf and scanned through it. Marsha had not held back on how bumpy life had been when Karis was little. Like me, Karis was born in London. Like Mom, Marsha went through the birth alone. Mick sent red roses and stopped by with a bottle of champagne but otherwise stayed away. It was news to me that later on in the seventies, when I first met Karis, Marsha's paternity suit against Mick Jagger was all over the papers. Had Karis read the articles? I knew she'd read *Real Life*, but I didn't push the famous-dads topic with her or ask the questions I still, after all these years, wanted to ask: *How did you forgive Mick? Is your life better now that he's in it?* I was proud of my restraint, as Karis was the only person I knew who'd been in my exact shoes but wasn't anymore.

Mick and Jerry Hall lived in Kensington, and Karis had her own key to their glossy white town house.

"Hello!" she called, letting us in. "Dad? Jerry?"

We'd been invited to celebrate Mick's birthday, but the dinner was a few hours away, and the house was quiet, just a muffled dance beat coming from upstairs.

"Let's go upstairs and see Jade," said Karis. Mick and Jerry had installed an elevator. I thought that was so fancy and was dying to try it, but Karis pulled me up the stairs.

Jade Jagger was Mick's daughter with his ex-wife, the fashion icon and human rights activist Bianca Jagger. Jade was born less than a year after Karis, but she'd led a very different life, always under Mick's care—

if only from a distance much of the time. Jade had gone to Spence in New York, but Mick wanted her closer to him, so she'd recently moved to St. Mary's, a boarding school outside London.

Jade opened her bedroom door in a black silk robe and a jewel-studded collar. She and Karis did the French double cheek kiss that posh English kids did naturally and I was never sure if I should do. Then Karis made the introductions.

"Lovely to meet you," Jade said, eyeing me.

"You too," I lied, eyeing her back. It was not lovely to meet Jade; it was stressful. But also thrilling, in the bone-chilling way meeting Jacqueline Bisset had been. Jade was stunning, with Bianca's almond skin and cascading sable hair, and Mick's pout.

Within seconds, the sisters were sprawled across Jade's bed— *a mattress on the floor, how edgy*—discussing their summer plans. Jade would spend her break at La Fourchette, Mick's château in the Loire Valley, and Karis would visit there in August. I perched on a windowsill, noting Jade's Scully & Scully desk and Indian-print curtains. Like the rest of the house, her room was chic and tousled— both urban and aristocratic. The epitome of relaxed elegance. Not that I felt relaxed.

Is Karis closer to her sister than to me? When did that happen?

Jade reclined on her velvet throw pillows, looking very Sophia Loren circa 1960. "What are you wearing tonight, Ione?" she asked.

I looked down at my baggy Esprit jeans and white T-shirt. I hadn't known we'd see Mick when I packed. "This?" I said.

Jade had no comment.

"Maybe she could borrow something from you?" said Karis.

"That's all right, I'm fine," I said. I wasn't feeling very fine at all but was learning quickly that here in England, one did not necessarily say what one felt.

Jade waved at her closet. "Oh go on, pick one."

Was I meant to accept the offer or decline? Deciding on the former, I riffled through the hangers, stopping at a whispery aubergine Ghost slip dress. Holding it up, I could already see it would look good on me.

"Not that one," said Jade.

Her clipped comment caught me off guard but then made me think, *Wow, maybe I do like her.* She'd spoken her mind, which I respected. But even more, I liked her defensiveness. It meant there was something to defend. Jade had a wounded quality about her, and boy did I want to protect anyone who telegraphed that. I hastily returned the sublime slip dress and picked the plainest thing I could find, a black cotton T-shirt dress that sort of worked with my Converse low-tops.

It was an intimate birthday gathering, just family, so I felt all the more honored to be included. A set table glimmered and the casually dressed butler poured champagne as we came downstairs. Mick was slender and catlike in violet slacks, a tailored dress shirt, and white saddle shoes. As he bounded over to greet us, I felt a ripple of nausea. Mick was known to make women lose their composure, not that I was worried I'd do anything ridiculous. I just wanted to make an impression. In the moment Mick took my hands and welcomed me, his vibe was startling and pure. But just as quickly, his attention was gone—alighting on someone else.

At dinner, I sat next to Mick's elfin-eared father, Basil "Joe" Jagger, a retired assistant schoolmaster and gym coach who said he was now tasked with keeping Mick in "tip-top shape." Mick and Jerry sat at the end of the table with their three-year-old daughter, Elizabeth, and her nanny. The youngest Jagger baby, James, was upstairs, asleep in his crib.

I didn't get to connect with Jerry at dinner, though I instinctively loved her for having helped bring Mick and Karis together years ago. Why hadn't my stepmother done the same thing? On top of being warm and generous, Jerry was the most glam mom I'd ever met—tall and slinky with great posture, and that iconic blond mane always swooped over one shoulder. She had a surprisingly goofy grin and a throaty drawl that was part rodeo queen, part royal queen. "Being Texan and all, I want ten kids," she said, diamonds flashing as she fed Elizabeth an apple slice. "Right, Mick?"

"Mind the pips now, Elizabeth," said Mick, instead of answering. (I loved how the English called seeds "pips.")

After dinner Karis, Jade, and I chatted in Mick and Jerry's bedroom while the grown-ups lounged in the living room a few stories below. I noticed a little plastic box beside their bed. It was a white noise machine. Did Mick need help sleeping? I'd always assumed the rich and famous had no cares in the world.

The next evening, we went to a movie in Mick's blue Ferrari, chauffeured by his beautiful driver-bodyguard, who I gathered was African French. The soft-spoken bodyguard often drove Karis to and from Mick's, and she clearly adored him.

It was fun to witness Mick doing normal-people things like buying popcorn and even drinking from a water fountain. He had possibly the world's most recognizable face, which he'd made no attempt to disguise, but somehow no one looked twice at him in the cinema lobby. When I asked how that was possible, Karis explained that English people were more laissez-faire about celebrities than were Americans.

As we crept into the packed theater for *Aliens*, Jade and Karis went first up the aisle, followed by me, then Mick, then the bodyguard. *Mick's going to sit next to me.* There were still ten minutes before the show. What would we talk about? It wasn't so hard to capture a powerful man's attention; as I'd learned from auditioning, all it took was a compliment (ideally sincere). I was preparing myself to be as fawning-but-chill as possible when Mick touched my shoulder.

"Would you mind popping ahead of Jade?" he asked, smiling down at me. "I'd like to sit next to my daughters."

I nodded, blushing. I was happy for Karis. I was.

A dreadful surprise awaited me back in LA. Usually, Mom's style was to shield my brother and me from bad news. But this time, she couldn't help herself. I'd been home all of ten minutes when Mom showed me the letter:

———— Legal Partners

PO Box ————
Abingdon
Oxfordshire

July 19, 1987

Enid Karl
———— N. Wilton Place
Los Angeles, CA
90068

Dear Enid,

Re: Paternity Test

I am writing on behalf of my client Donovan Leitch, who kindly requests that a paternity test be carried out to establish whether Ione Leitch is his genetic daughter. My client is firmly of the view that confirming Ione's paternity would be in the best interests of all parties.

My client is committed to reimbursing you for the cost of the blood test, which can be obtained through any of the conveniently located Los Angeles doctors listed on the attached page. Receipt for services can be sent to me.

My client hopes that this matter can be resolved amicably and looks forward to hearing from you shortly with your consent for a paternity test, so that we can get matters underway.

Yours sincerely,

———

Attorney, ——— Legal Partners

I stared at Mom, stunned. "Who *else's* would I be?"

She sighed. "He thinks it was this guy Nick who used to drive us sometimes."

Oh, God. Was a different stranger my dad now? What the fuck.

"Oh, Ione, don't look at me like that," Mom said. "I was so gaga for your father, I couldn't even look at anyone else. Take the test. We'll show him."

I looked at the letter in my hands. *Confirming Ione's paternity would be in the best interests of all parties.* Would it? Was this why Donovan had never wanted to meet me, had always insisted on calling me "the girl"? Had he *never* believed I was his?

I folded the letter and put it back in the envelope. I wished Mom had never shown it to me. She could have protected me, let me go on like before. But she didn't, and I knew why. She was being proud; she wanted me to take the test for her sake, not mine.

"Does Dono know?" I asked. I needed my brother. Needed him to tell me it was stupid and of course he was still my brother, not my *half* brother, and I should forget the whole thing.

Mom shook her head. "I've hardly seen him."

"Is he at the Zappas'?" I asked, plucking my car key from the hook by the door.

Mom nodded. "But, pussycat, you just got home!"

That was the thing: Lately, home was at the Zappas'.

For the past year, as Mom and Billy played out the final, unhappy scenes of their marriage, I'd spent all my non-working time with the Zappa family—Frank, Gail, Moon, Dweezil, Ahmet, Diva, and cousin Lala. It wasn't perfect there, but it was still a great escape from the heavy energy at Wilton Place. Dono had introduced me to them, of course. He'd met Moon at Flip of Hollywood, the coolest thrift store on Melrose. Dono worked at Flip, and Moon, still famous for her 1982 hit song, "Valley Girl," shopped there for Chinese slippers and poodle skirts. Dono and Moon had gone on a few dates, which segued into an all-consuming friendship.

Mom and I had dropped my brother at Moon's a few times before I was invited in. I'd burn with envy, watching him slip through a small iron gate in their hedge-lined wall. I had no idea what went on inside the Oz-like world my brother disappeared into. I just knew it was fun.

I got lonely when I wasn't working. All my old friends were busy with school, and my new actor friends were flaky, or working and hard to find. So you can imagine my reaction when the phone at Wilton Place rang with a summons: "I'm at Moon and Dweezil's," Dono said on the line. "Moon says to come over and hang."

Second to Sarah Pillsbury's faint-inducing announcement that I'd gotten *River's Edge*, it was the best phone call I'd ever received. You had to *be* someone to get that call. Moon and her brother Dweezil were very deliberate about who they invited over. When a young actor or musician appeared on their radar, they'd have their agent call the star's agent and ask if they wanted to come over. That's how young people in "the industry" found one another in the days before cell phones and DMs. In my case, of course, Dono had made the call. With him as a brother, I sometimes wondered why I needed an agent at all.

Like Charles Ryder falling under the spell of the Marchmains in *Brideshead Revisited*, I'd fallen in love with the Zappas, one by one.

Moon, the eldest at nineteen, was intense and organized, with a devastating wit. She was the mini-mom under the formidable mega-mom, Gail. When Moon wasn't stirring pots on the stove or (eternally) unloading the dishwasher, she was directing the rest of us in whatever art project, recording session, or performance-art piece she and Dweezil had come up with for that day. I was essentially her lady-in-waiting (a role I understood, after April) and lived for her approval. One time Moon called me funny, and I felt an inner swagger from then on. Because I was a shy person, my sense of humor often got lost in the noise, but nothing escaped Moon's radar.

Dweezil, seventeen, was a hunky, soft-spoken MTV VJ and actor-musician, known for his cameos in *Pretty in Pink* (with then-girlfriend Molly Ringwald) and *The Running Man* ("Don't touch that dial!"). He was the golden boy of the family, usually with a beautiful actress on his arm. I wrote his name over and over in my journal—the *D* luscious and decadent—and was actively trying to become the next actress on his arm.

Ahmet, the wild, grubby thirteen-year-old, reminded us of Max from *Where the Wild Things Are*. The poor kid had been called "Ahmet Vomit" so often he'd briefly changed his name to Rick. "But then they called him *Rick*," Moon would deadpan, shuddering, "so he changed it back again."

Diva, eight, my "little sister," refused to brush her hair and believed in magic.

Lala, the enchanting blond cousin, had a tragic Marilyn Monroe quality about her. She'd lived at the Zappas' since surviving a series of small accidents at her home in Santa Barbara.

But Gail, the powerful matriarch in strapless muumuus, didn't believe in accidents. She believed Lala's clumsiness was a cry for help—Gail's help, specifically. No one argued with Gail. While she was always smiling, there was pain and fierceness in her wide-set eyes. We were all on our toes under her stern, benevolent rule.

And then there was Frank, the elusive center of the Zappa universe. Like his kids, I was always on the lookout for Frank, though sightings were rare. He was a nocturnal creature: sleeping all day; composing and recording in his home studio, the "Utility Muffin Research Kitchen," all night. I didn't always understand Frank's music, but I got his genius and thought he was just so elegant and hot. Once, at some vampiric hour, he'd screened his absurdist "non-movie," *Uncle Meat*, for us. The other kids had watched intently, but I was the only one who laughed out loud, which made Frank turn to me, smiling under his mustache, and say, "*You* get it."

Twenty minutes after my horrible "welcome home" to Wilton Place, I was driving away again—pedal to the metal in the black 1975 BMW I'd recently bought with my acting money. On the passenger seat, under a rattling box of cassette tapes, was the lawyer's letter to show Dono.

Why had Donovan sent it? Why now? We didn't need his money anymore if that's what this was about. I'd turn eighteen in a year, so he only had a few more child support payments to make anyway. What was it to him?

I wound my way up Mulholland, then Woodrow Wilson, finally pulling up outside the Zappas' compound. The road was empty, but the canyon was rippling and alive. I sat on my hood and lit a shoebox joint, checking over my shoulder. I didn't smoke often—yet—partly because you couldn't at the Zappas'. It was no secret that Frank was staunchly against drugs of any sort, unless you counted the Winstons he chain-smoked. Anything stronger dulled the intellect and killed ambition, he believed. And because Frank was no ordinary father but something more like a cult leader to his kids, they were proud straight arrows too. Me, I was whoever they wanted me to be. Inside the compound, at least.

That's how it worked at the Zappas'. It was their world, and you just lived in it—taking part in their songs, films, and meals and turning on the old razzle-dazzle for the constant stream of new people who'd been invited to join the games. It was best not to come with your own agenda, other than to be as witty and creative as possible so they would keep you around.

I snuffed the joint in my car ashtray, stuffed the letter under the clean underwear in my overnight bag, and went to press the hidden buzzer.

Through the main gate, wrapped in creeping vines, was a spiral stair-case. There was only one way in, and it was up. At the top, I crossed the lonely rooftop tennis court no one ever used, then descended another staircase into the lush heart of the property. Following a twisty path through the grounds, I passed the guest cottages with their porthole windows and doors salvaged from old submarines, a couple of record-ing studios, and the still swimming pool.

It was an unusually cool, gray day. Normally the pool would be filled with young, pretty bodies bobbing in the water. You never knew who you might find there. That was part of the fun. Maybe it was Molly Ringwald on a pool float, pale and lovely as a forties Vargas girl. Molly and Dweezil were no longer together but still friends. Though newly famous, thanks to *Sixteen Candles* and *The Breakfast Club*, Molly was wonderfully un-stuck-up. I found her worldly and proper, in a vaguely old-fashioned way. A strong opinion would be

prefaced with "I suspect . . . ," and a mean ex-boyfriend wasn't an asshole but "not so very mature." Sometimes you'd find Eddie Van Halen
on a chaise longue, grinning around a cigarette. He was in his thirties
but looked twenty, with his new short haircut and tanned six-pack.
Drew Barrymore, another fixture, was twelve and in her *Little Girl
Lost* phase, always telling tall, provocative tales that she made sound
sweet, like a swearing toddler who feels the words but not the meaning
behind them. We were all protective of her.

I let myself into the house, a Tudor Revival mansion that held endless nooks, dens, libraries, studios, bedrooms, turrets, and towers. In
the airy kitchen, heavy metal blasted and Dono, Dweezil, and a few
gorgeous girls I didn't know—models, apparently—stood around a vat
of delicious-smelling soup, helping themselves. I'd been hoping to take
my brother somewhere quiet and ask what he knew about the chauffeur
and my identity, but Dono hardly registered me. One of the models, a
sun-kissed Christie Brinkley type, was yelling about her boobs. "They're
floppy!" she kept insisting. The boys protested. "Yes they are!" she cried.
"Does anyone want to see?" The boys raised their hands. The model,
braless, lifted her top.

"They're not *that* floppy," Dono said.

"Get me a spoon!" cried the model, still holding up her top. "I'll
put it under my boob and if stays put, they're officially floppy."

On any other crummy day, this scene would have breathed life into
me. I loved breasts, of all sizes, including my own. But standing at the
edge of the kitchen, I felt suddenly homesick. That was my brother,
but this wasn't my family. I missed the way it had been with Mom,
Dono, and me in that brief, blissful time between Mom's husbands
and depressions. I missed how we were simply us.

I wandered off to poke around the house, as I often liked to do.

There were two wings: one with living areas and bedrooms, the
other with Frank's office and studios. At the top of a spiral staircase—

Gail was obsessed with spiral staircases and had added so many it was starting to feel like the Winchester Mystery House—I followed the sound of Bulgarian choir music and the smell of cigarette smoke toward Frank's office. We weren't allowed to knock, but on the rare occasion Frank's office door was open, it meant he was open for visitors.

The door, sadly, was closed. I hovered outside, listening to the rise and fall of the choir. Moon once told me she recorded "Valley Girl" with Frank because it was the only way to spend time with him. Was any dad perfect? It was a sliding scale, for sure.

"Ione?" called a woman's voice. "That you?"

It was Gail, in the bedroom wing. She was leaning against the wall outside Diva's room, her bare feet covered in canyon dust and her ashy curls a wild halo. She looked exhausted.

"Diva's bath strike still on?" I said, hugging her. Gail was incredibly huggable for such a scary person.

"Day four," she sighed. Stepping back, she looked me up and down. "So, what's wrong with you?"

Gail was so like Moon—nothing got by her. She saw everything, including Frank's affairs. We all saw those. I was pretty sure his current girlfriend even slept over sometimes. I never heard Gail say a word about that, but she didn't hold back on much else.

"My father doesn't think I'm his," I said, bursting into tears. I rummaged in my tote, pulling out the letter.

Gail snatched it, then thrust it back in disgust. "What a dipshit," she said. "Have you ever seen a picture of him? That downturned mouth?" She put her hands on my shoulders and marched me to a mirror on the wall. "Look at yourself. You're his spitting image."

I peered into the mirror, searching.

"See?" said Gail.

I am, I thought, wiping my eyes.

"All those hippies going to India and singing about love and to-getherness, it's just a look for them," scoffed Gail. "Bunch of phonies."

I nodded, smiling a little. It meant something that Gail was on my side, angry on *my* behalf. Her protectiveness was exactly the medicine I needed.

I would refuse the paternity test. For better or worse, I was Don-ovan's. One day, he'd know it too. I'd show him, but not like this.

9

Love and Scar Tissue

1987–1988

There was me before Anthony, and me after.

The me before him was just a kid despite myself. I was sixteen-going-on-seventeen and throwing a rather epic joint party with my new neighbor Michael Fitzpatrick, who was my exact age and would later start the band Fitz and the Tantrums. We'd strung lights across the road between Michael's house and mine, a boom box on the sidewalk blasted *Licensed to Ill*, and people flowed from house to house, dancing on the lawns. I was in heaven.

On the sadder side, Flea was back with Loesha. She'd moved from Canada to be with him, and I liked her, intimidating as she was. So Flea was for sure off the table romantically, but I still wanted to be near him and part of the cool post-punk scene he'd introduced me to. Anthony Kiedis was in that scene, of course. Anthony, who apparently wanted to meet me.

Only someone with a fairy-tale view of the world would have been open to a setup with Anthony at that particular moment in his life. Especially if they'd heard the stories I'd heard. But I liked the idea of this dangerous, dark prince of a rock 'n' roller. I'd asked Flea to invite him to my party, not really thinking he'd come, fresh out of rehab.

But he did. I felt him before I saw him, a prickly sensation on my bare shoulders as I lay on the lawn with Johnny Rozsa, stargazing. Turning my head, I saw a lone figure on Dono's balcony, looking down at me. Anthony wasn't famous yet, but he was unmistakable from a flyer I'd seen for a Chili Peppers show with the Dead Milkmen. His long, ironing-board-straight hair and fringed suede jacket were odd, but he was muscular and fit. Healthier than I'd expected, for a heroin addict. Ex–heroin addict, I hoped.

I gathered my courage and went to him—weaving and greeting and hugging my way across my crowded living room, up the stairs, through the mini-party in Dono's bedroom, and onto the balcony. Anthony was still there, back turned to me, a lit cigarette burning close to his fingers. There was almost a force field around him, a pulsating energy warning, *Stay away*. Judging by his lack of company, it was working. But everyone needed connection. Everyone craved love. And I knew my love was powerful. If anyone could penetrate this enigma, it was me. I'd crack his spiky shell.

I tapped his shoulder and Anthony whipped around, smirking. I guessed we could skip the introductions.

"Are you having an okay time?" I asked.

"I believe I am now," he said.

"Cool," I said.

"Cool," he said, smirking some more. Was he mocking me?

Fashion sense aside—the fringed jacket was paired with striped board shorts and combat boots—Anthony was beautiful. Not much taller than me, but tall in presence. His warm olive skin and dirty-blond hair went very well together.

We talked for the rest of the night. Well, mostly he talked—in metaphors and non sequiturs, like a brainy beatnik poet, jumping so quickly from thought to thought I soon stopped trying to follow the threads and let the words wash over me—bits and bobs about tigers, music, cosmic equilibrium, and various colors of energy. Anthony was really into energy.

At one point he lifted his hand to the breeze. "Can you feel that, Ione?" he said.

I lifted my hand too. "I feel it," I said.

"That's what makes Hollywood so dynamite," he said. "That desert energy, blowing in. I can really get down with it."

Like me, Anthony had a slight lisp. I liked it on him. And I liked that he thought Hollywood was great and wasn't too jaded to admit it. But it was the thing about the wind that got me. I'd always had a connection with the Santa Anas. They brought up something in me, a wild yearning feeling.

Anthony finally stopped talking and was now staring at me with focused intensity, his eyes tracing my hair, my mouth, my neck, as if memorizing me, for later. I stared back at him. Who did he remind me of? I couldn't place it.

"Well, good night," I said, suddenly aware of my exhaustion. It took serious energy, trying to sync up with this guy.

"I'm going on a little tour tomorrow," he said, buttoning his *Midnight Cowboy* jacket at his chest. "See you when I'm back."

That was not a question, I noted.

Only as he walked away did it hit me who Anthony reminded me of: Carl, my first stepdad.

Prickly, macho, charismatic, controlling Carl.

I'd often wondered if Mom had sensed the trouble she was walking into with Carl. She must have seen the red flags, like I did with Anthony. And yet Mom went willingly. Just as I knew I would.

A few days after my party, Loesha, stunning in a plain white T-shirt, her head newly shaved, stopped by. We were sitting cross-legged on my twin bed, under my *The Harder They Come* poster, drawing and talking about boys. I drew a ponytailed girl, holding a baby. Loesha, who was now engaged to Flea, sketched a wedding dress idea. It was exciting having someone as hard-core as Loesha over, but it felt a little funny, as if we were playacting at being normal teen girls. With Loesha in it, my room looked too sweet and girly.

"You and Anthony would be good together," she said, crosshatching her wedding dress. "Your sweetness would balance out his intensity."

"Maybe," I said. I still wasn't sure about Anthony, though I couldn't shake the deep-down feeling that Something Big would happen with him.

As if she were listening to my thoughts, Loesha's pencil paused, and she smiled, quite roguishly. "I have an idea," she said.

Two hours later, Loesha and I breathlessly boarded a flight to Tucson, headed to that night's Chili Peppers concert at the Tucson Garden. We'd wanted to take my car, but Mom had a rare flickering of strictness and said it was too far a drive, she was putting her foot down. From her haunted expression, I could tell it wasn't just the drive but who was on the other end of it that worried her. Mom thought Anthony was bad news for me. It was written all over her face, but she didn't know how to say it. Billy had finally moved out and divorce papers had been filed, so there was no one to deliver the tough love in our household. Enid only knew how to give us the soft kind.

"Fine," I'd said, calling her bluff. "We won't drive, we'll fly. I have the money."

It was a short flight, just ninety minutes. I was giddy for the first eighty, relishing my autonomy and resourcefulness. I'd never bought my own plane ticket before. I'd felt so aloof and decisive, dialing the airline. *I'd like two seats on your next flight to Tucson, thank you.* I hadn't worried about the cost or imagined where we might stay the night even as I packed a little bag. Only as we came in for a landing and the desert lights flickered on below did the panicky feeling set in. What *was* I walking into?

We missed the show. By the time our taxi pulled up outside the stage at the Tucson Garden, sweaty teenagers were trickling from the exits. Loesha beelined for a back door. The band wasn't expecting us, but it didn't take much in those days for two underage girls to get backstage at a small rock show.

A crew member showed us the dressing room door, and Loesha threw it open . . . then froze. I was behind her and still registering what I was seeing—Flea and Anthony on two ends of a crummy sofa, each straddled by a girl—when Loesha rushed at Flea, fists balled. "Fucking asshole!" she screamed, whipping out of the room. Flea ran after her, while I looked at my feet, mortified. Anthony probably thought I was obsessed with him, flying here like some crazed groupie. He didn't even get off the couch, just sort of maneuvered the girl to the side. Was that a hard-on under his shorts?

There was a brief but eternal interlude while Flea and Loesha passionately argued outside the door and I must have made small talk with Anthony and the girls. Or did I leave the room? Either way, I disappeared.

Now it was two a.m. and I was in Flea's hotel room, listening to Flea and Loesha's pillow talk in the next bed. Flea was speaking in a tender voice I'd never heard before, telling Loesha no, she wasn't fat; telling her how beautiful and amazing she was. I could hear her softly crying, then it stopped. The sheets rustled. I heard kissing. *No, please, no.* I curled into a wheel, covering my head with a pillow.

"Hey." Loesha was beside my bed, touching my shoulder. "Why don't you go to Anthony's room?"

I sat up, hugging my knees and shaking my head. "Uh-uh. He's probably with that girl." Did she think I had no pride?

Loesha shrugged. Her makeup was raccoon-y from all the crying. "You came here to see him. I think you should see him."

I wanted to consider it an act of friendship that Loesha walked me down the hall and knocked for me. Anthony opened the door in shorts and a white muscle shirt silkscreened with Marilyn Monroe's face. The girl from the dressing room glared at me from the bed behind him, fixing the straps of her tank top. Hillel Slovak, whom I'd met before at Flea's, was lying on the other bed reading. I waved and he nodded with a half smile that I took as sympathy. The original Chili Peppers—Flea, Anthony, Hillel, and drummer Jack Irons—were all friends from Fairfax High School, class of 1980. But Hillel was different from the others, romantic and sensitive. I knew he had a heroin problem, just not how bad it was.

"We came to see you," said Loesha, already turning back to our room.

Unable to look Anthony in the eye, I studied Marilyn's face on his T-shirt; she was glancing to the side, as if watching Loesha walk away.

"Hold on," said Anthony, closing the door in my face. A minute later, the door opened and he walked the girl out. At the far end of the hall, they stopped and leaned against the wall, heads bowed and whispering, while I just stood there, snapping the black rubber bracelet on my wrist and wanting to disappear. Again.

Just when I thought I'd implode with mortification, the girl left and Anthony ushered me into the room. Hillel had turned off the lights and I was glad for the darkness. Not that I was ashamed or embarrassed, not anymore. I felt almost dignified entering that dark room. I felt powerful, come to think of it. Anthony had chosen me. I was, as Chrissie Hynde of the Pretenders sang in "Brass in Pocket," the song always in my head:

Special
So special.

It was deep and sweet that night. The Anthony who lay facing me on that hotel bed, hair fanned out on his pillow, was open and curious and almost soft. I could barely see the person I'd met on Dono's balcony. No defensiveness, no beatnik shtick. For hours, we lay there, shedding layers, words flowing into kisses flowing into words. For such a punk he had a hippie's heart. He stroked my face and said I was like an angel and I understood that we were falling under the same spell. Later I'd try Ecstasy and it would feel just like that night. What did we talk about? Everything. I told him about Wilton Place and Enid's poker games and my stepdads and my brother, the Great Connector. Anthony told me about his father, Blackie, lover of drugs and women, and his mother, Peggy, lover of Christmas and blackberry pies. And then, like it was Christmas in August, we shared all the things we loved: the Santa Ana winds, and my grandmother's arms, and perfect pieces of fruit, and George Clinton's rainbow-colored hair, and Marilyn Monroe's arched eyebrows, and the joy of a warm, still ocean, and getting comfortable after being shy and uncomfortable, and how BO on the right person was an aphrodisiac, and—

"*Please*," moaned Hillel as the dawn light filtered in. "Will you please, please be quiet now?"

Anthony and I giggled into our hands like kids at a slumber party. He pulled me closer under the scratchy polyester bedspread, his erection pressing into my thigh. I opened my legs, then closed them.

"I have a condom in my purse," I whispered.

I wasn't on the Pill, and needle users were at high risk for HIV. Even if it meant breaking the spell, I deserved protection and care. I still remembered this because I was still, just barely, on my side—the light side—of the looking glass.

I won't say the "me after Anthony" completely lost her innocence. I would find it again, at least. And we would have our share of sweetness and good times too.

We were instantly full-blown, instantly enmeshed. Being with Anthony meant living on his terms, but I didn't mind. I was between acting jobs and simply folded my world into his. For now, it wasn't such a big world. The Chili Peppers had just released their third studio album, *The Uplift Mofo Party Plan*, to not much of a bang. Anthony was broke and living with the band's manager, Lindy Goetz, in the Valley. I'd pick him up for latkes with applesauce at Canter's Deli, or sometimes we'd just drive around, shouting our life stories over the radio. Anthony was twenty-four but still didn't have a car, so we shared my new Toyota Corolla (I'd sold the old BMW for something more dependable). Anthony drove fast and reckless, and in no time I was driving like a maniac too.

Some nights we'd see a show—Fishbone, Mary's Danish, Thelonious Monster—at the Whisky or the Palace. When the Chili Peppers were the show, I'd get to watch from the sidelines. I didn't understand why Anthony and the guys liked to perform naked, with socks on their penises, but I respected their fearlessness. All the bands were genuinely great. I just wished there were more girls in them, and in the rooms in general.

I didn't see it in such feminist terms yet, but in the late eighties, the entire music industry—not just Anthony's LA post-punk sliver of it—was aggressively, obnoxiously hetero-male. The only famous girl bands then were the Bangles and the Go-Go's, who had to be adorable on top of outrageously talented to get where they did. To be a young, pretty musician's girlfriend was not quite like being a Playboy Bunny, but there were similarities: We were there to make the guys feel good, not to challenge them with our intellect and humor, the way college women surely did at parties. Sometimes I imagined I was a college woman, an anthropology major collecting data on the social interactions of drug addicts. I could never tell who was on what, but I could tell that Anthony's friends liked altered states as much as he did.

Sadly, Anthony's post-rehab sobriety hadn't lasted long. Right away, he'd started disappearing on binges—slow-motion heroin rampages that lasted for three days or so. He'd reappear looking worse than dead—a dead man resurrected, with picked-over skin and hollow eyes that wouldn't meet mine.

The binges terrified me. Each time, I'd imagine him out there on some filthy mattress in the cold and dark, quietly overdosing. The other junkies wouldn't notice till it was too late. Who would save him if I didn't?

And so my Falling for Anthony phase was quickly replaced by my Saving Anthony phase. Sometimes I'd drive all night looking for him, trawling the usual spots over and over: the corner of Sixth and Union, the market where he bought bleach for his needles, the Eat'n High Thai restaurant on Fountain, that apartment on Bonnie Brae where his favorite dealer lived with his grandma... Without Stevie Wonder's *Songs in the Key of Life* to keep me company on those lonely late-night drives, my soul might have extinguished.

One night, I enlisted Anthony's friend Bob Forrest to go looking with me. Bob was the lead singer of Thelonious Monster and a some-time heroin user. I didn't know him well but had felt tenderly toward him since the night we first met, when he told me, "I've learned every Dylan song and now what's left to do? I might as well just die." Bob Forrest wouldn't die; he'd get clean and start his own recovery center. But for now, he was in my backseat, strumming his guitar and point-ing out junkie haunts. Bob looked like a *Chinatown* detective in his trademark trench coat and fedora, but he wasn't acting very hardboiled. "I should get back," he kept saying, sounding nervous.

"But we haven't checked the Jumbo's Clown Room parking lot yet," I'd say, driving on. Or, "I just have a feeling about this underpass."

Finally, Bob leaned over the front seat: "Ione, trust me," he said, weary but firm. "There's nothing we can do."

I thought it was odd that Bob of all people had such thin skin. Only later would I get it: Bob wasn't being cowardly or indifferent to Anthony's plight. He just knew to let Anthony do his three days in whatever down-and-out place he'd chosen to match his down-and-out insides. Because, of course, the only person who can save an addict's life is the addict.

Anthony would have to hit rock bottom to quit drugs, just as I'd have to hit my own rock bottom to quit the feeling I had to take care of Anthony. The need to save him was an addiction in itself. I was hooked.

A couple of months and several disappearances into our relationship, I couldn't take the worry anymore. Maybe, with enough love and care and stability from me, Anthony would find peace and be cured! It was worth a try. Before I could change my mind, I picked up my pink princess phone and called Anthony at Lindy's. "I think you should move in with me at Wilton Place," I announced.

"Interesting," said Anthony. I imagined him weighing his options: to continue sleeping on Lindy's cheap-carpeted floor . . . or move in with me and be cared for, cooked for, and loved.

He arrived that night, a black Adidas duffel on his shoulder, a clean-smelling T-shirt on his back (long-sleeved, to hide the track marks), and his hair freshly washed. That he'd made the effort to pull himself together, if just for one night, touched me. I knew he wanted to make a good impression on Mom.

"So Enid's okay with it?" he said as I led him upstairs.

"Sure," I white-lied. Enid was not cool with this pursuit of mine but hadn't said a definitive no when I asked if Anthony could stay. I think she was trying to keep me close, just as I was trying to keep Anthony close.

In my room, Anthony dropped his bag and fixed his eyes on my new waterbed—a gift from Billy, who still came by sometimes with offerings from various film sets he worked on. "Never used!" he'd promised when Mom raised her eyebrows.

Anthony pressed the mattress; it gurgled and rolled. "Well, I think I can fuck on that," he said. And we did, constantly. Not always safely. I'd gone on the Pill but it made me feel sick, so I'd stopped, and we only sometimes used condoms. I worried Anthony didn't like them, and apparently, I wanted everything to be okay for Anthony more than I wanted it to be okay for me. Anthony didn't trick me. He never said he'd pull out all those times that he didn't. And I let him keep doing it, though I knew how unsafe it was. I was confused about why he came inside me but I didn't speak up. Anthony's sex drive intimidated me. It was massive, as was his sexual ego. If Anthony's sex drive had a soundtrack, it would be *Fun House*, the brittle, muscular Stooges album he'd turned me on to. He liked to brag that he only exercised in bed and onstage, though I saw him doing push-ups all the time. He was obsessed with making me come, and the pressure could be a lot.

When it was over, I'd lie in the candlelight looking at his new back tattoo of Native American–style wings and think, *Is this good? Am I happy? No, I'm not, but is anyone?* I was committed now. I couldn't go back.

Anthony wasn't just intense and competitive about sex. He was like that about everything. He couldn't go to the park with his friends without challenging them to a race or a handstand contest. Later, when Anthony and I adopted our dog, Leva, he'd insist on racing her against the other guys' dogs. I don't remember who won. His competitiveness was funny to me, especially his irritation that Flea had been the first to take me to the coolest make-out spot in LA, the Hollywood Forever Cemetery. "Of course he took you here," he'd say every time we went. "Smooth motherfucker." Flea and Anthony had a deep, strong bond. If they ever got truly cross it was always in the interest of making better music. Flea had even kicked Anthony out of the band the last time his drug use was holding them back. That had led to the recent rehab stint and the recording of *The Uplift Mofo Party Plan*. I admired Flea for putting his foot down, even knowing what Anthony might do. The Chili Peppers were everything to Anthony. Losing them could have been the end for him, but instead, he'd gotten clean for a whole fifty days and come back to work.

But Flea could do what he did because he was ready; he'd already hit his rock bottom with Anthony. I was still falling, still learning.

We spent the Christmas of 1987 in Grand Rapids, Michigan, where Anthony had lived as a kid before he moved to LA to be with his dad. His mom, Peggy, was as wonderful as he'd described; her brown eyes really did shoot love beams at everyone in their sight. Peggy and Anthony's stepdad, Steve, welcomed me with warm hugs and proceeded to show me the quintessential American Christmas of my hippie Jewish dreams. (We had a tree and opened presents at Wilton Place too, but in California it just wasn't the same.) I loved being with Peggy in the kitchen as she prepped for the holidays, filling me in on who was who in the family and friends circle. We made fruit pies and green bean casseroles while Steve watched football and Anthony went out "snowshoeing," but really visiting an old friend he hoped would have drugs. He was distracted by his addiction at times but clearly devoted to Peggy, and he seemed to be in a hopeful place. After five years of struggle, the Chili Peppers were finally moving on from being just a fringe local band to being played on KROQ. Tickets for the upcoming *Uplift Mofo Party Plan* tour were selling out and the record was sidling up the charts. I didn't have to buy Anthony cigarettes anymore and he could afford nice Christmas presents for his family. Peggy got an outdoor Jacuzzi, complete with a big red bow.

For Christmas dinner, I cosplayed the Perfect Midwestern Guest in a purple wool dress with a white eyelet collar. Peggy and Steve were traditional people, pillars in their community, and I wanted them to know I wasn't some young groupie Anthony had picked up four months ago and was just keeping around. I wanted them to love me above all the others. I wanted Peggy to call Anthony after we left and say, *"She's a gem. You're so lucky to have her."* I think she probably did. Peggy and I are still in touch today. She might be the best thing to have come from my time with Anthony.

The night we returned from Grand Rapids, I knew Anthony would want to get high. Sometimes being around loving people just made him feel inadequate, opening up a black hole that only drugs could fill. I couldn't compete with heroin, and I could see how hard it was to stop. If using was what kept Anthony alive, I was willing to help him.

"If you're going to do it," I told Anthony that night, trailing him out the kitchen door, "just do it here with me, where you're safe."

"I don't deserve you," he said, hanging his head.

"I'm coming with you," I said. In my pajamas and robe, I drove Anthony to meet a dealer on the corner of Wilton and Franklin Avenue. Then we came home and I watched, biting my knuckles, as Anthony shot up in my bathroom. The same bathroom where Karis and I used to stand on the tub's edge, lip-synching in the mirror.

That was the first of many times I went with him to score. He didn't like me tagging along at first, but then we discovered I had a sixth sense for the fuzz. One time we were parked in the Mayfair Market parking lot and Anthony had just smoked some dope; I got a weird feeling and put the tinfoil in my pocket seconds before a cop car swooped up. They searched the car and questioned us separately, and miraculously, we had the same story: We were just going to the market to get bagels.

Heroin would make Anthony remote but also snuggly. We'd curl up on the waterbed, listening to Stevie Wonder or other soothing stuff like Bob Marley's *Kaya* and Neil Young's *Harvest*, which reminded Anthony of Peggy and the innocent part of his childhood. Sometimes we watched old movies, and not just because I wanted to. Anthony had a thing for Veronica Lake and might have seen *Sullivan's Travels* as many times as I'd seen *The Blue Dahlia*. He liked it when I read to him—a chapter or two of *The Catcher in the Rye* as he drifted off.

But then there were the nights he shot speedballs, a mixture of coke and heroin. Those nights weren't sweet at all. I'd try to sleep while he crouched on my floor, drawing scary pictures. "Don't look at me!" he'd snap when I tried to pull him into bed. "I'm bad. I feel like a demon."

I'd look away for his sake, but it wasn't true. Anthony wasn't a bad person, he was just in a bad way. Wasn't that the case with all "bad" people? I knew Mom saw the goodness in him too, or she wouldn't have let him stay. Even so, something had to give. Dono was still living at home, and while he was too conflict-averse to come right out and say he disapproved of Anthony, I felt it. The tension between my brother and my boyfriend was thick and smoggy. We all needed some fresh air.

In the New Year, Anthony and I moved our joint belongings—his duffel, my three suitcases, and whatever else fit into the Toyota—into a quite glamorous 1940s triplex on North Orange Drive. I loved the apartment, with its original pink-tiled bathroom and Art Deco moldings. The electricity wasn't turned on yet, so Anthony bought an armload of watermelons, cut them in half, and shoved candles into them. I was disappointed that he shot up in the bathroom our first night there but relieved to be in our own space where we didn't have to feel embarrassed or ashamed about it.

The first week at Orange Drive went by in a surreal, fruity haze. We strutted naked through the empty rooms and went thrift shopping for dishes and a vintage cocktail shaker to match the house. I had grand visions of our housewarming party—me in black satin and cherry lipstick, pouring sidecars. I don't know who I thought I'd pour them for. My world-inside-of-Anthony's-world was shrinking by the day. Little by little, I was closing myself off to anyone who cared enough to question my choice in dating a junkie eight years my senior.

There would be no housewarming. Nine days after the move, Anthony went on tour, leaving me alone at Orange Drive. I'd known about the tour, of course. But my teenage brain, with its half-baked rational parts, hadn't considered what this meant for me. I was seventeen, all alone, and too proud to go home.

I tried my best to be a grown-up—decorating, cleaning, checking in with my manager about a handful of upcoming auditions, which I dreaded. What I dreaded the most, though, was being alone in that apartment at night. The neighborhood was pretty but there had been break-ins. Anthony had had an alarm system installed, which was always blurting false alarms: "Guest bedroom window open!" "Kitchen window open!" I'd jump out of my skin every time. I took to sleeping with Anthony's itinerary under my pillow so I could call his hotel to say goodbye while being ax-murdered.

The time there actually *was* an intruder, the robot voice remained silent. It was daytime, and I was standing at the kitchen table, folding laundry, when I felt that slow prickle on my neck. Someone was watching me. I turned to see a man in torn clothes, face pressed to the window behind me. *"Go away!"* I roared—truly, I roared—at the man. And thankfully he did. I don't know where that alpha voice came from, but I loved it, and I was jealous of it. I wanted to learn from it. I called the police, then Anthony. The police came and told me to get a dog and cover my windows with newspaper until I got curtains. Anthony called back from his hotel, girls laughing in the background.

"Maybe you should stay at your mom's," he said.

"No," I said firmly. If I went back home now, something told me I'd never regain the courage to be alone. "Where are you again?"

"Augusta," said Anthony.

"Augusta, Georgia?" I said. I'd found a letter he'd written but never sent, to a girl in Georgia. My heart had dropped when I read the last line: *I wake up thinking of you, and I like it.*

"That's the one," said Anthony.

I quietly hung up.

He was always cheating on me, and I was never surprised. I'd heard about the constant flow of women and drugs that had moved through the house where Anthony came of age. The stories were a little shocking, even to me, but Anthony was his dad's biggest defender. "It wasn't that he was this coldhearted user of people," he'd say. "He just had this insatiable desire to meet all of the beautiful girls in the world." I believed the same about Anthony. And as long as I was number one, I didn't care so much who he "met."

It was heroin, the one with the power, that I cared about. At least if he was having sex, he wasn't using under a bridge, which meant he was alive. Anthony wasn't my great love—I already knew this—but I loved him, and I still believed my love could fix him if I just loved him well and hard enough. I needed him to be okay, so I could be okay.

As much as I hated being alone, it was when Anthony came home on his first tour break that I started having anxiety attacks in the middle of the night. Startling awake, I'd jump out of bed and pace—up and down, up and down—the dark bedroom. Anthony was sweet and consoling, pulling me back to bed, stroking my hair, singing "Sun Is Shining" to me, low and gravelly, till I went back to sleep: "*To the rescue, here I am. Want you to know just if you can . . .*"

What was my problem? I wasn't alone anymore. He was here with me, not out there. Eventually, I figured it out. Anthony and I were having a lot of sex. I was keeping track of my cycles and avoiding the most fertile days, but we weren't being safe. Condoms weren't even a discussion anymore.

"I think we should get tested," I told him one night, staring at his black-winged back.

"I think so too," said Anthony—more quickly than I liked.

It was a nice doctor's office, the kind of place that didn't take insurance. Anthony could afford that now. I filled out the forms. *Reason for testing?* I bit my lip, checked: *Possible exposure to HIV.* The nurse who took my blood patted my shoulder, and I refused to let myself cry. She led me to a private meeting room, where the doctor frowned over my paperwork and proceeded to give me the gravest pep talk of my life. He would personally call me with the results, he said. If I was positive, he wanted me to know there were treatments on the horizon. He wanted me to know I could still have a life, of some sort.

Anthony drove the speed limit, for once, home from the doctor's office. I stared numbly out the window. All along Santa Monica Boulevard, pink-triangle SILENCE = DEATH posters plastered storefronts, next to the ones with AIDSGATE stamped across a demon-eyed Ronald Reagan. I loathed the president for his apathy as thousands died every year. But I'd been in denial too—despite all the dear Wilton Place friends who'd fallen ill and those we'd lost already: friends like the *Interview* magazine editor Peter Lester; our neighbor Ken; and Ken's lover, John, who'd driven to the desert and died by suicide after learning he was positive.

I'd risked my bright future for what? I didn't want a "life of some sort"; I wanted a big, beautiful life, full of movies and lovers and babies and friends and music and fun.

After an endless month (it could take that long then), the doctor called with our results. Holding the phone between us, we learned that the world would continue spinning: we were both negative. I melted with relief as Anthony snatched the receiver, his face lit up like a little kid's on Christmas. "Doctor, it's me, it's me, Anthony!" he said. "Do you remember who I am?" I guessed the doctor must have given Anthony the "life of some sort" talk too. Maybe he'd given Anthony a sterner lecture—about exposing me, perhaps. But now Anthony was redeemed. *See, Doc? I didn't fuck up. We're not sick.*

I understood Anthony's shame. I felt it too. The day after we'd taken our tests, I'd stopped by Wilton Place to see Mom. We were sitting at the kitchen table, and I saw her eyes flash to the needle prick in the crook of my arm. Her face turned ash white. "What's that?" she said, yanking my wrist for a better look. "Ione! Are you using heroin?"

"No!" I yanked my arm back. "I'd never! It was for an AIDS test."

Poor Mom. She didn't know whether to be relieved or terrified. The whole time I was with Anthony, I think she was equal parts both—relieved I was still okay, and terrified I wouldn't be.

I often wondered how my unfortunate adventure would end too. But it was true, at least, that I'd never, ever become a junkie, because junkies always resorted to needles and I would never do that. Heroin was "the worst drug in the world," the "crossing the line" drug, and needles were *so* gross.

All the same, I'd grown curious about heroin, now that it was in front of me so much. I wanted to know how the drug felt from the inside, why it was so bewitching.

"Can I try some?" I asked one night as Anthony laid his lighter and tinfoil on the bathroom sink.

Anthony looked horrified. "No," he said sternly.

"But you did it with Rebecca," I said, referring to his ex-girlfriend. I'd always been a little jealous that she'd gotten to share such an important part of Anthony's life with him, and I never had.

"Yeah," said Anthony, "but that wasn't good for her. I regret it."

"Come on," I said, rubbing his shoulders, "I'm curious."

Anthony flinched away from me, then packed up his stuff and left the room. I heard him walk down the hall and open the front door. "Don't ever ask me that again," he said, just barely loud enough for me to hear in the next room. The door softly closed, and I didn't see Anthony again that day.

I was becoming friends with Bob Forrest's girlfriend Patty. She was in her twenties, lean and sharp with a striking Louise Brooks bob. I liked hanging out with her because she understood exactly where I was at. With her, I never had to make excuses for Anthony or pretend I had my situation under control. Like me, Patty was fed up with her gifted, charismatic, untrustworthy boyfriend but kept on taking his shit because no one needed her like he did.

One night when Anthony was away, Patty invited me to a party at an artist's loft on La Cienega. I got all dressed up in my black Vivienne

Westwood hoop skirt and bustier from the Worlds End boutique on Kings Road in London. (I hadn't been to a proper party in ages, and punk was over but Vivienne Westwood was not.) As pretty as I felt, when Patty came out to my car in black jeans and saddle shoes, I second-guessed myself.

"Should I borrow some jeans?" I said.

Patty shook her head, buckling her seatbelt. "Fuck no. You're famous. You should be acting like it."

It was nice to be reminded that I was somebody in my own right, not just Anthony's girlfriend. Then we launched into dissecting our boyfriend dramas and I started forgetting that again.

"Literally minutes after confessing he fucked this girl," said Patty as I careened through a yellow light, "he shows me his new tattoo. 'But look! It's you. This proves I love you.' And I'm like, 'That's not me, that's a random cherub with blond curls, asshole.'"

I giggled, pulling into a vacant lot behind a warehouse with candles in the windows. As I killed the engine, Patty pulled a baggie of dirty-looking powder from her purse. I tried to act unfazed. I knew Patty snorted Bob's heroin sometimes, but she'd never done it in front of me.

Patty dipped a finger into the bag and sniffed it, then started to pack it up.

"Can I try some?" I said.

Patty shook her head. "I'd feel weird. You're too young."

"Come on," I pleaded.

"Fine," Patty sighed. "Just a tiny bit."

She slowly handed me the bag. The powder wasn't sparkling white, like Anthony's China White or the coke I'd done in junior high with April (in the Jonathan Club changing rooms, where better?).

I took a sniff, then felt a wave of nausea. "I'm gonna throw up," I said, reaching for the door.

Twenty minutes later, I was sailing on a dopamine river, gliding through the party, heads turning at the swoosh of my ravishing skirt. I did not regret the skirt one bit. I did not regret anything. Every choice I'd ever made, every path I'd ever taken, was utterly perfect. The kitschy short films playing on the white brick walls of the loft were perfect. The young art pioneers in their paint-splattered denim, drinking white wine from jam jars, were perfect. And me, I was perfect too. So completely at ease, talking to everyone, working the room like a star. It was as if I were born with one wing pinned behind my back, and now I was free. As if I'd lived my whole life *down there*, and now I was *up here*. All that time, I'd only been living half a life.

10

The Oldest Teenager in New York

1988

In the bathroom at JFK, I brushed my teeth, put on some eyeliner, and changed into fresh clothes.

"You're fine," I told the washed-out girl staring back from the mirror.

I'd just thrown up on the red-eye from LA, minutes before touchdown. I made it to the toilet in time, but my blanket was wrapped around my shoulders and I got some on that too. The stern stewardess who'd ordered me back to my seat as I bolted into the restroom was more affable when I wobbled out, clutching the balled-up blanket. "I'll take that, hon," she said, reaching from her jump seat. "Buckle up!" I clasped my seat belt just as we hit the tarmac.

At least I wasn't sick from heroin. Thankfully I was one of the lucky ones who didn't get hooked. The morning after my stupidly dangerous adventure with Patty, I woke up with a realization: The high of heroin wasn't meant for the living. I could wait for heaven, if there was one. Real life was hard, but it was worth it. I was strong, and I wanted to be happy. As glorious as I'd felt at the warehouse party, there was no way I could live a happy life chasing that feeling all the time.

Anyway, I thought my airplane episode had been airsickness. Lots of people threw up on planes. That was why they had barf bags, though it hadn't occurred to me to use mine.

I was visiting Anthony on tour. I was worried about him. I'd heard from Flea that he and Hillel had been disappearing, separately, between shows. I'd come to make sure he was okay.

I took a cab to his midtown hotel and called from the reception desk. As the phone rang and rang, I thought of the unthinkable: Anthony face-down on the hotel bed, his body cold and still. Was this it? The moment my worst fear became my reality?

"Yeah," said Anthony on the line.

I sagged against the wall, the fear rushing out of me like a ghost. "I'm here, downstairs."

"Don't come up," Anthony told me. "I'll meet you in the restaurant."

"Oh," I said, "sure." I assumed he was pulling himself together as he had a big press day to get to. The band was exploding and everyone wanted a piece of Anthony now.

I parked my suitcase next to a booth and sat with a coffee until he showed up wearing a Peruvian sweater a few sizes too big for him, his beautiful long hair in a smooth ponytail. I quickly scanned him for signs of post-binge wear and tear and was thinking he looked pretty good when I noticed the girl trailing behind him. She was beautiful, wearing a sparkly, off-the-shoulder minidress that was no daytime dress. He must have brought her back from last night's show. And now he was bringing her to breakfast. Anthony had never been so blatant before. Did he want me to know my competition? Was that why she was here?

Anthony casually introduced us, as if it were the most normal thing in the world that his live-in girlfriend and his one-night stand, if that's what she was, should meet. I was so confused these days, I didn't know what was normal anymore.

The three of us ate in awkward silence peppered with small talk, then Anthony signaled for the check and we all stood up and he kissed the girl on the cheek and me on the lips. I didn't reciprocate but lifted my chin after that. *Still number one.* Anthony took my suitcase and suggested that since the girl and I were both headed downtown, we should share a cab.

The two of us rode in silence to Vesuvio Bakery on Prince, where the girl worked. *Of course she works at a cool, rustic bakery*, I thought as we pulled up to the kelly green shop with golden baguettes stacked in the window. *Of course she sells handmade bread, like a rom-com heroine.*

"Thanks for the ride," said the girl, reaching for the door.

"Have a nice day," I said blandly. I wasn't mad at her. It wasn't her fault. I just felt so tired, and suddenly very old. I felt like the oldest teenager in New York, and that was probably saying a lot.

While Anthony did his day of interviews, I wandered the East Village, buying things to feel better: a Donovan CD I found at St. Mark's Sounds, a silk pajama top at Trash & Vaudeville, a book of Charles Bukowski poems for Anthony at the Strand bookstore.

Back at the hotel, I didn't bring up the bakery girl like I wanted to but lay quietly next to him on top of the bedcovers, listening to Sam Cooke. Anthony was in a deep Sam Cooke phase and naturally, I was learning to love and appreciate the King of Soul too.

The next afternoon, Anthony was headed to another city and I was headed to Harlem to stay the night with my friend Martha Plimpton.

Anthony hailed me a cab and embraced me in the open door, French kissing me with a zeal that I sensed was to compensate for our sexless night in the hotel. I let this go on until I got a little woozy and pulled away.

"You good?" he said, unsticking a lock of hair from my cheek. "You're all sweaty."

I nodded, resisting the urge to cover my mouth.

"I love you," he said, looking deeply, too deeply, into my eyes.

I nodded again but didn't say it back.

In the beginning, when Anthony and I started saying "I love you" to each other, I'd gone a little overboard. I'd said it every time he walked into a room, every time we talked on the phone, every time we said good night or goodbye. Finally, he'd said, "You know, you don't have to say it so much."

Horrified by my failure to read the room, I'd apologized a million times, then never said "I love you" again. I'd gone cold turkey on the "I love you"s.

"You can say it back to me sometimes," said Anthony now, his voice teasing and sweet, as if prompting a child.

"I love you," I said, feeling like one. The words sounded forced, but maybe I was just out of practice.

"That guy your brother?" said the taxi driver, leering in the rearview mirror as we drove away.

"What?" I said. "No!"

"How old are you?" he asked. I could still feel him staring. He was looking at me so much I started to worry we'd crash.

"Seventeen," I answered, gripping the hand rest. He was really big. We were on the West Side Highway now, speeding too fast past the midtown exits. Would he take me to Martha's or just keep on driving farther and farther north, into the woods?

"How old's your boyfriend?" said the driver.

"Twenty-five," I said. What I wanted to say was, *"Stop the car and let me out!"* But the Alpha Ione who'd scared off the peeping Tom at Orange Drive did not show up and I was stuck with People-Pleasing

Ione, who just sat there answering the man's creepy questions, not wanting to be rude. Because God forbid he *wasn't* planning to abduct me and I should hurt his feelings.

By the time I arrived at Martha's cozy railroad apartment, shaken but unharmed, all I wanted was to curl up and let sleep erase the last thirty-six hours from my memory.

"Are you okay?" said Martha, hugging me. "You look sort of . . . gray."

"Just a little carsick," I said.

Martha brought me a glass of water. "You can go lie down in my room." She pointed me down the narrow hallway. "When you're rested, I'll take you out on the town." She raised her eyebrows and gave me her impish smile.

I must have turned a shade grayer because Martha added, "Or we could stay in and cook?"

"That sounds really good, actually," I said. For the first time on my trip, I felt safe and cared for, which made me realize how much I missed home, and Mom. I couldn't think of the last meal I'd had at Wilton Place. I couldn't remember for the life of me why I'd chosen this lonely existence I was living.

From what I'd seen, Martha seemed to make only healthy, self-respecting choices. I'd admired her since we'd met a couple of years earlier in an audition room for *Shy People*, a serious film with Jill Clayburgh and Barbara Hershey. We were both up for the rebellious teen daughter part and had both been waiting for over an hour to audition when Martha stood up and told whoever was in charge that they'd better hurry up or she'd have to go. They called her right in, and of course, given her huge talent, she got the part.

Then we met again on the Chicago set of *A Night in the Life of Jimmy Reardon*, where Martha was visiting River. They were one of those yin-yang couples: River was more like me—daydreamy, warm, and a little flaky—while Martha, with her pearl-blond pixie cut and elfin features, was cool and solid and always in control, or at least it seemed so to me. She'd been famous since starring in *The Goonies* a few years earlier but wasn't crazy about the attention she still got for it. When people stopped her on the street and asked, "Are you the *Goonies* girl?" she'd say, "Yep," and keep walking. I imagined if I were in her shoes, I'd probably feel obligated to stop and chat with each person, lest they feel snubbed. Though Martha intimidated me a little, I felt a kinship with her. Maybe because she, too, had a strong single mom and a famous, artistic dad. Martha's father was the actor Keith Carradine, who'd played Brooke Shields's sugar daddy in *Pretty Baby*. It was still one of my favorite movies, though now that I was older, I realized the film was more complicated than I knew when I was a kid.

Martha's floor was scattered with black-and-white photography books and *New Yorker* magazines. A radiator under the window tapped and hissed and I stood close to it, peeling off my jeans and inspecting my new tattoo. I'd gone to the Chili Peppers' favorite tattoo artist, a Dutch guy known as Hanky Panky, and asked for a swan on my left hip. They called Anthony "Swan," ironically, for his ungraceful dancing style. My swan was unironically elegant and almost fully healed. I dabbed it with some moisturizer from a pot on Martha's dresser and crawled under her bedcovers with my Discman and new CD, Donovan's 1968 megahit, *The Hurdy Gurdy Man*. It pained me to listen to Donovan, but perhaps masochistically, I genuinely loved his music.

My father's voice was startlingly clear through my headphones— much clearer than it sounded on our old scratched albums at Wilton Place. I fast-forwarded to one of the prettiest songs, "Jennifer Juniper," and closed my eyes.

Jennifer Juniper, rides a dappled mare
Jennifer Juniper, lilacs in her hair . . .

Boy, if I felt crummy about the bakery girl, how must Mom have felt, listening to *that*? Jennifer was Jenny Boyd, the gorgeous, blond sister of the equally gorgeous and blond Pattie Boyd, George Harrison's wife. Jenny was in love with Mick Fleetwood, but my dad fell hard for her one weekend while he and Mom were visiting George and Pattie at Kinfauns, their cozy Surrey bungalow with a willow tree and roses and psychedelic murals outside. Enid had put on a brave face, trying to ignore Donovan's new infatuation. She loved Jenny, Pattie, and George. If she was going to lose Donovan, she didn't want to lose them too.

I sat up in Martha's bed, remembering another story Mom had told us about visiting George and Pattie. It might have been that same weekend, or another soon after, that Mom borrowed Pattie's expensive fur coat and proceeded to get sick all over it. Pattie sweetly waved it off. "It doesn't matter, darling, I have plenty more," she said, but Mom felt terrible. She was so flustered about the coat, she didn't stop to wonder if the sickness had been of the morning variety and she might be pregnant. It turned out she was, with Dono.

Throwing back Martha's covers, I looked down, placing both hands on my belly. Had it been more than airsickness, on the plane? Could I be . . . ?

Two weeks later, I found myself in a womb-pink Beverly Hills doctor's office, snapping my rubber bracelets and staring at the closed journal in my lap. I'd thought I might want to draw while I waited, alone, to have an abortion. But I didn't feel like drawing. I started to read old journal entries instead and came to the baby names page:

BOYS

Claud

Hercules

Béla

Oskar

Minx

Angel

Silver

Pal

Zully

Zulton

Leonardo

GIRLS

Birdy

Benny

Sappho

Milla

Delfine

Goldie

Matilda (Tilly)

Isis

Paloma

Harlow

Ione Junior

There were hundreds more where those came from. I'd been doing it for as long as I could remember—jotting down names for my future children. I was the type of girl who'd wanted a baby since I was a baby, who used to fantasize about finding a swaddled infant on my doorstep or catching a flying ghost baby with a butterfly net (that one thanks to Carl's bizarre reincarnation theory). But fantasizing was different from *seeing*. I couldn't see having a baby at this point.

Sitting across the waiting room was a woman, maybe thirty years old. She was reading the Bible, just my luck. Every once in a while she looked up, trying to catch my eye, but I kept my head down, avoiding her inevitable judgment. The constant scrutiny I faced in audition rooms hadn't thickened my skin one bit and I still wanted everyone I met or crossed paths with to like me. I cared what this Christian lady thought of me, even though I knew I was doing the right thing for myself.

While I regretted not being more careful, and putting myself in danger, I was taking care of myself now, making a choice that felt good and important for my future. I wanted to be young and also to keep working. I would not have a baby at seventeen, with someone who didn't want to be a dad, wouldn't commit to me, and had anger issues. Not to mention the heroin. And besides that, I was depleted enough from worrying about Anthony and worrying what people thought of us and worrying about my career. I was sure that adding a newborn to my list of things to worry about would be the end of me. I'd bring my dream back to life one day.

"On the bright side, I'll never get cramps again," announced the woman.

Who was she talking to? I looked toward the receptionist's desk, but there was no one there. I looked at the woman. She smiled, closing the Bible in her lap. "Sorry," she said. "I talk when I'm nervous. I'm getting a hysterectomy. Uterine cancer."

I must have appeared stricken because the woman waved her hand. "It's okay," she said. "This is a good thing! If all goes well, it's the beginning of the rest of my life."

I managed a flimsy smile.

"Can I ask why you're here?" said the woman.

I froze. No one but Anthony knew why I was here today, or that I was pregnant in the first place. I hadn't even told Mom yet. Not that she'd have been mad, but it wouldn't exactly bolster my case that I was doing just fine in my new life with Anthony.

"A termination," I said, looking out the window at the parking lot. Did that sound better than "abortion"? Somehow it was easier to say. More clinical, less emotional.

"Oh, I'm so sorry." The woman leaned forward in her womb chair, her face soft, empathetic, and without a trace of judgment. For a moment, I thought she was going to cross the waiting room divide and give me a hug. But then she leaned back again, and I was both relieved and a little disappointed.

"Thank you," I said, my eyes welling up. I was so touched and humbled by her compassion. It was more than I'd gotten from Anthony over the past two weeks. He seemed to think that by paying for me to have the "termination" at a nice Beverly Hills doctor's office instead of Planned Parenthood, he was being a mensch. He hadn't offered to be with me today, just guiltily dropped me off at the curb. To say nothing of the fact that after our AIDS scare, and the supposed new lease on life he'd gotten with the negative test result, he'd gone on using needles and having unprotected sex with me. And I'd consented to that. Other people in our group had unsafe sex and they were fine, I kept telling myself, using my teenage reasoning. Of course, I could see how irresponsible we were being. Whether Anthony could see it too, he obviously wasn't ready to grow up, to take care of himself and others, to make real adult choices. Anthony wasn't yet strong enough for all this.

But I was the girl—I had to be.

11

Say Anything

1988

"Cameron Crowe is looking for an ingenue," said Moon, her voice low and conspiratorial on the phone. "Come over Saturday. He should meet you."

"Wow, Moon, that's . . . wow," I mumbled, a little in shock. Cameron Crowe was that whiz kid who'd written *Fast Times at Ridgemont High*. This would be his directorial debut, and it was bound to be good. I was grateful that Moon wanted to connect me, to help me, after the disappearing act I'd pulled. It had been six months—as many as I'd known Anthony—since I'd seen Moon. She wouldn't have liked my dating a drug user. Avoiding her disapproval, and Frank's and Gail's, I'd gone cold turkey on the Zappas.

"It's a great, great project," said Moon. "Cameron's talking to Jennifer Connelly and Elisabeth Shue, but I told Nancy to tell him it should be you." Nancy Wilson (from the band Heart) was Moon's friend and newly married to Cameron.

"Jennifer Connelly?" I said. Jennifer was the closest thing I had to an archrival, though I'd never met her. We'd started acting at around the same time, had a similar look, and were always up for the same parts.

"She's brilliant," said Moon, "but you're the one for this. Wear something pretty."

I arrived at the Zappas' in full ingenue mode—soft makeup, opal stud earrings, my hair brushed loose and wavy. I'd chosen a coquettish white eyelet dress that made me feel like Nastassja Kinski in *Tess*. Moon and Cameron were in the kitchen, where everything always happened. He was cute for thirty, with his shaggy bangs and rumpled button-down.

"Cameron Crowe, Ione Skye," said Moon, encircling my waist. She smelled almondy and shower-fresh, like always. I had missed her smell, her appraising gaze, and maybe most of all her possessive way with me, which made me feel safe somehow.

Cameron and I mumbled awkward hellos, then froze, heads bowed, like statues in the White Witch's garden in Narnia. This was new; I had yet to meet a director as shy as me, though many indeed are introverted.

Moon gave me a little nudge, unfreezing me. I flipped my hair and smiled. "I'd love to hear about your movie," I said.

Now Cameron looked at me. "Well, it's called *Say Anything*, and it's a love letter to young love and music and the city of Seattle and—" He stopped. "What it is, it's a story about real people."

"That sounds good," I said, trying to keep my cool. I wanted to be one of Cameron's real people more than anything.

When *Fast Times* came out in 1982, I'd gone to see it in the theater three weekends in a row. When I watched it again to prepare for our meeting, it was as good as I remembered. Even better, actually, because this time around, I was old enough to relate. Like me, the main character, Stacy (Jennifer Jason Leigh), was having sex that she wasn't totally prepared to be having. Like me, she'd messed up and had to get an abortion. And like me, she wasn't ashamed or traumatized by it. She was okay, but she wanted to do better. She wanted to grow.

Surely, *Fast Times*'s empathy for Stacy and her friends had a lot to do with the director, Amy Heckerling, but it gave me confidence in Cameron too. He cared so much, he'd gone back to high school, posing undercover as a student, to research the book that became the movie.

The confidence was mutual, I guess. By the end of our meeting in the Zappas' kitchen, I'd been invited to audition for *Say Anything*.

A few weeks later, I pulled up to the 20th Century Fox studio gate and rolled down my window. "I'm here to see James Brooks," I told the guard, with relish. James L. Brooks, the genius cocreator behind *The Mary Tyler Moore Show* and *Taxi*, among many others, was executive-producing Cameron's movie, which I was here to audition for, again. On my first audition for the part of Diane Court, I'd played it too-cool-for-school, clearly disappointing Cameron. He didn't give a damn about being cool. Which was why he was so great, and why his script was so great. "Just put your heart into it," he'd said when he called to offer me a second chance. "It's okay to want this, you know."

I did want it, so badly I'd sabotaged the audition. I still did that sometimes, when the stakes were high. If I didn't care, I couldn't get hurt, so I'd barely prepare. In a recent audition for *Steel Magnolias*, set in Louisiana, I'd read my lines with a British accent. In my nervousness, I half-read the character descriptions and somehow deduced the film took place in England. I hadn't expected the great Sally Field to show up to read with me. What if I disappointed her? Might as well get it over with. A few minutes in, Sally's confused expression and the strong Southern twang she was doing stopped me cold. I switched accents, but it was already over. I went home and wrote and rewrote a groveling apology letter for not respecting

Sally's time. Whether she'd forgiven me or not, I was having trouble forgiving myself.

Nerves aside, I still loved an old-fashioned movie lot. Arriving at James L. Brooks's totally historic office bungalow—it had once belonged to Fred Astaire, and Will Rogers before him—I did a double take. Was that short, jolly man shaking James's hand . . . ? Of course it was. No one else looked like Danny DeVito.

"Break a leg, kid," he told me, heading out.

The audition felt almost enchanted, as if the spirits of all the Hollywood greats I'd ever loved, living and dead, were right there with me, backing me up. *Deep is the way*, they silently coached me. *No faking. No indicating emotions. Have fun! Play!* And I did. I tapped into all my teenage angst and longing and disappointment and hope and gave that reading my all. It was go big or go home, and I did not want to go home.

"I got the part," I told Anthony, kneeling over his sleeping body. He smelled rough. I kissed his cheek, stroked his greasy hair.

Anthony was the first person I'd wanted to tell when I got the news, but he'd been on a binge, so I'd gone home to Wilton Place for a few days and savored the news with Mom. On the third day, the day Anthony usually came back to me, I went home and found him in bed, sleeping it off.

"Are you hungry?" I whispered, gently shaking him. "How about Canter's?" I'd get some food in him, then we'd take an easy bike ride or go to the beach. I wanted to feel the sunshine on my face and be a normal teenager, just for today.

Anthony didn't move or make a sound.

"Anthony?" I pulled back the covers. A used syringe was tucked halfway under the mattress, the cap on the floor. So he wasn't sleeping off the run, he was on the run? I sat there awhile, staring out the blue-sky window, then curled myself around my boyfriend, meeting him where he was, like I always did.

Now that I was on board, Cameron threw himself into wooing his top choice for the male lead, John Cusack. (I heard Christian Slater was runner-up.) John was twenty-one and more than almost famous for movies like *The Sure Thing, Stand By Me*, and *Better Off Dead*. Tall and boyish, with dark questioning eyes, John was perfect for the outsider-hero part of Lloyd Dobler, an aspiring kickboxer who woos the untouchable class valedictorian, Diane. The problem was John didn't want to go back to high school. He'd done his fill of teen rom-coms and was reluctant to do another, even one with a script as good as Cameron's.

One afternoon when Anthony wasn't around, I invited Cameron and John—Johnny to everyone who knew him—to Orange Drive so I could help Cameron charm Johnny. I'd bought a six-pack of good beer with my fake ID, and the three of us sat in my sunny kitchen— me on the counter, Johnny on the floor, Cameron in a chair like a grown-up—and talked about the movie.

Cameron did most of the talking, pouring his heart out about the three-year scriptwriting process. I learned that *Say Anything* had started with the germ of an idea from James L. Brooks. He'd seen a father and daughter crossing a street together in New York City, and something about the way the father touched the young woman's elbow, guiding her, moved James. *What if that caring father happened to be a crook?* he wondered. Could Cameron write about that? Intrigued, Cameron started by writing a ninety-page novella in the voice of the girl, Diane. To get her perspective right, he spent hours in Seattle malls and diners, chatting with kids over burgers and shakes. He also drew inspiration from his overachieving mother. Lloyd's character was inspired by a kooky guy named Lowell who lived down the street from Cameron and was always stopping by, interrupting Cameron's writing to talk about kickboxing.

"I get it," said Johnny. "This isn't a John Hughes movie where kids talk like caustically hip forty-year-olds. I wouldn't be here if it was." (I happened to love John Hughes movies but forgave him for this remark. God, he was confident.)

"Smokin'," said Cameron, grinning. "So why are you here?"

"To get my question answered," said Johnny.

Cameron pushed back his chair, opening his arms, like, *Give it to me*. "What question?"

"Why should *I* do this movie?"

I looked from Johnny to the director, who ran a hand through his hair, carefully considering his answer. *Please let it be the right answer.*

"Because you get to be a warrior for optimism," said Cameron.

Johnny just smiled, but it must have been the right answer because days later, he signed on for the part—on the condition that he could help develop Lloyd's character and dialogue. What chutzpah! I had ideas for Diane, too, but would keep them to myself. I couldn't imagine asking to write my own lines. Partly because I didn't have the experience Johnny did. But also, back then, an ingenue was an ingenue. I felt it was my job to be pretty, mysterious, and poetic, not to push the boundaries of what my character could do or be.

Say Anything was set in Seattle but mostly filmed in real locations around LA—all a short commute from Orange Drive. Each morning the cute skater dude assigned to be my driver would pull into my driveway with a cheerful honk. If Anthony was home, the ghost of me would kiss him goodbye, then drift out the door. Somewhere along the way, with all the hiding I'd been doing from my old friends and my sweet, wholesome former life, I'd forgotten where I'd put my real self. I could hardly remember who I was before Anthony. But on the drive to work, I'd start coming back to myself, remembering. And by the time I arrived at the day's shooting location—often the picture-perfect Windsor Square Colonial that served as Diane's house—I'd be so excited for whatever was ahead, I'd feel engaged and almost human again.

It was impossible not to come alive around this cast and crew. The cinematographer was László Kovács, who'd shot films like *Paper Moon*, *The Last Movie*, *Easy Rider*, and *Five Easy Pieces*. It was like being filmed by God himself. Kovács had been brought on by our legendary producer, Polly Platt. Polly was James's partner at Gracie Films. They'd worked together on *Terms of Endearment* and *Broadcast News*, and he called her his directing mentor. No one was more inspiring than Polly. She was one of the few female power players in an industry largely stuck in the 1950s when it came to women. Blunt and hard-driving, she kept the production running like a Swiss watch—a vintage Patek Philippe, maybe, in line with her low-key, impeccable taste.

I revered Polly from day one, and the more I found out about her from Cameron, the bigger my fangirl crush grew. She'd once been married to the director Peter Bogdanovich, with whom she'd made masterpieces like *What's Up, Doc?*, *The Last Picture Show*, and *Paper Moon*. Polly was either uncredited or billed as the production designer on those films, but it was whispered that she'd directed them as much as Bogdanovich had. Not only did he like to keep her in his shadow (typical), he'd infamously left her during the filming of *The Last Picture Show* for the film's much younger star, Cybill Shepherd. Polly and Peter had a toddler at the time and she was pregnant with their second child. Maybe I was projecting, thinking of Mom, but I felt I sensed Polly's lingering anger over that betrayal. Talk about channeling pain into creativity. She'd since made a slew of incredible movies. I couldn't believe it when I learned she wrote and produced *Pretty Baby*.

Why did that movie keep popping up in my life? Maybe it was a message: to value myself as a whole person, not just a pretty baby.

According to Cameron, *Pretty Baby* was Polly's critique of the sexualization of young girls in Hollywood. I would have liked to ask her about that but was too intimidated. We were all a little afraid of Polly, even Cameron. But the two of them had chemistry. They had fun.

At first, I'd worried that Johnny and I might not click that way. What could a hippie Jewish girl from the Hollywood Hills possibly have in common with an Irish Catholic–raised boy from suburban Chicago? I'd imagined he might be a little stiff and square, a know-it-all, like the jocks I knew in middle school. But it turned out Johnny was as weird and open-minded as I was. Right away, I felt a sweet friendship building between us.

I knew how important that relationship was to the film and threw myself into nurturing and protecting it. I wanted to be Johnny's person and felt a bit jealous of his other close relationships on set. The actress Lili Taylor was John's old friend from Chicago, and he was always talking about how great she was. She was great, of course. Who could ever forget her scene-stealing turn as the lovesick, guitar-strumming Corey Flood, belting out *"Joe lieeees when he crieeees"* at the party? Then there was John's sister Joan, who played his onscreen sister, Constance. She was another born-funny person, with brilliant comic timing and the elastic face of a mime. We only had one scene together and I was too shy to try befriending her, but I was always watching her, marveling at how bold she was, how unafraid to take up space.

Sometimes I got the feeling I was supposed to do the opposite.

Trailblazing as Polly was, there were some Hollywood rules she wasn't willing, or able, to buck. One day she caught me dunking a donut into my hot chocolate–laced coffee at the craft services table. "Watch all the snacking," she said, waving a finger. The next day, the costume designer left a pair of Playtex Secrets shapewear (what we had before Spanx) for me to wear under my costume. The Secrets were not, as the ads told us, "a beautiful alternative to holding your breath." I hated wearing them. They gave me a stomachache and flattened out the curves I liked along with the ones I didn't. Still, I wore them without complaint.

Faking Diane's academic brain was another thing. I was much more at home playing brats and bitches and bad girls than I was Diane. Could a ninth-grade dropout be believable as a valedictorian? I knew my tentativeness was coming through on camera, but Cameron, as a first-time director, seemed equally tentative about addressing it. Instead, to my horror, he hired an acting coach to work with me on a particularly tough scene where Diane learns that her doting father—played by the endlessly patient and respectful John Mahoney—has been pilfering from the residents of the retirement community he owns. I didn't understand Diane's devastation over this. At least her dad was providing for her.

Begrudgingly, I worked with the coach in my trailer. He told me it didn't matter that I couldn't relate to Diane's angst and to let go of the substitution method, for now. Substitution is when you recall a personal experience that evokes the same feeling your character is experiencing—like when I imagined protecting Dono from Carl in order to play a fiercer Pauline in *Napoleon and Josephine*. It's a common way that actors tap into an authentic emotional response, but it's not always the answer. "Don't overthink it," said the coach. "Just be vulnerable and playful. Bring your humanity and imagination to the scene, and serve the story!"

In other words, he gave me permission to relax and let the character flow through me. We shot the scene, and it must have done the trick because Cameron let the coach go. Then he asked me to do some coaching of my own.

He needed my help convincing Johnny to say "I love you" in the scene where Lloyd lays his heart on the table, moments before Diane breaks up with him. The "I gave her my heart and she gave me a pen" scene.

"But Lloyd *has* to say he loves her," I told Cameron. "That's what makes the rejection so painful."

Cameron nodded gravely. "Your mission is critical," he said. "Don't let me down."

I suppose we both understood that it wasn't a matter of life and death to get this scene in our beloved movie right, but to us, it felt like it.

I found Johnny in his trailer, eating mini peanut butter cups from a Halloween-sized bag and working on Lloyd's great social-ist monologue about not wanting to sell, buy, or process anything sold, bought, or processed. "Safe European Home" by the Clash was blasting so loud the windows shook. I squeezed into the miniature banquette seat across from him, helping myself to a chocolate, then another.

"We're so alike," yelled Johnny, watching me eat. "We'll both be like Orson Welles one day."

Wow, he thinks we'll both be great auteurs, I thought. *That's nice.* But then I realized he meant fat like Orson Welles. I stopped popping the chocolates and turned down the music.

"Have you ever said 'I love you' before?" I said.

Johnny put down his pen, stretched out one leg. He was so tall, a "big hulking blob of charisma," as Cameron once joked, and muscular from all the kickboxing training. A bandana was still tied around his ankle, a costume touch Johnny had come up with himself. I'd thought it looked silly before, but it was growing on me.

"In character, I've said it plenty," Johnny answered. "That's my point. 'I love you' has been said a billion times, in a billion movies. That's why it's a cliché."

"What about in real life?"

Johnny shook his head. "I've never been in love. At least not till recently."

I spun out on that for a moment. Was Johnny in love with me? As our romance had grown on camera, a real attraction had grown as well. I felt it all the time and knew he did too, but we'd just let it be on film. Did he want more? Did I? Was *I* in love with *Johnny*? Could I fall in love with an actor? I'd thought not. As much as I enjoyed flirting with actors in their trailers, I preferred musicians when it came down to it. Seeing someone reading a script was too close to home. I'd thought I loved Keanu, but that was just a crush, in retrospect. And Flea was a musician at heart. I'd often thought I could fall in love with River Phoenix, if given the chance. Because River was also a musician, and just magic . . .

"I've thought about saying it to Susannah," Johnny said, bringing me back to earth.

Right. Johnny had mentioned a date with Susannah Melvoin, the backup vocalist and dancer for Prince. Apparently, she'd inspired Prince to write "Nothing Compares 2 U." I hadn't known Johnny also found her so very incomparable. Along with my jealousy, I felt happy for Johnny, and I told him so. Then I asked him to reconsider the "I love you" scene.

"Maybe you can think of her when you say it," I suggested, though I hoped he wouldn't.

"Thanks, but no," said Johnny.

I pressed my foot against his. "Say it for me, then."

We had a brief, thrilling stare-off, and I thought we might kiss, but we didn't. That would come later, years later.

Meanwhile, Johnny relented and we filmed the breakup scene with Lloyd's "I love you" intact. I didn't feel he was saying the words to Susannah, I felt he was saying them to me—both Diane-me and Ione-me, who, in that moment, were the same.

———

The day Anthony came to the set, I kept him away from Johnny. I didn't want my fantasy boyfriend to see how my real boyfriend treated me—like an insignificant if sometimes pleasing little girl he let tag along on his scorched-earth path through the world. Our messed-up power dynamic had been recently pointed out to me by Amelia Fleetwood, who was becoming a close friend (one of the few I had left). "Why do you always walk two steps behind him?" she'd asked. I didn't have an answer, as I hadn't even noticed I was doing that. I had noticed that Anthony was extremely possessive. It might not end well if he saw the affection between Johnny and me. Jealousy made Anthony cruel.

Once, at a Lakers game, I thought I saw Crew Sinclair across the stadium. "That looks like the first boy I ever had sex with," I said, squinting. Anthony said nothing but poured his soda on my lap, then stood up and left. I waited, wet and sticky and in shock, till the end-of-game horn blew, then followed the swarm down the bleacher stairs, through the hallways, and out into the night. When I finally found our car in the lot, Anthony, or some robot replacement of Anthony, sat stiffly in the driver's seat, staring straight ahead. "Don't ever say something like that again," he said, so cold and expressionless I decided I'd better not say a word.

That was not the Anthony I introduced to Cameron on the front lawn of Diane's house. The Anthony who showed up that day was friendly and polite. I knew he admired Cameron's early work as a teenage *Rolling Stone* journalist who'd written passionate profiles of Black Sabbath, Led Zeppelin, and David Bowie. By the end of their talk, Anthony had agreed to license a Chili Peppers song for the *Say Anything* soundtrack.

As much as I wanted to insulate my work from my relationship, I'd been pleased when Cameron asked me if he thought Anthony would be into the soundtrack idea. I wanted something good to happen for Anthony. He'd been using a lot and seemed beaten down. You can hear it in "Taste the Pain," the song Cameron ended up choosing (it plays in the scene where Lloyd is driving around and jams a pack of matches in his tape deck). Anthony had written it on our living room floor, after a binge.

As Cameron had told me the day we met, *Say Anything* was very much a love letter to music. Throughout filming, there were endless discussions about what song should play when Lloyd boom box–serenades Diane outside her window. At the time, no one knew the scene would become iconic, but we knew it was significant—the "Romeo under the trellis" moment, as Cameron put it. He'd originally written the scene while listening to Billy Idol's "To Be a Lover," so that song made it into the first draft of the script, but we all knew it wasn't right. After weeks of exchanging mixtapes, Cameron and Johnny decided Lloyd would blast "Turn the Other Way" by Fishbone up to Diane's window.

Johnny and I were scheduled to film our respective sides of the scene on separate days, which I was glad about. Johnny was being cynical about the whole thing. He thought Lloyd's grand romantic gesture would come off as cheesy. "Why does he have to hold the boom box up?" he kept arguing to Cameron. "It makes him subservient. I want to try it with the box on the car beside me and I've got my arms folded and I'm defiant. She broke up with me! I'm pissed!"

Cameron felt certain that Lloyd should be all in, not holding on to his cool by sitting down, but he agreed to shoot the scene both ways to keep the peace. (László later confessed to Cameron that he hadn't bothered to load film into the camera for Johnny's version; he was that sure Cameron was right.) Initially, they filmed on the street outside Diane's house, but Cameron wasn't happy with the footage. Later, we were doing the 7-Eleven scene where Lloyd brushes glass out of Diane's path (a nod to the movie's origin story), and László noticed a tree-lined stretch of park across the street. "That's our boom box spot!" he said. "Quickly, before the sun goes down!" The crew rushed over to set up the shot, and with minutes to spare, Johnny did the scene, wielding his portable stereo like a dare. The mixture of heartbreak and defiance he brought to the moment made it perfect.

Well, almost perfect. When Cameron reviewed the footage, he realized the funky, raucous "Turn the Other Way" made Lloyd come off less as a thinking teenager's heartthrob and more like a crazed Fishbone fan. So the song search began again. Eventually, Cameron would have an epiphany while listening to his wedding mixtape. When Peter Gabriel's "In Your Eyes" came on, he knew it was the one. Three other films were vying for Gabriel's big song, but Cameron went to the mat to get it, and the rest is history.

My side of the boom box scene was quiet, contemplative. Onscreen you see me lying awake in bed, my pretty room glowing with dawn light. Lloyd's song begins to play from outside and I briefly sit up, then fall back on my pillows, conflicted. Diane won't go to her window, like Juliet. She loves Lloyd, but he can't be right for her. Can he?

In reality, the street outside Diane's house was empty and quiet. It was nine or ten at night, the corner streetlight shining through the window. That might have been the only lighting we used. Cameron often directed us through music, and tonight he played "Child of the Moon" by the Stones, "Buckets of Rain" by Bob Dylan, and "I Want You" by Elvis Costello to set the tone. The songs were a perfect gateway to Diane's love story—melancholy, but not outright tearjerkers. Diane wasn't supposed to cry for Lloyd. She was sad and confused but holding it together. I smoothed my nightgown and sighed, picturing Lloyd outside my window, fighting for Diane like I wished a boy would fight for me.

"Cut," said Cameron, emerging from the shadows. "And that's a wrap."

One late night that June, Bob Forrest called, crying so hard he couldn't get words out. I stood in the dark living room, clutching my pajama top where my heart would have been if it lived outside my chest. "What is it?" I said. "Is it Anthony?" It was Anthony, I knew it. He'd gone to meet his dealer and hadn't returned.

"It's Hillel," Bob sobbed. "They found him at his place . . ."

We'd just been to Hillel's the week before. He and Anthony were both a little strung out, but Hillel made his usual spaghetti aglio e olio and we had a nice quiet evening, listening to jazz and not saying much because we didn't have to. I loved being with the two of them together. Hillel softened Anthony's edges where I couldn't. One of Anthony's most cherished possessions was a little brown paper box that Hillel had given him, for his birthday, I think. On it, Hillel had written: *Anthony, you think what I feel and understand what I say. I love you.*

Bob hung up and I stood in the dark, holding the empty phone till I heard Anthony rev into the driveway. He didn't come in . . . and didn't come in . . . I thought he might be fixing. *Don't leave me alone with this.* I ran outside and saw him hunched over in the front seat, a plastic THANK YOU shopping bag crumpled next to him. *No, no, no . . .* I pressed my palms to the window and he looked up, startled. There was an open notebook in his lap, a pen in his hand. He was only writing in his notebook, a song probably.

Anthony threw open the door, taking me in his arms. "What is it?"

"Come inside," I said into his chest. "You need to call Bob. Right now." I couldn't be the one to say it.

Anthony dialed the phone, his warriorlike shoulders slowly curling around the blow of Bob's news. Then he straightened, hung up, grabbed the THANK YOU bag, and strode to the bathroom.

"You're doing that *now*?" I said, following him.

Anthony whipped his head toward me with a look so anguished that I understood. Of course he was shooting up. He'd just lost his best friend. Who wouldn't numb that blow if they could?

> *On the day my best friend died,*
> *I could not get my copper clean.*
> —Red Hot Chili Peppers, "This Is the Place"

Hillel's mother came by one day soon after. I don't think she was fond of Anthony; she thought he'd been a bad influence on her son. But maybe she was looking for answers. "I was massaging his feet the other day," she said, trembling on the edge of our sofa. "He looked bad, and I wanted to do something to help him. He liked me to rub his feet." She put her face in her hands and I fought the urge to hug her as she didn't even know me. Hillel had told me both of his parents were Holocaust survivors, but I still wondered how they would survive losing such a beautiful son. Anthony touched Mrs. Slovak's shoulder and told her nothing she did or didn't do could have changed things for Hillel, that it had been up to him.

It was the same thing Bob Forrest had been telling me all along. I thought of Bob in the backseat of my car the night we'd trolled LA's grubbiest corners for Anthony: *Trust me, there's nothing we can do*, he'd said. Only now, sitting with Mrs. Slovak—who had taught Hillel how to paint; and watched with pride as he picked up his first guitar, a gift given for his bar mitzvah; and let him play it deep into the night because it made him so happy—did Bob's sad wisdom start to sink in: Some things love couldn't fix.

12

Meeting the Sunshine Superman

1988

... to take your hand, along the sand
Ah, but I may as well try and catch the wind
—Donovan, "Catch the Wind"

The summer I filmed *Say Anything*, my brother made a discovery: Our father did not still live in England, as we'd thought. In fact, he lived in Joshua Tree, a two-hour drive east of LA. He and Linda and their family had been there for years.

We found out thanks to Dono's girlfriend, Susanna Hoffs from the Bangles (he was always dating someone fabulous). One day Dono called to speak with Susanna at the recording studio where she was working on the album *Everything*. "Guess what?" said Susanna. "Your dad's recording in the room next to mine."

Dono, the outgoing Leo, hung up with Susanna and called the studio right back, asking for Donovan. My brother hadn't seen our dad in more than a decade. The last time was at Donovan's concert in

1977, but somehow, he harbored no resentment about this. They exchanged numbers—Donovan's with a 760 area code, not a +44—and soon Donovan invited us both for a visit.

My brother was lit up about the invitation, but I'd taken some time to come around to it. I was surprised and angry. It felt more forgivable for Donovan to ignore us from faraway England than to do so from 140 miles down the highway.

Still, how could I say no? I'd been waiting for this moment my whole life.

Now, exactly one week before my eighteenth birthday, I was standing at the top of my stairs like a girl before her first prom, my stomach in knots.

"How's this?" I asked Dono.

Dono looked up from the couch, where he was stretched out watching MTV. It was nice to see my brother relaxing at my house, even if it was only because Anthony wasn't home—he was on tour, again. Dono rarely relaxed. He was still the same Dono as ever, always chasing the next big party, club, woman, project. His movie *The In Crowd*, a sixties dance musical, had come out earlier that year. It was a small film, but Dono was huge in it; his dancing just flew off the screen. I was so proud.

My brother deemed my carefully chosen outfit—white lace shirt, long flowy skirt, and wedge sandals—"a little dressy for the desert," so I ended up in black jeans and a thermal shirt with a floral print, my hair pulled into a messy ponytail. I didn't want to look dressy, like I was trying. I wanted to look accidentally pretty, like I had *not* been waiting for this moment my whole life.

In the car, I nervously wiped off my eye shadow and took my hair down again. It was a tangled mess, not even accidentally pretty. My father was a hippie, but still. I made Dono stop at a 7-Eleven, where I bought a cheap plastic comb to smooth out my knots.

We had always taken turns being the strong one and today it was Dono's turn. Back on the road, he popped in the Smiths' "This Charming Man" and soon had me singing passionately along.

"Tell me about Dad," I said, feeling better. Dono was practically a Donovan scholar, but I'd always tamped down my curiosity in a stubborn *If you don't want to know about me, I don't want to know about you* kind of way.

"He sounded good on the phone," said Dono. "His upbeat self. He's really great. You'll see."

"I mean, why'd he disappear?" I said. "From fame, I mean."

All these years, Donovan had been making music. He still toured and had turned out some interesting New Age and Celtic rock albums, plus a couple of movie soundtracks. But the hits had stopped soon after I was born. It used to disappoint me that my school friends didn't know my dad's name the way they knew Karis's dad's. Maybe Donovan was never as big as Mick Jagger, Bob Dylan, David Bowie, or John Lennon, but he'd sure had lots of hits. I'd always wondered why they stopped. Was it bad business decisions, or maybe he burned a few bridges back in the day?

My brother the optimist thought Donovan's retreat from the spotlight was mostly intentional. He'd read an interview where Donovan said his life had changed with that 1968 Beatles trip to visit the Maharishi. Stardom and topping the charts seemed meaningless after that, so he'd simply stopped playing the fame game and found his spiritual side. With Linda.

"Huh," was all I had to say to that. Our dad was only twenty-two when he went to India, twenty-four when I was born. It seemed an awfully young age to lose interest in fame. But I could relate to having a push-pull relationship with the spotlight. Maybe we were similar?

Donovan's chosen family consisted of Linda; their two daughters, Astrella and Oriole; and Linda's son with Brian Jones, Julian, whom

Donovan had adopted. They lived a few miles past the sunbaked main drag of Joshua Tree, up a steep dirt road.

"Linda's father built the house from a kit," said Dono, stopping the car at a two-story log cabin with carved moons in the shutters. What a strange sight, that Vermont-y, Lincoln Log house plunked down in the dry desert—nothing but yuccas and spiky Joshua trees for miles. Even stranger was the sight of our father on the front porch, dressed all in black like Johnny Cash. Where was his tweed cap? His brocaded fur coat? He was playing a beautiful deep-blue guitar decorated with stars and a white crescent moon like the ones on the house. I recognized that guitar, from the cover of *Cosmic Wheels*.

Donovan gave us a smiling nod and came down the steps, strumming a folksy tune.

"Hello," I called, approaching him.

"The boy's hung himself from the tallest tower," Donovan replied, sing-speaking the words.

Dono and I traded looks. Should we stop smiling? Look sad? What boy? Impulsively, I stepped forward and embraced my father across his guitar. He stopped playing and, after a moment, returned the hug. His brown curls smelled of sage and smoke. *I'm touching my father for the very first time*, I told myself, breathing him in. This couldn't be real.

Next out of the house came a slim brunette woman with a sideways, childlike smile and long, long, long hair. Linda, obviously. I felt an instant repulsion toward her; I couldn't help it. This was the woman who'd had my father all these years. She was followed by two brunette girls whom I'd seen pictured in articles about Donovan, my half sisters. They weren't much younger than me and we all looked so alike, we might have been triplets.

I'd known about my half sisters my whole life, but they'd only recently found out about Dono and me, from a picture of us on our

Scottish grandparents' bookshelf. I knew this because my grandma Winnie had told me in a letter: *They were terribly cross not to have known all these years*, she wrote. *They didn't speak to your dad for a week.* We weren't close with our grandma and grandpa Leitch like we were with Grandma Tillie and Grandpa Benny, but at least we knew them. When I was six and Dono was nine, they'd reached out to us, wanting to meet. They'd paid for us to fly to Spain—all by ourselves, an adventure in itself—for a vacation with them. Then we'd visited their home in Scotland, where our strict grandpa Donald played Donovan records as we sat quietly under the bronze Donovan bust on the fireplace mantel. It had been a somewhat traumatic trip.

"I'm Astrella," said the friendlier looking of my half sisters, "and that's Oriole." Astrella had pale skin, straight hair, and bright blue eyes that seemed hungry for connection. Oriole was taller, with long waves like mine and loads of silver jewelry. She seemed a little angry—not at Dono and me, I sensed, just in general.

"Sorry about Don's song," said Oriole.

Then my half sisters spoke at once, as they would do for the rest of our visit, explaining, in overlapping sentences, that a friend from their school had hung himself from a bell tower and it wasn't the first suicide and wouldn't be the last given the speed epidemic and how lacking in excitement the desert was.

The girls seemed oddly unfazed by this terrible event, but maybe they'd detached from their emotions, like I was doing now. I could feel it happening as we stood there in the blazing sun—the numb euphoria of leaving my body, the world around me becoming unreal, my fear and anxiety now many times removed . . .

Donovan walked with a slight limp as he led us inside. The house was desert-toned and spare, softened with sheepskin throws and half-burned candles everywhere. As Linda proudly showed us around, I oohed and aahed and my brother tossed her softball questions: How long did it take her dad to build it? Did she know Harrison Ford was a carpenter? Were those pine or redwood beams? Dono cared nothing about carpentry but knew how to keep things going. I felt a little guilty that we were flattering and fawning over Mom's mortal enemy like this, but my brother and I always got extra charming when we were uncomfortable; it was just automatic. Also, we were no dummies. Linda called the shots in Donovan's life. We needed her vote.

"Let's all sit and do some healing," said Linda in the kitchen. The round wooden table was set with six glasses of water, some high-end trail mix, and a skinny wedge of Parmesan cheese. It was nothing like the lush offering Enid would have served—fresh mangoes from the farm stand, juicy tomato slices with basil and mozzarella, hunks of dark bread smothered with Brie . . . I would have to push Enid and her food out of my mind if I wanted to enjoy these people.

"The nuts are delicious!" I gushed as Donovan strummed another song and my stepmother hovered over us with a Sony Betacam. I wondered why she was filming us. Was it because this meeting mattered to them and they wanted to remember it? Or was it her way of controlling the situation? Maybe a little of both, I decided.

Our dad was shy and strange like me. As he strummed and hummed, I snuck glances at his face, looking for bits and pieces of myself. We really did have the same mouth, as Gail Zappa had pointed out not long ago. And the same turned-up nose too. When he sang, his face lit up and I saw sparks of Dono in his eyes. Donovan's music was mesmerizing, but I didn't want to be mesmerized. I'd been waiting seventeen years to have a conversation with my father. I had a mental list of things to ask him about. Easy questions, not the ones I most wanted to ask. Not: *Why did you leave? Why didn't you ever contact us? DID YOU REALLY THINK I WASN'T YOUR DAUGHTER?* I couldn't risk scaring him off like that. I wanted my brother to have a father. *I* wanted to have a father. I'd start small, ask about his favorite books and music. Once he was comfortable with me and saw how smart and thoughtful I was, he'd surely want to see me again. We'd get to the big stuff.

Eventually, my father put down his cosmic guitar and I leaned in to start the interview, then leaned back. My father was already talking—or was it soliloquizing? riddling?—about all sorts of things. What I managed to comprehend, over the next twenty minutes or so: Donovan was really into the legend of the lost city of Atlantis; he dug the poetry of Sappho (*"Me too!"* I wanted to say, but didn't get an in); he had acquired both his limp and his love of books from having polio as a kid; he took credit for starting the sixties hippie flower power movement; and most important, Donovan wanted to save the world with his "bohemian manifesto of change," which preached a kinder, gentler way of living on Earth.

And then, just as suddenly as he'd started talking, my father stopped, stood up, and sauntered down the hall to the bathroom.

He and Linda and Oriole kept doing that. Every twenty minutes or so, one of them would disappear into the bathroom and the smell of hash would fill the house. Clearly, they were seeking relief from the awkward situation, and I didn't blame them, I just wished they'd offer me and Dono some. Did they think we were squares? That we'd judge them?

"I smoke pot!" I blurted, to clear that up.

Everyone nodded, visibly relieved. Oriole pulled a joint out of her pocket and we all went to the porch and got stoned. It broke the ice.

"Have you been to see *River's Edge*, Don?" asked Dono.

I shot my brother a look, shook my head. It was sweet that he wanted to lift me up, but I didn't mind letting our dad stay in his world, and I didn't want to put him on the spot. What if he'd hated the movie and that was why he hadn't said anything?

"Can't say I have," said my father with his lovely lilting accent. "We don't get to the cinema much. Or is that a play?"

And there went my fantasy of Donovan staring up at me on the big screen, filled with remorse. He hadn't even seen the reviews, which wasn't that surprising. I'd seen no newspapers or magazines in the house, just sketchpads, books, and tarot decks.

When the sky was turning pink and stomachs were audibly growling, Linda signaled the end of healing time. "I'm so glad we did this," she said.

"Yes, yes," said my father, a sadness crossing his face. "I'm only sorry it took this long. We wanted to meet, but your mother was just so angry. It made it difficult."

This threw me. Hadn't Mom desperately wanted us to know our dad? It had been Linda standing in the way! As the story went, Enid had once called Linda and pleaded with her to bring Don around to seeing us: "I'm no threat to you," Mom had said. "I know you and Don are happy together, but think of the kids." Linda had turned a deaf ear, and nothing had changed.

Now I wondered: Had our dad really wanted to see us, and Mom was so angry she'd scared him off? Did she play *any* part in how badly things turned out?

A dry wind had whipped up, and our shirts blew on our backs as we hugged goodbye. My father's hug was better this time. Letting me go, he pointed to a distant mountain range, where lens-shaped clouds hovered like flying saucers. "Like celestial sentinels," he said, "guarding the wilderness below."

"Indeed," said Linda, tucking into his arm. As much as I disliked her, I could see why she was the one for Donovan. He'd found a muse who understood his riddles *and* took charge of his life. Mom would have wanted Donovan to lead and would have followed him almost anywhere, but not into the clouds. Enid loved her bohemian life, but in her heart, she'd always be a matter-of-fact Jewish girl from Queens, and thank God for that.

I couldn't face my empty apartment on Orange Drive that night. Dono dropped me at Wilton Place, where I found Mom sitting on the front porch in a distant, downcast mood. Our trip to the desert had clearly hurt her, though she didn't say so. She didn't say anything at all. Having always absorbed my mother's pain, I absorbed it then, and my sympathy for my father snuffed out like a light. I didn't know how to love them both at once, so for now I'd love only Mom, the one who'd earned it.

PART TWO

Womanhood

13

I'm Crazy About You
1988-1989

Of all the big things that happened the year I turned eighteen, the biggest was meeting the first great love of my life, Adam Horovitz.

As always, Dono was the connector. He and Adam's sister, Rachael, then a film publicist, had become close while filming a remake of *The Blob* in New Orleans. (Dono had a big part and made it almost to the end before getting blobbed.) "Rachael's the best!" Dono kept telling me. "We just get each other, like you and me. She feels like family." Back in Los Angeles, he invited Rachael and her famous brother to Wilton Place for dinner. (Anthony was *not* invited.) I could not wait for that night to come. My brother and I were mutually obsessed with the Beastie Boys' one and only album so far, *Licensed to Ill*. Back when we both lived at home, Dono would put on "Rhymin & Stealin" and we'd headbang to the epic Led Zeppelin drum breaks, screaming *"Ali Baba and the forty thieves!"* at the top of our lungs. I knew the Beastie Boys got shit for being white rappers and some people took their jokey-nasty lyrics too seriously, but I didn't care about any of that. To me, the album was all good energy. And I was going to meet the cutest one of its creators!

Rachael, and Adam too, really did feel like family. We got one another's dry jokes and retro movie references, and their warm, funny, New York–ish vibe reminded me of Mom and my grandparents. Adam was twenty-one, the same age as Dono and his friends, which made him feel like another brother. Except that I was insanely attracted to him. I was so lovestruck at dinner, I hardly spoke. Adam was quiet too—nothing like his brash, swaggering Ad-Rock persona. But our connection was undeniable. Over Enid's shepherd's pie, we snuck shy glances, and when we hugged goodbye I thought the whole house might explode with our chemistry. My grandpa Benny always said he knew he'd marry my grandma Tillie from the moment they had their first date at the movies. I wasn't thinking of marriage in that moment, I was thinking, *This is the most attractive, charming, wonderful person I've ever met.*

After that, Adam would often stop by Wilton Place when I happened to be there—probably no coincidence. Sometimes we'd sit close on the living room couch and let the backs of our hands touch. It had become clear that we were mad for each other, but we were trying our hardest to be "just friends." Adam had been dating Molly Ringwald, but they'd drifted apart romantically. I think he was waiting for me to leave Anthony, which I wasn't ready to do yet. Despite all the turmoil in our relationship, despite Anthony's cheating and occasional cruelty, I wasn't ready to quit him. I'd taken such a bold leap, leaving home and moving in with an older man. If I just walked away, what was it all for? It felt wrong to leave my Anthony project unfinished—especially at this sensitive juncture . . .

Not long after Hillel's death, Anthony had gone back to rehab and gotten clean again. My worst nightmare was that he'd relapse if he found out I was falling in love with Adam. People thought Anthony was indestructible, but I wasn't convinced. I was bound by a strange belief that I *had* to be with him to keep him safe.

So for months, Adam and I never did more than hug and touch hands.

Then one beautiful September day—*just a perfect day*, as the Lou Reed song went—everything changed.

I'd wrapped *Say Anything* and would soon leave for London to film a new movie, *The Rachel Papers*. Anthony was in Northern California doing a show—one of the band's first without Hillel. After the longest summer of my life, filled with more drama and heartache than I'd ever imagined I could hold, I woke up on this sunny morning and decided that today, damn it, I would be a normal, frivolous teenage girl—not a babysitter or a breadwinner.

Dono had pulled together a big Sunday brunch at Duke's Coffee Shop next to the Whisky. There were probably ten of us, all smushed around a long table, eating oozy, delicious omelets and fluffy French toast with weak diner coffee and taking turns sneaking out back to smoke pot. I don't remember who exactly was there that day, only that Adam was sitting across the messy table, the toes of his green shell-top Adidas touching the toes of my black pointed flats.

After brunch, Adam and I peeled off from the group and drove to Aron's Records, where, like Duke's, you often saw musicians and celebrities and other Hollywood types. No one ever hounded Adam or asked him to autograph a copy of *Licensed to Ill* at Aron's, though people recognized and loved him. I was too stoned and in love to shop, but Adam went straight to the "C" bin and selected three Elvis Costello albums: *My Aim Is True*, *Almost Blue*, and *Blood & Chocolate*.

The pasty cashier flipped through the records, squinting beneath his pompadour. "You gonna sample these?"

"Nope," said Adam. "They're for Ione."

I floated right through the acoustic-tiled ceiling when he said that. Out in the parking lot, he handed me the bag.

"These albums are dope," he said with an adorable shrug. "I think you'll love them."

I hugged the records to my chest, my heartbeat so loud it drowned out the Sunset Plaza traffic. "Are you crazy?" I said. "Of course I'll love them. I'll listen to them on the plane. I mean, not the records . . . I'll make tapes!"

Adam laughed. He looked like a fifties matinee idol with his thick, cropped hair, brooding eyebrows, and white T-shirt. When he crossed his arms, his Silver Surfer tattoo poked from his sleeve.

I put the albums in my trunk. They'd have to live there till I returned. Anthony wouldn't open the trunk—unless he sensed the records' powerful romantic energy and investigated. I pictured him calling me in London: "Since when do you like Elvis Costello?" he'd say. *Since Adam*, I'd think. Maybe I'd even say it.

After the record store, Adam and I went to Wilton Place, ostensibly for a snack. I opened all the windows and we sat on the sofa, enjoying the breeze, fingers just touching. Our bodies inched closer, till our thighs touched and Adam made a frustrated *argh* noise and pulled away, running his hand through his hair.

"That was fun today," I said. "I told you LA was great." The Beastie Boys were die-hard New Yorkers, just temporarily in LA to record their second album. Adam liked to talk shit about avocados and all the fucking sunshine, but I was convinced he was secretly falling in love with my town.

"Okay, fine, LA's nice," said Adam, "but I still don't feel at home here." He turned to look at me with his deep brown eyes. "Except, I guess when I'm with you."

And then we just couldn't restrain ourselves anymore.

It was terribly romantic, like any kiss that's been repressed and repressed for the sake of decency. Remembering it now, it was like the end of an opera, when the yearning Tristan chord finally resolves. It was the most consequential kiss of my life so far. I felt restored. And then ruined. Everything I'd ever wanted had come true with that one kiss. But I wasn't ready to keep it. I hadn't hit rock bottom with Anthony yet.

So I walked Adam to his car and we promised once again to stay friends and only friends. I watched him pull away and closed the door behind me.

The next morning, I went to Mom's room for the scoop on Warren Beatty. They'd gone out the night before, and she'd come home impressively late. Enid had been sleeping with Warren on and off since the 1950s. He had a photographic memory and still knew by heart her parents' number in Queens, from when she was a teen. (Can you imagine how many women's numbers were stuck in Warren Beatty's head?) Every seven years or so, he'd get Mom's new number from my grandparents and call her up for a date. Mom had hardly dated since Billy, but she never could resist Warren.

Normally, Mom and I would avoid getting into the details of her love life; I never asked and she never told. But this was Warren Beatty! Mom was just getting to the part about how, for some reason, they'd done it in his car, when the phone rang. It was Anthony, calling from a hotel.

"I dreamed you kissed someone last night," he said accusingly.

I almost dropped the phone. Was Anthony psychic? It was practically an invitation to come clean and just say it: *Yes, I kissed someone! He makes me happy and I love him and want to be with him, not you.*

But I was a coward, so I said, "That's weird. Where's your show tonight?"

After the kiss, I did what I always did when I felt distant from Anthony: went to see him perform. It was usually the best medicine. Watching him from the stage wings, my depleted heart would fill with pride and admiration. *He's a star, and he chose me*, I'd think. Then I'd be into him again. Wash, rinse, repeat.

The show was in Oakland, a six-hour drive from LA. I sped like a maniac to get there in time. I wanted to see Anthony backstage, to make sure his psychic dream hadn't derailed him. I needed confirmation he was still okay, still clean.

There was a void in the dressing room without Hillel. The band was trying out a new guitarist (they hadn't yet found John Frusciante), and I felt sorry for the guy, trying to fill those magic shoes. Still, things were looking up. Anthony was clean and clear-eyed and had not brought any girls backstage, if only because he was expecting me. Flea seemed back to his old self, beaming like the sun. He and Loesha were married and expecting a baby any day now.

Anthony liked the fancy Pierre Cardin attaché I brought him, a guilt present. (I'd thought it seemed so chic and Florida-gangstery, like something Carl would have had.)

"Thank you, my beautiful, smart, sexy, loyal girl," he said, ravaging my neck with kisses.

I pushed him away, pretending to be ticklish. Anthony often said nice things like that, but he'd never called me "loyal." My loyalty had always gone without saying. Was he giving me a message? Did he know? I tried to look into his eyes and see what was really there, but he was already turning away, heading for the stage.

Anthony was spectacular that night, strutting and leaping around in hot-pink baseball pants and no shirt. His arms were smooth and golden, his hair shone in the spotlight, and his scattershot rapping was forceful and commanding. But this time, the medicine wasn't working. I admired Anthony's music, but it didn't bring me joy. None of this brought me joy.

Sometimes when Anthony went to an NA or AA meeting, I'd go to an Al-Anon meeting. There was this woman I'd see there, the mother of a drug addict. Once, when it was her turn to speak, she talked for her allotted time about the hell she'd been through with her kid. Then she looked right at me and said, "I'm his mom, so I can't leave him. But if you don't have to be with an addict, my advice is don't. Get out of it. Live your own life."

She made it sound so clear-cut, but I thought that was kind of like saying to an alcoholic, "If you don't want to suffer, then just don't drink." Easier said than done. Possibly reading my skepticism, the mom approached me after the meeting with a book recommendation. "It's called *Codependent No More*, by Melody Beattie," she said. "Do you want to write that down?"

"I'll remember," I said. "Thanks."

For *The Rachel Papers*, in London, I would temporarily escape my real-life love triangle for a fictional one. It was a decent screenplay, adapted from a really good, if sexist, Martin Amis novel about a wily university student, Charles Highway, who methodically lures the girl of his dreams, Rachel Noyce, away from her smug boyfriend. The plot, in summary: Boy stalks girl, boy gets girl, boy and girl shag (a lot), boy discovers girl is not a projection of his fantasies but an actual human being, boy is disillusioned, boy dumps girl. Basically, my worst relationship fear writ large. But in the end, Rachel doesn't take it so hard, and rightly not. She's rich, educated, beautiful, and great in bed. Imperfect or not, she's totally out of Charlie's league.

I was thrilled to be working with Dexter Fletcher, who played Charlie. I'd loved him in *The Elephant Man* and *Bugsy Malone*. He was so cute—the only actor I'd ever had on my wall, in fact. All through middle school, Dexter—bare chested, lush lipped, and holding a big, sexy basket of fruit—had watched over me from my *Caravaggio* poster, and now here we were, pretend lovers. I felt just as privileged to work with James Spader, Jonathan Pryce, Jared Harris, Bill Paterson, Michael Gambon, Eric Stoltz (who'd also had a cameo in *Say Anything*), and

our suave English director, Damian Harris (son of the famous Richard Harris and brother of actors Jamie and Jared). Best of all, Amelia
Fleetwood had a small role, and we got to run around London in our
downtime. Spending that time with Amelia, away from Anthony,
helped me reconnect with the carefree girl I'd been before him.

Rachel Noyce was twenty, two years older than me. It's rare for
teen actors to play older characters, but I looked a little older and felt
it, as I always had. Rachel came easier to me than Diane Court had
in *Say Anything*. She was smart but not a bookish valedictorian, and
her posh life, filmed mostly in the mansions and town houses of the
director's friends, was so much fun to drop into, right out of my high
school fantasies.

Then there was the sex part. To quote the movie, "Sex was Rachel's
Disneyland," so there was a lot of shagging in *The Rachel Papers*. For
days on end, we filmed graphic, buck-naked love scenes. Thankfully,
I had lots of experience pretending in the sack. In real life, I didn't exactly love sex like Rachel did. It wasn't my Disneyland but a way both
to connect and to feel important. My body was responsive, but with
every boy I'd been with so far, a part of me was acting, too concerned
about being appealing and too afraid of being judged the way Charlie
judged Rachel to really lose myself. Orgasms never came easy.

I didn't mind being naked on camera. I was feeling good about
my body, thanks to a juice cleanse I'd done to prepare. (When
tempted to cheat—I'd discovered Hobnob biscuits!—I'd just imagine Polly Platt waving her finger: *Watch all the snacking.*) Most
important, I liked and trusted Dexter, Damian Harris, and our
cinematographer, Alex Thomson, who'd filmed movies like *Excalibur*, *Year of the Dragon*, and *Labyrinth*. Everyone involved was
professional and kind, and it gave me a sense of control that the
love scenes were tightly choreographed, down to each caress and
emotion: *Charles and Rachel kiss. He caresses her neck. She moves*

on top, unbuttoning his shirt. They roll over. Charles puts Rachel's left arm over her head. As Rachel and Charles begin to make love, Charles feels grateful, then amazed, then comfortable . . . , and so on.

The only uncomfortable moment was when Dexter brought his tough Cockney model girlfriend to set. You weren't supposed to do that, especially not on a closed-set day. As Dexter and I rolled around in the sheets, she glared from the back of the room, chain-smoking Silk Cuts. Was she going to lose it and beat me up? I closed my eyes and thought of Adam.

A part of me was always thinking of Adam. The Kiss had made me weak for him. We'd been sneaking around a little, before I left for London, meeting at Wilton Place or the field under the Hollywood sign to bask in each other, and kiss and touch some more. It hadn't gone further than that. Partly because of my one-sided, infuriating loyalty to Anthony, and partly because as light and effortless as our connection was, it was still fine and fragile.

After London, I flew to New York for an audition with Woody Allen. Sorry—a *meeting* with Woody Allen. My new manager, Arlyne Rothberg, kept stressing that it was "just a casual meeting, *not* an audition." She might have been trying to take the pressure off, knowing how gaga I was for Woody's films. Arlyne was a bigwig in the business who also managed Diane Keaton and Carly Simon, so I believed her when she said: "He notoriously doesn't talk in meetings or auditions. Expect him to say nothing."

Fortunately, I had a whole new wardrobe to show off. I'd loved my clothes in *The Rachel Papers* so much that I'd purchased several outfits from the production. (A small digression: Actors are prone to being both sentimental and sticky-fingered, and many nab or buy costume pieces as souvenirs to remember their work by. I'd just met John Malkovich at a dinner party in London, for example. He was weirdly sexy with his lisp and tiny teeth and small devilish eyes, but what sent his magnetism over the top for me was the French lace cravat louchely tied at his neck. He'd worn it in *Dangerous Liaisons*, which he'd just wrapped.)

I felt my *Rachel Papers* costumes similarly worked for me. There was something transformative about the jewel-toned ensembles that Marit Allen, the costume designer, had chosen for Rachel. Wearing them in the movie, I felt closer to Rachel. Wearing them in real life, I felt like myself, but elevated.

For my non-audition with Woody, I wisely chose a Rachel Noyce red wool skirt paired with black pumps, a hot-pink short-sleeved sweater, and a puffy black headband. When I'd first laid eyes on this outfit I must have given Marit a surprised look because she said, "There's no such thing as mismatched colors if the hues are complementary. Trust your eye." Marit taught me so much about style.

So there I was, in my complementary hues, ready to intrigue Woody Allen. The meeting was in a velvety brown room off the lobby of his Fifth Avenue apartment building. The curtains were drawn against the bright afternoon sun, so it took me a minute to register him, slumped on the edge of a leather Chesterfield sofa, legs crossed. Through his thick black glasses, he stared flatly into the distance, as if he hadn't noticed me. I looked around for a chair.

"Where do you go to school?" he said.

He's talking! He must like me. Should I stand? I'll stand. I crossed my arms, uncrossed them.

"Oh, uh, I don't, anymore. I went to . . ."—I was about to tell him Hollywood High but changed my mind, remembering Woody liked shiksas—"Immaculate Heart. A Catholic school."

"What do you like to do?"

"I, uh, like drawing?"

"What's your favorite film?"

Had I ever seen a film? My mind was blank. "*Manhattan*?" I tried.

Woody nodded, just barely. There was a moment of silence.

"Well, thank you," he said softly. Or did he only sigh?

A woman rose from a chair in the corner, showing me the door.

"Thank you," I mumbled with a small bow.

And that was it.

I crossed Fifth Avenue to Central Park, sat on a bench, and put my head in my hands. Woody had talked to me all right, and it had completely thrown me for a loop. So much for my aloof Rachel Noyce persona. I'd come off like an insecure airhead. *Manhattan*? He probably thought I was a kiss-ass, picking his own movie. If only I'd said *The Year of Living Dangerously*, or *Fanny and Alexander*, or *8½*, maybe he wouldn't have sent me away. There went my hope of being Woody's next Mariel Hemingway.

Something good did come out of that day. I realized there was nothing interesting about being a human mirror. My own opinions were worthwhile. Woody must have thought so, or why else would he have asked for them? I was someone worth talking to, and I was going to start acting like it.

Adam happened to be in New York too, but I wasn't sure I'd see him. He'd dipped his toe into acting and was busy promoting his upcoming movie, *Lost Angels*.

Since I wasn't available, Adam had been dating around—fabulous women like Heather Graham, Winona Ryder, and Moon Zappa's cousin Lala Sloatman. The actresses I wasn't so worried about, as gorgeous and accomplished as they were. "I care about them," Adam had told me on the phone, "they're just not you." But Lala was more recent, and she had this bewitching combination of beauty, openness, and vulnerability that made people, including me, want to take care of her. Everyone fell hard for Lala.

I was packing for my flight home to LA when the hotel phone rang. It was Adam's brother Matthew. Adam was in the hospital. He'd had some kind of seizure during a photo shoot when the strobe light flashed. He was asking for me.

I raced to the hospital and into Adam's room. He was sleeping, and Matthew stood at his bedside with a doctor. The doctor was explaining that Adam would have sore muscles and need lots of rest because post-seizure, you feel as if you've just run a marathon. This doctor spoke only to Matthew, not acknowledging me. To him, I was just some teenage girl who'd barged in, not family. But I felt *so much* like Adam's family. I felt like everything all at once—his partner, his mother, his sister, his friend, his lover. Why weren't we together? My heart was bursting, I loved him so much.

When Adam woke up, it was just me in the room. I went to his side, taking his hand. They'd given him a sedative and he was really out of it. He looked surprised to see me. "*Ioneeeee*," he said, all dazed and goofy and vulnerable, "I'm crazy about you."

"*Shhh*," I said, smiling, "I think you're supposed to rest."

His eyes drifted closed and I thought he'd fallen back to sleep, but then they fluttered open again. "Crazy about you," he repeated.

"I know," I said, tears in my eyes. I was about to say it back, but then Adam started to have another seizure. I ran to get the nurse.

That was the last time I got to see Adam before I left. They gave him another sedative and I had to catch my plane, so I left him a note that said *I'm crazy about you too. See you soon. xo Ione*

At the airport bookstore, I saw that book the Al-Anon mom had rec-ommended. It was impossible to miss, front and center in the best-sellers section: *Codependent No More.*

Hmmm, I thought. I bought it.

Then the entire flight home was one long *Ohhh.*

The book said, in a nutshell, that codependency comes from a fundamental human desire to "save" others, which we think is a selfless desire, but often, it's more of a selfish one. For a codependent person (usually a woman), giving equals having control, and having control equals safety. She gives and gives to her partner, telling herself she can change them, even when the writing is on the wall that she can't. But she's afraid to walk away because what she fears more than anything is being alone. At her core, she fears abandonment.

When I returned to Orange Drive, I shoved the book behind some shoeboxes in my closet. Not to hide it from Anthony—he was on the road again—but to hide it from myself. I didn't want to think about it for a while. Reading *Codependent No More* was a bit like looking into one of those magnifying mirrors that shows your face super close up. I'd never seen myself this way before, but it was definitely me, and I wasn't as sweet looking as I'd thought.

The next time I saw Adam, I'd just taken a heroic dose of psychedelic mushrooms. Wilton Place was back to its original self that night— warm and alive and free of marital strife. Mom was hosting her weekly poker game and the screen door kept slamming with new people stopping by. A friend of Dono's had offered the mushrooms. "Sure, why not?" I'd said. I was staying over anyway.

I happened to be on day five of the same nine-day juice cleanse I'd done in London for *The Rachel Papers*. (It was 20 percent about being healthy, 80 percent about being thin.) I'd already gained back the five pounds I'd lost that time, plus a couple. I always ended up gaining weight after a diet.

Anyway, a handful of mushrooms on my very empty stomach resulted in a very strong trip. I was lying outside on the grass, bonding with Billy's agave plants, when Adam showed up at Wilton Place. He came toward me and I thought he must be a hallucination, he was just so dreamy. I whooshed to him like a magnet, and we hugged and hugged in the porch light.

Then we were in the living room with Dono's crowd, watching
Baby Doll, a great old Elia Kazan movie where Carroll Baker sleeps in
a baby-doll nightgown in a crib. My sense of hearing was off the charts
and the rustling cotton fields in the movie merged with the laughter
from Mom's poker game in the other room, forming giant sound waves
that said, *Ooh, ahh, ooh, ahh.* "Can you hear them?" I asked Adam.
He was mostly sober and could not. The others had left us alone and
Adam was stroking my hair and I felt everything I'd been bottling up
since I met Anthony spilling out of me. For the next millennium of
my mushroom trip, I locked Adam into a revelatory purging of my
relationship guilt and shame. He patiently heard me out, only interrupting once to tease, affectionately, "You have a lot to say."

"I do," I sighed. And then, a voice in my head spoke up, clear and
confident, like the voice that had scared off the Orange Drive peeping
Tom. Slowly, so I would pay attention, it said: *You don't have to take
care of Anthony anymore. He is not your job. You are not a nurse.*

"I'm not a nurse!" I told Adam.

"That's true," he said.

"It's my job to take care of me," I said.

"Straight up," he said.

I stood and took Adam's hand. He followed me upstairs and into
my old bedroom, where we went to bed together for the first time, and
a new day began. I could not go back to Anthony's world after that.
My heart was too full. I would not fit.

14

Nineties Daydream
1989–1991

Once I'd had my psychedelic codependent-no-more epiphany, I could not wait to act on it. The very next morning—well, afternoon—I kissed Adam at the door, watched him drive away, then went to find Anthony's tour itinerary.

"What did you just say?" said Anthony on the phone. I'd caught him at his hotel, somewhere in the Midwest. As usual there was laughter and music in the background. Maybe he hadn't heard me, or maybe he couldn't believe his ears.

"I think we should break up," I repeated. "I love you, but I think it's best." Could it really be this easy?

Anthony was hurt, but he didn't fight it. He'd probably been ready to end it himself but just hadn't bothered. And why would he? I'd made it so easy for him to have his cake and eat it too.

A few days after that, a limo pulled up to Wilton Place. I watched from my bedroom window as Anthony got out, wearing red basketball shorts and a red tank top and gripping what looked like a trophy. He lumbered up my front steps, left the trophy on the doorstep, and drove off in that long black limo.

It wasn't actually a trophy that he left but an Art Deco lamp we'd seen at the flea market. The base was a nude woman, holding up the round glass bulb. Anthony hadn't left a note, but I knew him so well I felt I understood his parting message: *Remember the beautiful times we shared, not just the ugly ones.*

I did remember the good times, but I wouldn't miss Anthony. I'd try to put him out of my mind, naively believing I could simply erase all the pain and anxiety of our relationship now that Adam had rescued me.

A few months later, Anthony would send me a letter—and one for Mom too. He was working the Twelve Steps and making his amends, which means being very specific about your wrongs and regrets and taking full ownership of them. Anthony covered a lot of territory in my letter—including a few events I'd done my best to block out. He apologized for all the worry and hurt he'd put me through, for his jealousy, for cheating, for criticizing my body and saying other unkind things, and for the time he poured his drink on me at the Lakers game.

Reading Anthony's amends, seeing what I'd put up with for two years spelled out on paper like that, I'd think of that Joan Didion line about how "it was distinctly possible to stay too long at the Fair." Was the fair ever a good place? Why had I abandoned myself there? Could I trust myself not to do it again? Eventually, it would sink in that my relationship with Anthony had fucked me up a bit.

All the same, I'd harbor no grudges toward Anthony, especially after his heartfelt apology. And I kind of liked that lamp. There was something so pure and hopeful about that bare naked lady, holding the moon. She reminded me of dreamy things I used to like as a kid. I took her with me when I moved into a new house, with Adam's friends Sato Masuzawa and Max Perlich.

I'd been living with Sato and Max for a couple of weeks when Adam and I went to Le Parc Hotel for a rooftop swim. I was floating in his arms in the shallow end, feeling utterly surrendered and in love, when Adam said, almost urgently, "You should live with me. I've waited so long for you."

I looked up at my boyfriend-slash-savior, with his wet eyelashes and pleading expression. Maybe I needed some "me time" to get to know myself again. That would probably be healthy. But then again, this was Adam, asking me to move in with him. What if this was my big chance at happiness, and I blew it? To hell with that.

"Okay," I said. "Let's do it."

I moved into Adam's 1930s apartment on Stanley and Hollywood Boulevard that night. It was glorious, with a huge balcony, floor-to-ceiling windows, and instruments and stereo equipment everywhere. I even loved the portrait of Mushmouth from *Fat Albert* hanging over the mantel.

The Beastie Boys' second album, *Paul's Boutique*, had come out that summer, a couple of months after *Say Anything* was released (to great reviews and so-so ticket sales). I thought *Paul's Boutique* was genius, with all its crazy beats, loops, and samples of everyone from James Brown to Afrika Bambaataa to Johnny Cash to the Beatles to my dad (the drumbeat from "Hurdy Gurdy Man" is on "Car Thief"). But *Paul's Boutique* was too complicated and weird for the mainstream kids who'd loved *Licensed to Ill*. Like *Say Anything*, it would be a sleeper hit. The bright side, for now, was that the record tour had been downscaled, which meant Adam and I got to spend lots of time together in LA.

It felt like one long daydream. Adam was in one of the biggest bands of our generation, and I had just starred in *Say Anything*. We were the perfect amount of famous—dancing backstage at Sonic Youth, wearing free clothes from Adidas and the Beastie Boys' X-Large brand, and throwing house parties where our old friends mixed with Hollywood hotshots. At the same time, we could go completely

unnoticed when we wanted to. It helped that the press was mellower
then. There have always been Hollywood gossip columnists, but
tabloid culture was still an innocent little baby compared to what it
would explode into when Paris Hilton hit the scene. The paparazzi
didn't yet stalk celebrities outside restaurants or in the streets for
"just like us" candids. There was no *In Touch Weekly*, *OK!*, or *TMZ*
yet, and most importantly, no Internet.

Publicity mattered, of course. Most every movie or show release
came with the obligatory press tour, which I was always happy to do.
Interviews were much more fun than auditions. I liked talking about
the filmmaking process and analyzing myself out loud. I'd been such
an internal kid, I longed for people to know me. I felt ready to be seen.
But the real me rarely was. No matter how grounded and thoughtful
I was in interviews, reporters couldn't resist portraying me as a wide-
eyed ingenue. For example, the opening lines of a *Chicago Tribune*
profile headlined "Surprised Star":

> *Ione Skye seems a little bit lost. She's not quite sure where she's going,
> and she's rather mystified to be where she is. She's so delicate that she
> seems almost fragile, so beautiful even without makeup that she seems
> unreal, and so apparently surprised by her circumstances that she
> seems almost like a fawn, frozen by the headlights of an automobile.*

It was one thing to be infantilized by the press, but another to be
objectified . . .

One day, Adam and I met up with Dono and the other Beastie
Boys, Mike Diamond (Mike D) and Adam Yauch (MCA), at Jerry's
Famous Deli in Westwood. We were outside, flipping through maga-
zines on the newsstand, when Dono said, "Whoa."

He was holding *Celebrity Sleuth*, an adult magazine that show-
cased stills of actresses in sex scenes. And there I was, frozen in a

full-frontal nude moment from *The Rachel Papers*. I spun on my heel, feeling as if my clothes had been ripped off me, right there on the sidewalk. I didn't mind doing nude scenes when I was prepared and making the choice myself, but to show the image so flatly and out of its original context was demeaning. While it was nothing compared to the exploitation some young actresses were subjected to, it sucked.

"Hey, don't be upset!" Dono came running after me, the magazine in his hand. He flipped through the pages. "Look, Diane Keaton is in here from *Looking for Mr. Goodbar*. Diane Keaton!"

I laughed. It did make me feel better to be in the company of the great Diane Keaton. And then Adam, Mike, and Yauch came over and hugged me and I felt much better.

I adored those Beastie Boys. They loved to goof around but were smart, considerate, and not chauvinistic at all, surprisingly. I thought it was cute how enmeshed they were, for guys. Yauch was twenty-five—the oldest and wisest of the group, with a beatnik goatee and a soft, deliberate drawl. Mike was the son of big-time New York art dealers and actually quite sophisticated behind the bad-boy act and the giant VW insignia he wore for show. He was often quiet, with bursts of fun and wildness. Adam, my Adam, was the darling sweetie pie: touching, funny, and up for fun but very, very private.

The Beastie Boys may have thrown off their party-boy personas, but they still liked to party, in a chill way—lots of weed and mushrooms. Compared to the Chili Peppers' scene, which had felt welcoming enough but often tense in the shadow of Anthony's and Hillel's addictions, the Beastie Boys' scene felt much more open and fun, fun, fun. There was always some activity going on: group road trips to the desert; nighttime games of Red Rover at "the field," our favorite park, under the Hollywood sign; and endless hangs by the pool at "Club D," Mike and his girlfriend's Spanish-style villa.

Mike and Yauch had the coolest girlfriends, Tamra Davis and Lisa Ann Cabasa. Tamra, Mike's girlfriend, was in her late twenties and had already been married—a real grown-up. She was a music video director who'd worked with Depeche Mode, the Smiths, and Young MC. She also grew killer pot and cooked delicious healthy food for all of us. Lisa Ann was a stunning actress with parts in the upcoming *Wild at Heart* and *Twin Peaks*. She was more in the starry-eyed-teen phase of life, like me.

Sometimes when the band was recording, I'd drive to the canyon to be a rock girlfriend with Lisa Ann. She and Yauch rented one of the original Laurel Canyon log cabins from Carrie Fisher. The big draw of that place was the old clawfoot bathtub that sat in front of the living room fireplace. We'd build a fire, eat some mushrooms, slip into the delicious hot water, and let the rolling revelations begin. Sometimes the revelations were more like affirmations.

"We're powerful," Lisa would say.

"We're dope," I'd agree (I'd started talking like a Beastie Boy, couldn't help it).

"Like, think of all that we've accomplished," Lisa would say. "We act. We make art. We make our own money. We walk our own paths."

"We're our own women," I'd say.

Then we'd dry off and make a pot of herbal tea, maybe sketch or paint for a bit. By then the mushrooms would have faded and we'd feel slightly less powerful, slightly more afraid when strange cars passed on that lonely mountain road.

"Meet up with the boys?" one of us would say.

Lisa and I often carpooled to the Beastie Boys' recording studio, G-Son, in Atwater Village. They'd bought and tricked out an old ballroom next to a plumbing shop called Gilson's. The "I" and "L" had fallen off the sign, and someone had painted in a little hyphen to spell "G-Son." It was like the Beastie Boys' version of Andy Warhol's Factory, a creative hive where something was always happening, day or night. Aside from the recording studio, there was the X-Large clothing label and the Grand Royal record label and magazine (I contributed a comic strip, and Adam and I posed for a photo shoot as Joey Buttafuoco and Amy Fisher). The boys shot videos in the back alley and shot hoops in the inner courtyard, where there was also a skateboard ramp.

To be close to Adam, I started painting a mural on the lounge room wall. I'd page through skateboarding magazines and comics and whatever was lying around G-Son until I'd see something that gave me a certain click inside, and that's what I'd paint. First came a Vaughn Bodē–style Cheech Wizard, then a *Spy vs. Spy* character, then my best likenesses of the people around me—Adam, Lisa Ann and Yauch, Mike and Tamra, the record producer Mario Caldato Jr., even my half sister Astrella, who stopped by sometimes. Lisa Ann added a psychedelic mermaid, and various friends tagged their names. The mural grew and grew, spreading like a forest from wall to wall to wall, until it pretty much consumed the whole space. The more I painted, the further acting fell from my mind. Sometimes I forgot I was an actor at all.

My manager, Arlyne Rothberg, had been leaving me messages, but I'd been avoiding her since a disastrous audition I'd done for *Mystic Pizza*. The director had really wanted me, but I'd let him down, phoned it in. "Try again," he'd pleaded, "just give me something!" But it had felt, in that moment, as if I had nothing to give. I was nineteen and had been working consistently for four years. I wasn't exactly burned out, just extremely distracted. My commitment to acting had been derailed by the fun of living inside the Beasties' world, where I didn't have to go to bed early and wake up early like a grown-up and all I did was play. And the deeper I fell into my rock-girlfriend life, the scarier it was to imagine putting myself out there for auditions.

Then one day Josh Richman, my friend and nemesis from *River's Edge*, came by G-Son. I was in my paint-splattered jeans, a little high, and perfectly content to be working on my mural, until Josh said, "*This* is what you do every day?"

I was proud of my mural and my decisions, till I saw them through his eyes. Where would I put my creativity when there were no walls left to paint?

Not to give Josh too much credit, but it was one of those moments when an offhand remark, at just the moment I needed to hear it, struck a chord.

I stopped ignoring Arlyne Rothberg's calls and made three movies in 1991—all with inspiring female directors. (Only about 12 percent of directors are female today, and back then they were even rarer.)

In *Gas Food Lodging*, directed by Allison Anders and costarring Fairuza Balk, Brooke Adams, and James Brolin (also featuring Dono in a supporting role!), I played my favorite kind of role, the Angry Fuckup. The film was shot in dusty Deming, New Mexico, and I got to wear round-toed cowboy boots just like the real Deming teens, work in a real diner for practice (I was a terrible waitress), and do lots of yelling and door-slamming. It was incredibly cathartic, coming off two years of bottling things up with Anthony. I'd never felt so confident in a role before.

After *Gas Food Lodging*, I had a small part as Rob Lowe's character's girlfriend in *Wayne's World*. The director, Penelope Spheeris, was known for switching off between big-budget studio projects and underground films, like I was starting to do. I'd loved Penelope's *Decline of Western Civilization* documentaries about punk and heavy metal kids, as well as her movie with Flea, *Suburbia*, so I jumped at the chance to work with her. Though a "girlfriend of..." role wasn't exactly one I could sink my teeth into, just being in Penelope's presence was empowering. She'd grown up in a chaotic, violent family of carnival performers, which might have given her the grit it took to climb as high as she did in the man's world of movie directing. But Penelope was always positive. I remember her telling me, "When bad things happen to you, you can get pissed and negative, or you can turn it into something creative and help people."

The last movie I made that year was with two women I already knew and loved, Tamra Davis and Drew Barrymore. I was so happy when Tamra asked me to be in her first film, *Guncrazy*—especially when I found out Drew was starring. We'd been crossing paths for years and had always had a nice connection. *Maybe we'll become besties*, I thought hopefully. Drew was in a great phase of her life. No longer a "little girl lost," she'd risen from her traumatic childhood like a phoenix. On set, she quietly compelled everyone around her to rise up too. But Drew and I would never become close friends, sadly. Sometimes I wonder if I remind her too much of her chaotic younger days and she'd rather look forward. You can't force a friendship.

Between my work and Adam's recording and performing schedule, we went to New York every chance we got. I'll never forget the first time he took me. Adam had two apartments in the West Village—one small loft off University Place that he paid for with his new money, and a humbler family place in a brick low-rise farther west on Washington Place. Adam's parents had divorced when he was three. His siblings had chosen to live with their dad, the playwright Israel Horovitz. Adam had chosen to live with his artist mom, Doris, on Washington Place. She'd passed away a few years earlier, and Adam still grieved for her.

Washington Place was Adam's Wilton Place, a museum of his childhood. Of course I wanted to stay there. Adam preferred it too. He missed his mom so much, and her warmhearted spirit was all over that apartment—you could feel it radiating from her oil paintings on the walls. There were framed family photos everywhere too. One showed baby Adam sitting on Doris's lap. She had tousled black hair and squinted into the sun with a wry half smile just like Adam's. In another photo, he was about six, wearing corrective shoes and standing by the Fire Island ferry. That one made my heart explode. I'd never been so entranced by a boyfriend's childhood pictures before. I wanted to reach through time and embrace that boy with the corrective shoes. I loved him as intensely as I loved the rock star version of Adam who existed now. Looking at those pictures, I knew I wasn't with Adam because he was a star and he'd chosen me. I was with him because I couldn't imagine a better person existed in the entire world.

Adam's old bedroom was a stripped-down version of what it once had been, like an Arthur Miller stage set of a boy's room. I remember a mattress on the floor, a record player, a softball bat leaning against the wall, a Mets pennant, and a film poster for *Sweet Smell of Success*. There was a white sheet tacked to the window that we never pulled back. On the other side, the sun arced and fell and engines idled and kids raced, sneakers slapping the pavement. Adam's beloved Manhattan was right outside the window, saying, "Discover me," but we were too busy discovering each other.

We spent our first three days together in New York in Adam's room—talking, writing, drawing, looking at pictures, making mixtapes, and having sex. The more I showed him of myself, the more he liked me. It felt safe to be myself around him.

By accepting me so completely, Adam was a game changer for me, sexually. Before him, sex was like eating hot buttered toast when you have a cold and it tastes like cardboard. But now I could taste the deliciousness of sex, because I was in my body, not in my head, critiquing myself or worrying that I wasn't ready or safe. It was so natural with Adam. I was beginning to understand how bonding sex could be.

On our third evening of nesting, Adam bolted upright in bed. "Oh, snap, Nick's mom's gallery opening!"

I sat up, catching my naked body and wild bedhead in the mirror on the door. All of Adam's New York friends would be there, and I wanted to meet them. I hoped I'd fit in. In LA, I traveled with the Beastie Boys' posse, but it was my home turf. I had Dono and Wilton Place and all the best brunch spots to bring to the table. Here, it was just me.

"Should I dress up for the art show?" I asked.

Adam shook his head, pulling me from the sheets. "It's casual."

I had not packed for a cold walking city and grabbed Adam's big puffer jacket as I followed him out the door and down to the sidewalk. The cold wind off the Hudson cleared my foggy head and heightened my nervousness. I was about to meet Adam's best friend, Nadia Dajani, a prospect way more intimidating than any audition.

Nadia and Adam grew up together in a different New York than I was seeing now. The city was rough and full of flavor in the seventies and eighties. They were independent kids, home by dinner, then back out to punk shows at Irving Plaza or CBGB. From everything I'd heard about Nadia, she was sharp and street-smart and cooler than cool. The one thing they disagreed upon, Adam said, was the Mets (Adam) versus the Yankees (Nadia).

At the Paula Cooper Gallery on Wooster Street in SoHo, Adam took my hand and we zigzagged through the sea of grown-ups with their plastic cups of chardonnay, out a back-room window, and onto a fire escape. Nadia, Nick Cooper (the Beastie Boys' first manager and Paula's son), and Dave Skilken, another close childhood friend, were huddled against the wind, smoking and passing around a comically large cheese wheel Nick had swiped from the party. I recognized Dave and Nadia from the Beastie Boys' "Fight for Your Right" video, where they'd dressed up to look like "nice kids." In real life they were good, outgoing kids from nice families but tough and edgy by choice. I hoped my LA-ness didn't stand out.

Adam introduced me around, one arm slung over my shoulders. Nadia was friendly but clearly sussing me out. She wore big hoop earrings, black eyeliner around her dark eyes, and her long black hair in a sleek ponytail. Nick wore a Bad Brains T-shirt under a moth-eaten cardigan. Dave was cheery and buoyant in chino floods and a London Fog trench coat about ten sizes too big.

"Fly jacket," Adam said. "That's what's up."

"Expensive wino, that's my look," said Dave.

"Walter Matthau in full effect," said Nick.

I cuddled into Adam, beaming at their strange banter. I thought these New York kids were so witty and urbane, like Dorothy Parker characters but for the 1990s.

Soon, we crawled back through the window and marched through the chic gallery crowd and into the SoHo night, in search of pizza.

As the guys jaywalked across Houston Street, Nadia linked her arm through mine, holding me back. We stood for a moment, staring up at the traffic light. I hopped on my toes to keep warm, but Nadia seemed oblivious to the cold.

"Don't hurt Adam," she said quite suddenly.

I stopped hopping and faced her. "I wouldn't!"

"I mean it," said Nadia. "He's good and rare. He's like a brother to me."

"I know," I said. "I'd never hurt him." And I meant it from the bottom of my heart. I never wanted to leave Adam or do anything but love him. I could even imagine us growing old together. It was crazy how much we clicked. It was like Adam would write in his song "Get It Together":

Ad-Rock down with the Ione . . .
Because she's the cheese and I'm the macaroni

"Okay, good," said Nadia, walking on. She seemed reassured, but I was shaken, and I didn't know why. Deep down, I must have known I'd screw it up.

15

King Ad-Rock and I

1992

We drove in a caravan—Adam and I at the helm in our olive-green Range Rover (ashtray stuffed with joints and roaches, wedding mixtape in the cassette player), followed by my bridesmaids, Zoe Cassavetes, Amelia Fleetwood, Karis Jagger, Lisa Ann Cabasa, and Rachael Horovitz. The sky blazed blue and the Pacific stretched out below as we wound higher into the oak-studded mountains, through the vineyards and Arabian horse farms toward Santa Ynez, where the Reagans and Michael Jackson had their ranches. Tomorrow, Adam and I would marry at a dreamy 1940s estate.

Some of our friends thought we were too young. I was only twenty-one and Adam twenty-five. But for us, it felt like the safe thing to do, the grown-up thing, a way to cement our commitment before we entered the daunting waters of a long-distance relationship. Adam was going on tour for the Beastie Boys' new album, *Check Your Head*, and I'd soon leave for England to start filming the TV series *Covington Cross*, my first medieval period drama. I was excited to take fencing and archery lessons and run around London on the weekends. But not to be apart from Adam. The show was at least a five-month commitment, and we both felt anxious about being separated for that long. Though we worked like grown-ups, when it came to relationships we were so green. We thought marriage was like a magical hall pass—permission to skip the messy, experimental, soul-searching part of our twenties and jump straight into stability, monogamy, and safety. With our commitment sealed on paper, no distance and no one could tear us apart.

For me, getting married was also a way to individuate from Mom without having to go out into the world on my own. I could cut the rope and set sail right into a cozy, intellectual new family, the Horovitzes. I didn't realize all my childhood baggage would come along with me.

The estate we'd rented for the big event was straight out of *The Philadelphia Story*, just perfect. Adam and Rachael went to check out the horses while the other girls and I ran around oohing and aahing at the Old World charm of it all. I half expected to bump into Katharine Hepburn in the drawing room, fluffing up the flowers for me, or gliding out the French doors on the way to tennis or drinks on the patio.

"I call this room!" pronounced Zoe from upstairs. I found her in a classic boy's room, wallpapered with faded Americana scenes of kids pulling red wagons and throwing footballs.

I cranked open the casement windows and we both leaned through, looking out on the lawn and rose gardens and golden hills beyond. Zoe lit a joint and we passed it back and forth, each hit amplifying the sensation that we'd landed in a Gilded Age fairy tale.

"I've always wanted to get married," I said dreamily. "I've always loved playing house."

Zoe narrowed her feline eyes. "You know this is real life, right?"

I shrugged. "I know."

Zoe was technically correct. But then again, who said real life couldn't be a little bit like playing house? To me, that was still the ultimate hallmark of happiness: when being awake was as good as a fantasy or a really great book. And that's what it felt like with Adam.

Zoe (daughter of Gena Rowlands and John Cassavetes) had grown up in a sprawling house down the road from the Zappas, who, sadly, weren't coming to the wedding. We'd drifted apart during my Saving Anthony phase, and I wasn't good at salvaging my old friendships when things got weird. While I missed the Zappas, now I had Zoe and her equally glamorous and sarcastic sister, Xan. "When I saw you in *Say Anything*, I could tell we were alike. I knew we'd be friends," Zoe had told me once as we sipped wine on her sunporch. That had thrilled me.

Like any wedding through the eyes of the bride, mine went by in a colorful blur. I remember only one distinct moment from our rehearsal dinner in the wood-paneled guest cottage. Adam and I were glued at the hip—he in a light blue mod suit and I in a creamy bias-cut tea dress—making the rounds from table to table. We stopped to talk to the old family friend who would marry us: the famously liberal gay judge "Baby" John Ladner. Baby John looked sheepish as he said: "I feel I have to tell you, no wedding I've performed has ever lasted."

"Ours will," I assured him. Adam ran a hand through his cute Caesar haircut, then pulled me closer.

The next evening, my bridesmaids and I gathered with Dono and Adam's best men, Mike D and Yauch—almost comically dapper in their top hats and tailcoats—under a massive oak tree at the garden's edge. Karis, my maid of honor, flitted about, smoothing the lace on my Victorian wedding gown and fluffing my veil. The evening was warm and dry, crows squawking in the trees. I'd told myself I wouldn't smoke pot before the ceremony, but when Lisa Ann wandered over with a joint, I thought, *Just one hit*. I never could pass up a joint. I felt dazed but so happy. In pictures, my eyes shine.

It felt right to be walked down the aisle by my brother and my dogs (Julius, named after Adam's grandfather, and Leva, whom I'd won in the Anthony split). I hadn't invited Donovan to the wedding. About a year after our big meeting in Joshua Tree, I'd written him a letter asking point-blank: "Why did you abandon me?" He didn't write back. Then, about a year after that, he and Linda came to LA and invited us to meet at their hotel restaurant. "Don wants you to hear our side of the story," Linda had said on the phone. "We'll talk it through, and I'll film it. Then we can all heal." Thankfully, she abandoned the idea of filming, though I wished she hadn't come in the first place. I didn't need her healing talk. Healing, for me, would be a real, intimate conversation, just between Donovan and me. That wasn't what I got. My dad was quiet and bashful. He didn't have much of a story to tell after all, but I realized I didn't mind. I had Adam and didn't need Donovan's approval so much anymore. I could be content to love my dad more as a mystery than a man.

Now Adam and I stood under the trellis of white roses and blue hydrangeas that was our wedding altar, flanked by our small ring bearer and flower girls—Adam's twin half siblings, Oliver and Hannah, and Flea and Loesha's daughter, Clara.

"Hey, buddy," Adam whispered, squeezing my hands.

"Hey, buddy," I whispered back. The Horovitzes were all "buddy" to one another, and I was part of the family now.

Adam's top hat tilted at a jaunty angle and he looked happily stoned. Those warm brown eyes . . . I would live the rest of my life smiling into them. Our babies would have those eyes and my down-turned mouth—their grandfather Donovan's mouth. They would grow up under the watch of this kind, talented, gentle man. They would know their father's love, and my love, right from the beginning. For them, love would feel safe. With Adam, I felt so safe.

Baby Dono, Dad, and Mom living on the Isle of Skye right before Mom got pregnant with me, 1969.

Mom and me with twin bed heads, 1972.

Out of the dark Connecticut woods and into summer days in Topanga, California, with Smoke the dog.

People were always welcome to hang out at
Wilton Place, making my childhood fun and
cheery. That's me in the back, holding Season
Hubley and Kurt Russell's son, Boston.

Mom's feather jacket and metallic
green Elton John platforms
complete my disco look.

With Karis Jagger and her mom,
Marsha Hunt, looking like I
have zero idea what to do with a
marshmallow.

Me and Dono with Mom
(looking like a tragic Tennessee
Williams heroine) on the day she
married Billy. Los Angeles, 1982.

Channeling my best Brooke Shields in the famously sultry light of the Griffith Observatory.

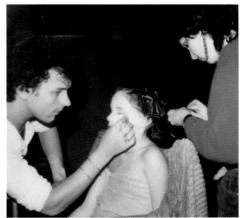

My first job was posing for an album cover. I felt more relaxed and happy getting makeup and hair done than getting called on in school.

Who knows how this living room performance was received, but in my mind I was Leslie Caron in *Gigi* or Natalie Wood in *Gypsy*.

I really took to modeling/ disassociating early.

Modeling on train tracks in downtown LA, with makeup artist Paul Starr's smoky eyes.

Living in a material world. With Elexa Williams Nicholson and Vanessa Hopkins.

Your typical, traditional family photo. Dono, me, Mom, and stepdad Billy.

Here is my brother Dono on his seventeenth birthday, dressed like Hugh Hefner for a memorable pajama party.

I had an early understanding of the immense power of striking a fierce pose while flanked by fabulous gay men. With John Deacon and Johnny Rozsa.

Pastel *Less Than Zero* vibes for me and Dono.

Believe it or not, Dono and I are dancing to the same song, "Just Can't Get Enough" by Depeche Mode.

My eighteenth birthday party in Bronson Park with my wonderful bestie, Moon Zappa.

Dweezil trying on the pants I picked out for him with Moon and Gail. Can you tell I had a crush?

Californication.

Loesha Zeviar, Flea, Grandpa Benny, me, and Anthony Kiedis. Wholesome fun at a friend's pool in Hollywood.

Another fun party at Wilton Place. Dono and Michael Fitzpatrick doing silly headshot faces. My bookends: Flea and Anthony.

Keanu and me sharing a smile during
an on-set photo shoot for my first film,
River's Edge. With Crispin Glover,
Roxana Zal, Phillip Brock, Josh
Richman, and Daniel Roebuck.

As if Keanu wasn't dreamy enough,
he was also incredibly sweet with
Tammy L. Smith, the young actress
playing his little sister.

Running our lines for
the first day of filming
River's Edge.

On the set of *A Night in the Life of Jimmy Reardon*. If River hadn't felt like a brother to me, I would have been in love.

On the set of *Say Anything* with legendary cinematographer László Kovács. I was so in awe when I found out he shot *Easy Rider* *Shampoo*, and so many other great films. Here he is showing me a tric to help when the key light is too bright.

My *Say Anything* costar John Cusack and I were always genuinely curious about each other. That never went away.

Very close and cozy on the set of *Say Anything* with John Cusack, Cameron Crowe, and John Mahoney.

The cast of *A Night in the Life of Jimmy Reardon* was five teens, including me and Matthew Perry, all running around a hotel together during our off hours. So fun.

Filming *The Rachel Papers* in London with James Spader and Dexter Fletcher. The stylish, well-written adaptation made for a fun, confidence-building shoot.

Dream for an Insomniac. A few months before Jennifer Aniston booked her role on *Friends*.

Drew Barrymore and I met in the early eighties. Here we are on set during a 1920s-themed party sequence in *Fever Pitch*, directed by the Farrelly Brothers.

With Adam Horovitz I felt completely safe for the first time. I didn't know how to be happy unless we were together.

Dono, Adam, and me in the West Village after I cut my hair shorter than their

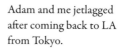

Adam and me jetlagged after coming back to LA from Tokyo.

Enid, mother to all, including Adam at the time.

Wedding dinner corniness.

Even though I was too young, I loved being married. Santa Ynez, 1992.

Me and my bridesmaids: Lisa Ann Cabasa, Rachael Horovitz, Karis Jagger, and Zoe Cassavetes.

Martha Plimpton is always cool, even wedged between her ex River Phoenix and her date at my first wedding.

With Amelia Fleetwood
in vintage slip dresses in an
Old Hollywood daydream.
We would dress up and take
pictures of our inspired visions.

Fashion week 1995, sitting with
Sofia Coppola at the Marc Jacobs
show before hitting a bunch of
clubs and parties. An inspiring
whirlwind of fun.

Dressing up and getting into
trouble with Lala Sloatman
while our men are on tour.

Dono and Gwyneth Paltrow, unconsciously coupling.

Lovable, funny, smart Jenny Shimizu and me at a charity event.

With Jenny at Dono and Kirsty Hume's annual New York Halloween party.

Listless at the Chateau Marmont. Alice Temple, Amanda de Cadenet, Amelia Fleetwood, and Rachel Williams.

Meeting my father for the first time at his house in Joshua Tree. His wife, Linda, on the right.

Underneath all the nerves, I felt happy.

Catching the wind with my dad near his home in Ireland.

In my house in LA with my father, building our relationship.

So nice when you realize you and your oldest friend are pregnant at the same time. Me and Karis with our first babies, Kate and Mazie.

Peaceful, happy days with baby Goldie and Ben Lee.

With Kate. The one thing I always knew was that I wanted to be a mom.

First holiday card with both girls in our blended family.

The family gets bigger and photobombs Kirsty's photo shoot. Top row, left to right: Dono hugging Kirsty; my little brother, Jack, with Mom; me holding Pop Up; Ben; and David Netto with Liz and their baby, Madelyn. In front is Kate with Dono and Kirsty's daughter, Violet.

Me visiting the Beastie Boys' G-Son Studios and posing by the remains of the mural I painted.

Endless Lust, oil painting, 2004.

Sad Parents, pencil and oil pastels, 2011.

Mama in Mexico, an oil painting of one of our trips to the Rosarito Beach Hotel, 1998.

As we prepared to take our vows, Baby John said, "A great group has gathered here today. It's nice to see so many old friends. Adam and Ione, take a look at all those smiling faces."

We turned to face our guests, seated in folding chairs on the lawn— one hundred fifty faces beaming up at us. One hundred fifty witnesses to the promise I was about to make. To be worthy of Adam, forever. I gripped his arm, suddenly lightheaded. Suddenly afraid. *There's nothing to be scared of*, I told myself. But my bouquet, a cascade of white roses, shook in my hands and my knees were literally knocking beneath my long skirt. Could everyone see?

Mom gave me an encouraging nod from the front row. She looked radiant in a loose string of pearls, her wavy hair coiffed into an elegant pouf. Sitting beside her was my newest (and forever-after) stepdad, Richard. She'd found the right match this time around. A born-and-raised New Yorker, like Mom, Richard was tall, handsome, and a good provider—a Harvard-trained lawyer and entrepreneur. He was the stepfather I'd always needed: calm, stable, a great listener and advice giver. Adam and I had paid for the wedding, but Richard had gifted us a weekend's worth of champagne for all, as well as the stunning champagne diamond earrings I wore now.

In the row behind Mom and Richard sat Anthony—still with that intense, intelligent stare—and his wonderful mom, Peggy. Anthony and I had stayed friends, mostly because we were both close to Flea. It was a little weird that he was there, but since his bandmates were invited, Adam and I had decided to invite him too. I was happy to see Martha Plimpton and River Phoenix, who'd broken up but remained friends. River looked out of sorts, unshaven and frowning behind his dark sunglasses. He gave me a little wave. In the first row on Adam's side of the aisle sat his father and brother with Nadia Dajani, who was now a good friend of mine (though

she still made me nervous, as very strong women tended to). Dave
Skilken, Adam's childhood friend, should have been sitting next
to her, but we'd lost him a year earlier to an overdose. His drug
problem had been a secret, at least to me. I'd thought, *I know drug
addicts. I know what someone in real danger looks like.* But now I
know you never know.

That night, while we danced under the stars to Prince and Stevie
Wonder and Parliament and the Clash, our friends snuck into our
room and did some decorating. When the party finally ended, Adam
and I fell onto our downy bed, scattered with rose petals. Exhausted
as I was, I worried it would be bad wedding etiquette not to consum-
mate our vows. I sat up, wriggled out of my dress, and tossed it onto
a chair. Adam clawed off his dress shirt and fell back on the pillows.
Eyeing me deliriously, he ran a hand up my thigh, tracing the edges of
my white lacy underthings.

I flung a leg over him. "Should we?"

"You want to?" said Adam.

"I'm kind of beat," I admitted.

"Me too," said Adam. Then, "Hey, buddy?"

"Yeah?"

"We did it," he said.

I nuzzled closer. "We did it," I affirmed. And then we fell asleep.

The next day we drove to the airport, cans rattling and white rib-
bons flying behind us. Following Rachael's advice, I'd dressed up for
the plane in a tailored Agnès B. skirt suit and hat. I was less confident
than I looked—deflated and a bit lonely, as I often felt when a big
night with friends came to an end and I was alone with my thoughts
again. Only I wasn't alone, of course. Adam was by my side, and in the
same downcast mood, it seemed. The weather had shifted overnight,
from clear to gray and ominous. Now it was drizzling—the windshield
wipers keeping time to a slow Sade song.

As we waited for our flight to Venice, Italy, clinging to each other across the hard plastic chairs like puppies seeking warmth, I thought about Baby John's warning—that none of the couples he'd married had made it. It hadn't bothered me at the time, but now I wondered if it was a bad omen. An announcement came over the intercom: "Would Adam and Ione Horovitz please meet their friends at Steak and Ale restaurant?" To our delight, Rachael, Amelia, and the Beastie Boys' former tour manager, Sean Carasov, aka "the Captain," had come to see us off with a drink.

"I wish you could come with us!" I told Rachael. Usually, I loved being alone with Adam: us against the world. But I wasn't sure we were ready to have an adult honeymoon, just the two of us. I didn't want to be separated from our friends quite yet.

Rachael laughed. "That would be fun," she said, "but it's your honeymoon! You two need time to yourselves, to decompress."

"You're right," I told Rachael, mustering a smile. "Of course!"

If my wedding memories are a blurry watercolor, my honeymoon memories are a stack of Polaroids—a series of nostalgic moments, with gaps in between: our first glimpse of the floating city on the boat ride from the airport; Adam suavely ordering "*due Bellini, per favore*" at Harry's Bar; a flurry of pigeons erupting in St. Mark's Square; a kiss on a bridge on a two a.m. walk . . . I felt too shy to utter more than a "*grazie*" now and again, but Adam was the kind of person who sounded charming trying (apologetically) to speak at least a few words of the local language. In Japan, where the Beastie Boys were big, he'd mastered the phrase for "I'm an ugly American tourist."

From Venice, we traveled to the Amalfi Coast and the hilltop city of Ravello, where we had a room with a view of the Tyrrhenian Sea. The first day there, we ate spaghetti alle vongole and drank limoncello with dessert, feeling like kids pretending to be grown-ups.

Then we went to see the celebrated and magnificent views. Back at the hotel, I took a long bath while Adam sat in the window nook, writing down a song idea. That Polaroid will never fade: Adam writing in the window, tanned and shirtless, his boxers peeking up from his baggy pants.

On our second day in Ravello, we meandered along the cobblestone streets, hand in hand, washed in the scent of citrus, jasmine, and the sea. At the city's edge, we stopped to lean over a warm stone wall, looking down on the pink rooftops and sparkling water. Silverware chimed on a restaurant patio and bocce balls thunked in a park across the road.

It was all so slow and lovely and picturesque. But I couldn't help feeling a bit antsy, a bit bored of sightseeing and eating pasta, as delicious as it was. I sensed Adam was itching for some excitement too. Maybe we should have brought Rachael and Amelia and the Captain along, after all. Rachael would have expertly guided us through Peggy Guggenheim's collection in Venice and found the most in-the-know places to eat. The Captain would have been drinking us all under a café table at this very moment—pausing, as a rule, to run a mile after every drink. Amelia would somehow find Ravello's secret underground club, where we'd dance all night to Brasil '66.

Adam shaded his eyes, turning to look up at a clock tower behind us. "Whoa," he said, "it's only one fifteen."

"Wow," I said, peering up at the clock. "Time goes slow here." We'd slept till eleven that morning, fooled around, had coffee and pastries in bed, then left the hotel for our stroll. We had dinner reservations for that night at the hotel restaurant and absolutely no idea what to do with ourselves until then.

I pulled a mirror from my purse and reapplied my lipstick, thinking, *Now what?* An idea sprang to mind.

"Hey," I said, "do you wanna go to London a day early? Amelia's there. She's having a party at her flat."

Adam grinned at me. I grinned back.

Was it a red flag that we cut our honeymoon short? I didn't think so. Besides, it was a super-fun party.

16

The Door to Alice

1993

After an excruciating five-month separation while I filmed *Covington Cross* in England and Adam toured, we returned to LA and moved into a Snow White–sized cottage with whimsical cupolas on Wonderland Avenue in Laurel Canyon. Our back garden had mountain views, a tiered brick patio, and a guest cottage with its own wood-barrel hot tub. That was where Amelia, who was now my very best friend, stayed when she wasn't at her boyfriend's. Mom had finally parted with Wilton Place, and she and Richard lived right next door, in a modern house that Richard had built for them—a cozier, homier version of Carl's angular masterpiece in Ridgefield. Lisa Ann and Yauch's log cabin was just a few doors down. We kept the cats and dogs inside after dusk so the coyotes wouldn't eat them but rarely locked the front door.

For three halcyon months, we were joined at the hip. It was all play and no work, just hanging with friends, eating good food, smoking blunts from morning to night, and being creative. Adam practiced guitar and made beats while I read and painted in thick, rich oils, copying photographs from my real and fantasy lives: Dono and me in the garden at Wilton Place; Mom sunbathing on a bright yellow blanket at the Rosarito Beach Hotel in Mexico; two sailors kissing; a red room from a Bergman movie. I learned by studying artists I admired and didn't crave formal instruction. Realism was out of reach, but I didn't mind. My style was impressionistic, crude, and whether I meant it to be or not, sensual. When friends saw the paintings, they said I had "it," and I believed them because I loved my paintings too.

But when Adam began spending long hours in the studio to record *Ill Communication*, I felt a little abandoned (my go-to feeling). I hadn't worked in the months since returning from England and it wasn't enough to follow Adam to the studio anymore. I'd finally covered every free wall with murals. I was antsy.

Fortunately for me, Dono had burst onto the New York fashion scene. After seeing my brother in *The In Crowd*, the photographer Steven Meisel had cast him in a Dolce & Gabbana ad, and things took off from there. In the spring of 1993, I left Adam to his recording and flew to New York to watch Dono walk in Anna Sui's runway show, modeling a black velveteen coat and busting out his pop-locking skills at the end of the catwalk. We then spent the rest of Fashion Week running around the chilly city with Dono's model friends—from hotels to shows to parties to dinners to nightclubs. One night, Dono invited Zoe Cassavetes, Sofia Coppola, and me to dinner at Kin Khao in SoHo with Katie Ford, the copresident of Ford Models. By dessert, she'd signed us all as clients. Dono was a real model in his own right, but Sofia, Zoe, and I were more of a package deal, as the children of celebrities (nepo babies before nepo babies were a thing).

We only booked one job, with Dono and Sofia's brother Roman, for an H&M campaign shot by Bruce Weber. It was thrilling to work with one of the greatest fashion photographers in the business. Bruce almost whispered his instructions, as if conserving his powerful energy. His assistant even held his heavy Hasselblad camera for him while

Bruce just pushed the button. The slow-motion click of a classic analog camera. Delish.

Once it occurred to Dono that he might actually be able to *date* the models he worked with, he went on a mission to woo his big crush, Kate Moss—and by God, he succeeded. After possibly the best first date ever, to see Nirvana perform on *MTV Unplugged* in New York (I got to play third wheel and tag along), Dono and Kate were briefly an item.

Though the relationship only lasted a week, it marked a new phase for Dono and me: Now we were hanging and clubbing with the *super-*models. I'd never liked going to clubs before. As a teen, I would beg Dono to take me to the best LA hot spot, Power Tools, then want to leave after three minutes, uncomfortable and overwhelmed by the scene. But now I couldn't stay home.

It was dawning on me that in my hunger to live a big life, packed with big experiences, I'd skipped a few stages. I'd jumped straight from girlhood into a grown-up career and a heavy adult relationship with Anthony, and then jumped again, into a life with Adam. At twenty-two, I had my own version of Mom's rock-wife dream life, with a beautiful home, travel, nice restaurants, and successful friends. But I'd missed the in-between years of going out and being young and careless and stupid, even.

I was making up for that now. The model scene was great, great fun and kept me occupied while Adam was in the recording studio, which would be 24/7 for much of 1993. That year, I'd bob between LA, New York, London, and Paris, having a wild, superficial time. I loved watching the magical model creatures act like children, having tantrums as they exercised their power. A model could throw a champagne glass across Raoul's in New York or Davé in Paris and everyone thought, *Ha-ha, how cute.* There were no consequences for anything in their world. So why not do a little coke when they offered? As with heroin, by some marvelous miracle, I dabbled and never got hooked.

I was especially intrigued by Kate, with her disarming Croydon accent. She and Naomi Campbell were besties at the time. Once, Dono and I flew with them from New York to London, just to go to a party. Kate and Naomi arrived at the airport nail-bitingly late yet completely serene in their big sunglasses. They whisked Dono and me into a private lounge, where we hastily smoked a joint before boarding and taking our first-class seats. Naomi and Kate were so glam, with their beautiful hair and makeup. They wore silky eye masks on the plane and Kate lit a cigarette. When the flight attendant said, "Ms. Moss, there's no smoking on the airplane," Kate replied, "I'll put it out in a minute," then took a few more leisurely puffs before dropping the butt in her glass of sparkling water. When we landed in London near midnight, Kate's driver whisked us to Groucho's, where we ordered scrambled eggs and champagne and I felt very chic and "bright young things" but, at the same time, painfully lonely without Adam.

The next evening I took the red-eye back to LA to see him. But he'd just been called to New York to record with Q-Tip at Tin Pan Alley Studios, and our planes all but crossed. Unable to be alone with myself, even for an afternoon, I drank three cups of coffee, put on a red X-girl minidress, and went with Amelia to a daytime party.

Echo Park was still eclectic and overgrown then. The party was at a charmingly run-down Streamline Moderne house that looked like a mini ocean liner from the Art Deco days. On a broken-up cement patio with monster weeds sprouting through, a few clusters of hip, alternative people stood around smoking and nodding along to something slow and trip-hoppy. It was the height of the Courtney Love heroin-chic era, and half the girls looked like Tennessee Williams heroines with brick-red lipstick and disheveled slip dresses. Then I saw the most incredible-looking person. Her being and clothes—Dr. Martens oxfords, low-slung Levi's, and a ribbed white tank—were masculine, but she was clearly a woman. She had bleached, close-cropped hair;

a pert, perfect nose; and cheekbones like James Dean. Staring at her, I forgot to breathe.

I peeled my eyes away and went to find Amelia.

"Who is *that*?" I whispered, tilting my head at the androgynous beauty. She was surrounded by a group of women also dressed like boys, who hung on her every word as she talked—a cigarette and a beer bottle in one leather-cuffed hand, the other in her back jeans pocket.

Amelia laughed. "That's Alice Temple. She's a bit famous in London. Everybody's in love with her."

I felt inexplicably crushed. Everyone was in love with Alice Temple? How could that be? Hadn't I discovered her? As if I were the first girl ever to be struck by a beautiful tomboy. No, "struck" is an understatement. I was walloped, clobbered, electrified by her androgyny. I didn't know if I wanted to have her or *be* her.

"A model?" I asked.

"Model, musician, BMX champion, Boy George's ex–best friend, the list goes on," said Amelia.

"Introduce me," I said.

Amelia gave me a curious look but took my wrist and led me toward Alice and her circle.

It was a short exchange, just polite hellos. She had nervous energy and spoke softly, with the stretched vowels of a posh English accent. Seeing her up close—her winsomely crooked teeth and smiling, light-sapphire eyes—I understood why she was surrounded by hangers-on. One of them, a too-skinny girl with a shaved head and a druggy glaze to her eyes, stepped between me and Alice, whispering something in her ear.

I watched, transfixed, as the druggy girl led Alice away and into the house. What was this yearning in me? An image glimmered in the back of my mind and I reached for it: April?

Suddenly, I was fourteen again, with April, queen of the Aprils, in a moonlit room in Hancock Park. She was lifting her Lacoste shirt, looking over her shoulder, asking for a massage. I saw myself straddling her, flushed with longing, then shame. Those feelings had faded away as our friendship grew distant, but had they ever really left me? I loved my female friends deeply, almost romantically at times, but not sexually. Not like this.

Alice had stirred something in me that I didn't quite understand but couldn't ignore. I sensed that I'd pursue her, and that it would be dark and scary, like falling down the rabbit hole. But I was so compelled by my curiosity, I didn't care if it hurt. Or who it hurt.

This might be the moment to make a confession: I was a serial cheater. Before Adam, I'd fooled around on every boy I'd dated, all the way back to middle school. Not that I'd had so many relationships, at twenty-three. But I'd had four serious boyfriends and betrayed them all. This habit—an obvious sign of my deep insecurity and need for validation—was something I'd never liked about myself, but I always thought that once I fell deeply in love with someone, I'd stop. Then I met Adam and fell head over heels and got married and thought *for sure* the problem was solved. But my cheating was never about my partners, it was about me.

The day after the Echo Park party, I tried calling Adam at Tin Pan Alley but he'd just left for a dinner break. I pictured the Beastie Boys having grilled cheese and pints in a cozy New York diner and felt terribly lonely. *Do you miss me?* I asked Adam, telepathically. Imagining his reply—*Of course I do, Buddy*—wasn't enough to stop me. Burning with shame, I called Amelia to get Alice's whereabouts.

She was staying in Silver Lake with another blue-bloodish, artistic girl, Fiona, whom I knew a little. Amelia was going to head over there later, so I now had a reason to "swing by" casually. I drove to Silver Lake in a state of terror, excitement, and disassociation.

At Fiona's scruffy-chic bungalow, Alice and two other girls sat around a coffee table, being blasé. The others ignored me, but Alice greeted me with a cheeky smile. "Hey."

"Hey," I said, dropping my bag like I belonged. I couldn't think of what else to say so I took a seat and started leafing through the *i-D* magazine on the coffee table.

I was getting a low-energy hangover vibe and felt very much outside of this little group, who seemed to have all kinds of private references and vague plans that needed to be made. Then I noticed a Visine bottle on the coffee table, the label crossed out in felt-tip, and I thought, *Huh*. One of the girls nodded to Alice, who casually picked up the eyedropper bottle and sauntered out of the room. *Ohhh*. Alice and her friends were into heroin. I'd once seen a friend of Anthony's cook it and use an eyedropper to squeeze the liquid into his nose. It grossed me out.

Cheating motivations aside, you might think that after what I went through with Anthony, I would've taken that as my cue to walk out of there and go find my sweet, loving, non-addicted husband and fun, vibrant friends. Alas, no. Instead, I dug deeper into my magazine, as if in a waiting room, waiting for my turn with Alice.

She returned and, at last, sat next to me. I told her Amelia and I had been friends for years but really got close when I lived in London doing *The Rachel Papers*. I was trying, transparently, to let her know I was relevant.

"You're married to Adam Horovitz, right?" said Alice.

It felt like a punch. I didn't want to hear her say Adam's name. He was sacred, hypocritical as that sounds. I just smiled.

"He's brilliant," said Alice, as if she got what I was up to and was letting me know she wanted no part in hurting him.

"Yes, he is," I said, looking at my hands. I wished she wouldn't talk about him. I was really trying to compartmentalize, so I could follow Alice's siren call and still live with myself. Her pull was so strong, it was already drowning out my life.

For the next few weeks I went to see Alice at Fiona's whenever Adam was recording. I don't remember us talking a lot. Heroin is not a talky drug, and Alice was having a big heroin moment. She and her friends cooked it, smoked it, snorted it . . . It was all I ever saw them do, though somehow they managed to model or play in bands. Alice had a band called Eg & Alice, and I bought their really good New Romantic CD, playing it on my drives to and from Fiona's bungalow.

At least they didn't use needles, I told myself. (At least not yet, as far as I knew.) They didn't go off alone to shoot up in cars or under stairwells like Anthony had. This was different, a social thing, a nineties thing! Alice and her friends all looked so . . . "healthy" wasn't exactly the right word, but they looked hot. They had nice skin, nice things, nice shoes. Regardless, I was so dead set on knowing Alice, I'm sure I would've hung about and chased her no matter how heavy her scene.

At first, I didn't partake. Just being in the same room as Alice was as good as being on drugs. But soon I started finding reasons why I should take a drop, a smoke, a sniff, here and there. I ignored the dark vibes, my sinking heart, and the stark knowledge of how addictive this all was, and I joined in.

One night when Adam was pulling an all-nighter at G-Son, I invited Alice to a small hang at Lala's place. Lala (Moon Zappa's cousin) was engaged to Chris Robinson from the Black Crowes. They lived just down the hill from the new house that Adam and I had recently bought and were having renovated—a 1960s Case Study with a heated pool and extra rooms for the family we'd have one day. Not that I was thinking about my husband or my home or my future children or the future, period, that night at Lala's. I was a natural at compartmentalizing.

Alice showed up alone—no hangers-on for once, just Alice, looking like an Italian *paninaro* scooter boy in Stone Island jeans, Timberlands, and a fluorescent-green Naf Naf hoodie. I couldn't see how she or anyone would not be seducible in Chris and Lala's decadent rock star house with its velvet sofas and antiques and Moroccan textiles. Not to mention the drugs.

We all took something called Mandrax—like a quaalude, but not as good, I'm told—and Alice and Amelia languorously danced while Lala and I played dress-up in the vintage cornucopia of her closet. The drug was hitting and my limbs felt slow and syrupy as we emerged, dressed in shimmery seventies designer dresses. The next thing I knew, we were crawling into bed with Amelia and Alice. Amelia and Lala began making out, just for fun. Sexual fluidity was starting to become cool. It didn't make you gay or bisexual—unless you were bisexual?

Either way, I was happily falling into this very free, very nineties girl scene, where everyone went from house to house, hanging out and sleeping with one another. It was likely that later on Alice would go to another party and be with a different girl, and I didn't care.

I decided to take control, running my hands over her arms and belly and taking in the bloom of her spicy cologne as she grew aroused. And when I heard a small, low sigh as she lifted her hips, I felt triumphant. Not just because I'd made the inimitable Alice Temple come, but because now I knew who I was.

Back in middle school, April had convinced me that what I'd felt for her wasn't real, that our "Bye, Bi" sign-offs were just a joke. That us being "dykes" was a joke. It was easier that way. But it didn't feel like a joke now.

Once I'd piqued Alice's interest, there was a brief, ecstatic (for me) window where she wanted to see me both in bed and out in the world, without drugs. I naively thought this was fantastic. I loved being with Alice, and in the moment—with all thoughts of Adam pushed deep into my horrified subconscious—our affair felt almost innocent, almost pure.

She was so special, like no girl I'd ever met. I was soaking her up, learning from her. I learned from Alice's example—she never claimed to know the best way to live or doled out advice—that it was okay to be my whole self, to explore this new dimension opening up in me. And explore I did.

I could see why gay boys often went so wild when they came out. I felt born again. Or like an Amish kid embarking on Rumspringa. Except my rite of passage was a secret, a betrayal. It felt so good, sometimes I forgot to hide it.

One afternoon I stopped by Mom and Richard's with Alice. Alice and Mom chatted a little while I raided the pantry, and then we sat in the garden, tossing grapes and crackers into each other's mouths. I left her in the garden to get drinks and found Mom standing in the kitchen window, a pensive expression in her eyes. She must have been watching us, watching me falling all over myself for this girl.

I grabbed two cans of Hansen's soda from the fridge and went to the window, where we both stood a moment, looking at Alice, who'd taken off her T-shirt and lay sunning on her stomach. Except for the thin black line of her bra, she looked like a beautiful boy.

"Isn't she great?" I said, holding the cold cans to my flushed cheeks.

Mom looked at me, alarm in her eyes. "I can see the appeal, but Ione, you're married! Adam's obsessed with you! Have you talked about this?"

Mom had never once been so forthright with me, about anything. I was so taken aback, I couldn't speak, just shook my head and ran down to the garden.

Telling Adam about this would make it real—that is, a real threat to our marriage. I could not imagine a life without Adam. But at the same time, I could not imagine a life where I would deny all these new feelings, this new side of myself. I didn't have the communication skills or guts to come out to Adam, let alone to tell him *that*. Neither of us was good at talking directly about our feelings. I won't speak for him, but my parents hadn't exactly modeled healthy communication or emotional intelligence for me. Donovan, it seemed, was good for fifteen minutes of emotional intimacy before retreating, and Enid was never one for directly confronting hard issues. Plus, she'd cheated on both her previous husbands. Not that I'm blaming Mom or Donovan, or anyone but myself, for my choices.

I wonder to this day how much Adam knew. I suspect he knew everything but chose to look the other way as long as he could. The only conversation, ever, that I can remember us having about my straying was cautious, almost coded. It was a few months after I'd started running around with Alice, and in the flush of my excitement about being bi, I'd hooked up with a couple of other girls too.

Adam and I were in our West Village apartment on the night of our sort-of big talk. We'd just flown in from LA that evening. He had an early recording session at Tin Pan Alley and was lying on the bed, writing lyrics. I was buttoning up my leopard coat—headed to Bowery Bar with Dono, Shalom Harlow, and Amber Valletta.

"Sure you don't want to come?" I said.

Adam shook his head, dropping his notebook by his side. He reached out his hand. I took it, and he pulled me to sit on the edge of the bed.

I sat very, very straight, as Adam seemed to weigh his thoughts, his brow furrowing.

"I did all this," he said. "I already went to the clubs. I already did that."

"I know!" I said, keeping my voice light. "It's no big deal!"

Adam sighed. "It is a big deal, though."

"It is?" I swallowed a funny taste in my throat, acid and metallic:

fear. I was playing dumb. Whether he knew I was straying or not, my constant going out obviously annoyed him. It was straining our marriage, even if we never talked about it.

"I just think maybe you need to be alone to explore this."

What was "this"? Was he talking about the partying or the girls? If he knew about the girls, I didn't want him to say it. *Don't say it. Don't make it real.*

I shook my head. "I don't need to be alone. Really!"

He looked at me, waiting for more.

What could I give him? What would save me? Not the awful, awful truth, but not a lie, either. It was one thing to sneak around, another to outright lie. I wouldn't do that.

"Just give me a little time?" I said, my eyes pleading. "Please, can you hang in with me? I won't be like this forever, but just for a while?"

Adam sat back on the pillows, studying my face. "Okay."

I could hear the vibrant sounds of New York outside. Then the door buzzer sounded from downstairs. I went to the window and waved to Dono and the supermodels in a waiting town car.

"Go," said Adam.

"You sure?" I said.

Adam didn't answer. The car honked. I kissed him, and I went.

17

Earthquakes

1993–1994

We were still in New York, on Washington Place, when my cousin called me with the news.

"Did you hear?"

"What?" I asked, cradling the phone as I paid the Zen Palate delivery guy at the front door.

"River died," she said. "He overdosed, at the Viper Room."

I stood there, holding the steaming takeout bag, my cousin's voice faraway now.

"Ione? Ione? Are you there?"

I hung up, loathing my poor cousin for giving me the news, as if it were her fault. Adam took the food. "What is it? What happened?"

River was his friend too. When the shock wore off, we'd both be furious about his death.

A world without River was inconceivable. And so was the way he'd died. River wasn't heavy into drugs. Was he? Like me, he enjoyed wine and cigarettes and dabbled in harder stuff now and then. But he didn't recklessly tempt death like the real addicts I knew. How did this happen? Soon, the terrible details would be everywhere: River had been planning to perform a song or two that night but never made it to the stage. He told our friend Bob Forrest he was feeling bad, and minutes later he fell to the sidewalk outside the club. The paramedics came and took him away, but they couldn't save River. He died from an overdose shortly before two a.m. on Halloween morning.

I cried myself to sleep in Adam's arms that night, images of River swirling in my head.

River and I had kissed once, at Wilton Place, a few years back. When in town, he preferred staying with friends over nice hotels. Mom set him up on a futon in the little office we used as a guest room. We ended up in there together, talking for hours. I can't remember about what. We both felt heavy that night. He seemed to have the weight of the world on his shoulders. The eldest of four kids, he was the one who worked constantly. I knew he felt pressure to be a good role model.

Stretched out on the futon, we turned on our sides to face each other, noses almost touching. River's wire-frame glasses had skewed to the side, so I gently removed them. We stared at each other for a while. River's right eye was almost blind and a little lazy, and he slowly blinked to focus on me.

He moved closer, tucking my hair behind my ear. We started to kiss, sweet and slow. He had the softest hint of a mustache above his perfect lips.

As nice as that kiss was, we soon fell asleep, spooning. River and I felt like brother and sister. I don't think we were meant to be lovers.

Later, when Adam and I were in our early days as a couple, we had a plan to meet up with River, but he didn't show, so we drove around looking for him. We found our friend walking barefoot down Sunset Boulevard. His long bob hung in his eyes and his favorite embroidered tunic was frayed at the hem. If you didn't know him like we did, you might have thought he looked unwell. Nobody walks in LA, of course. But River didn't follow the LA rules. As we pulled up alongside him, River turned with a big open smile, as if he'd been expecting us to come along at just that moment. He jumped into the backseat, gave our shoulders a squeeze, and cheerfully asked, "Where to?"

I can't remember where we went, but it doesn't really matter. Wherever you went with River, *he* was the place.

The last time I saw River was in Malibu, about six months before his death, give or take. Bill Richert, the much-beloved director of *Jimmy Reardon*, had rented a place in the mountains and invited some friends up to hang. When I arrived, River and Bill were smoking cigarettes on the deck. River was full of prankster-ish energy that day and had the sudden urge to roll down the mountain. "Let's do it!" he cried, throwing his arms around Bill. "You too, Ione?!"

River could be so moved by life, you wanted to join in with anything he was inspired by. For a moment I thought I should just jump into the clouds with him and forget who I was. But that was one steep, unforgiving mountain. As much as I appreciated River's spontaneity and punk-rock abandon, this felt dangerous. I smiled and shook my head. But Bill, who was middle-aged and a little heavyset, never could resist River's charm. So off they went, hooting and hollering and tumbling down. *Ouch! Ouch! Ouch!* I thought, grimacing as I watched. Somehow they emerged from the sagebrush and chaparral with only a few superficial cuts. Bill was bedraggled but beaming. River glowed like a shamanic Rimbaud.

Mom and I held a small memorial for him—one of several that friends and family members would hold—in Mom's garden.

River's middle name was Jude, after the Beatles song. But we couldn't bring ourselves to play "Hey Jude" at the service. It was just too sad, so we played "I Am the Walrus" instead. As our little group stood in a circle, sharing stories about River, Max Perlich nudged Adam. He pointed at the hillside, where two paparazzi were scampering through the trees. Adam nodded, and the two ran up the hill, yelling at the paps to beat it. Then all hell broke loose. Punches were thrown, Adam confiscated the videotape, and the paps called the police. Adam ended up being charged with a misdemeanor and sentenced to probation and community service. It was a bad scene that only happened because Adam was so angry and undone over River's death. We all were.

That night, as I dragged myself to bed, cried out and leaden, my eye caught a worn purple paperback, stacked at the edge of our messy bookshelf: Hermann Hesse's *Siddhartha*—the copy Flea had given me a long time ago. As promised, it had blown my mind—when I was ready for it, in my late teens. Remembering that River was named for Siddhartha's beloved river of life, I pulled the book down and flipped to my favorite underlined passage:

> *The world was so beautiful when regarded like this, without searching, so simply, in such a childlike way. Moons and stars were beautiful, beautiful were bank and stream, forest and rocks, goat and gold-bug, flower and butterfly. So lovely, so delightful to go through the world this way, so like a child, awake, open to what is near, without distrust.*

Yes. It was perfect. That was my friend River.

We were still grieving, still finding our balance, when the second quake came, a couple of months later. At 4:31 a.m. on January 17, 1994, the infamous Northridge Earthquake shook our cottage with a rumbling roar, throwing Adam and me out of bed.

"What the fuck?! What the fuck?!" exclaimed Adam.

The adrenaline coursing through me was oddly calming. I crawled across the shaking floor, grabbed Adam, and heroically (I thought) pulled him into the bedroom doorway. That's what we'd been taught to do in earthquake drills in elementary school before they changed the protocol to "drop, take cover, and hold on."

Less heroically, as we stood swaying and clinging to each other for dear life, I let out a big, terrified fart. Mortified, I pinched Adam's nose and held it till the shaking stopped, then ushered him into the dark kitchen.

"Wait, why'd you hold my nose?" he said, flicking a dead light switch.

"I didn't want to gross you out," I said. Even believing we might die, I couldn't bear the thought of grossing Adam out.

"That's so you," he said, almost smiling.

Outside, car alarms wailed and a neighbor shouted over and over again for his dog.

"The animals!" said Adam, panicking again. "Leva! Julius!"

When the dogs and the cats, Clancy and Fuki, were accounted for, we surveyed the damage. Only a few things had fallen off the shelves, but the Snow White cottage felt crooked, unsafe.

"Let's get out of here," I said.

We pulled some layers over our pajamas, looking very grunge, and wandered next door, where Mom and Richard sat in their garden, wrapped in blankets and drinking whiskey. Mom handed us blankets and Richard filled our shot glasses. "Best to stay outside," he said, "in case of aftershocks."

It wasn't long before the four of us were joined by Adam Yauch and a few other pajama-clad neighbors.

"We should do an earthquake fashion shoot," someone joked.

We all laughed, but as the morning wore into afternoon and Mom brought out sandwiches and a second bottle of Glenfiddich,

I couldn't settle. It was as if a silent alarm were flashing inside me, warning that any second, the other shoe would drop, and life as we knew it would end. Or had it already? Was this the other side? As my friends traded earthquake stories, I kept a stiff smile on my face. I could hardly hear what they were saying over the white noise in my head.

The earthquake must have broken something in me. The months of self-loathing, of splitting myself in two to hold everything together—one Ione for Adam, another for Alice—had left me depleted, paranoid, and fragile. No wonder I'd cracked.

For the next several months, I rarely left the cottage or spoke to anyone, especially not Alice. I didn't want her to see me like this, and at the same time, I'd stopped needing to see her. The spell had been broken. It seemed I'd tumbled to the darkest depths of the rabbit hole and now I was stuck there, trembling in the dark. Was this how Mom's frozen episodes had felt? She hadn't had one in years and I didn't have the words or voice to ask her.

This wasn't just the blues, it was "the mean reds," like Truman Capote described in *Breakfast at Tiffany's*: "The blues are because you're getting fat or maybe it's been raining too long. You're sad, that's all. But the mean reds are horrible. You're afraid and you sweat like hell, but you don't know what you're afraid of."

I *thought* I knew what I was afraid of. I had a long list of new and paranoid fears. Aliens, for starters. I'd never believed in them before, but now I was pretty sure they were real and plotting Earth's destruction. My beloved *Twilight Zone* reruns were too spooky to watch now, too close to home. I was also newly afraid of fire. Every gas station I pulled into was about to blow up. Every intersection was the imminent scene of a fiery crash. And earthquakes, obviously.

Of course, what I really feared wasn't aliens or explosions. It was losing control. If the very ground we walked on wasn't to be trusted, if highways could swallow buses, and babies sleeping in their nurseries could be crushed, and five-million-dollar houses could topple down hillsides, who was I to think my beautiful life with Adam would always be there for me? Who was I to think I had any control at all?

Adam and our friends could see something was very wrong, but I wouldn't let them in. "I'll be fine," I'd try to reassure them. "I just need to smoke less pot." Once or twice I considered talking to a therapist, but letting a professional into my head felt like too big a risk. Wouldn't they be obligated to lock me up or medicate me if I revealed such crazy thoughts?

In lieu of therapy, I had the British comedy show *Fawlty Towers*, with John Cleese and Connie Booth, as well as the Mel Brooks film *High Anxiety*, which I watched on repeat. God bless Mel Brooks for turning anxiety into art. It gave me a wisp of hope that one day I'd be able to do the same. Getting outside, close to the ground, also helped. Lying in the grass in my wild backyard, staring up at the swaying trees, my panic level would dip from a ten to a five. But every time a dreaded aftershock hit (they went on for months), I'd shoot up to ten again.

Except for the time Mick Jagger was in town. To cheer me up, Karis invited me along to visit her dad, who'd separated from Jerry Hall and was staying with his girlfriend, Carla Bruni (the Italian French model and future First Lady of France), at a rented house in the upscale "Bird" streets. I'd had no appetite since the earthquake and barely touched the antipasto and pretty lemon tea cookies on the coffee table in their plush living room. I was dripping with admiration for gorgeous Carla. I could see why Mick chose her: She could have anyone, just like him. She was *sooo* pretty. So charming and tidy and composed. I couldn't believe she was only twenty-six, just three years older than me.

As Mick went to top off my champagne, the glasses rattled on the tea tray and a few drops spilled onto my hand. Another aftershock.

Mick, eyebrows raised in surprise, calmly held the champagne bottle
aloft like an airplane steward in turbulence. When it was over, he
laughed and said, "Good fun, LA!" and went back to filling my glass.
It wasn't the biggest aftershock we'd had, but it wasn't the smallest.
And yet I hadn't dived under the coffee table for this one. True to my
special brand of magical thinking, I must have felt Mick's presence
meant nothing bad could happen. As if the force field of his fame
and importance would not allow it.

Sadly, I couldn't keep Mick as my good-luck charm. As soon as
Karis dropped me back home, the mean reds returned with a ven-
geance. I waved goodbye and walked up the front path, my heart
slowly erupting into flames.

What was this? Why couldn't I fix it? Dono told me Belinda Car-
lisle of the Go-Go's had had a bad reaction to the earthquake too, and
had picked up and moved her family to France. Maybe that was the
answer? Maybe LA was the problem, not me.

"Let's just leave," I said to Adam that night, trying to keep the
desperate edge off my voice. "We could rent a place in Paris, or move
to New York for a while!"

"Ione, I can't," he said. His tone was unusually cold. "I have to
work."

I knew Adam was still deep into recording *Ill Communication*, but
the pointed way he said "I have to work" stung me. Was I too much?
Too needy? It was the first time I'd ever felt unsupported by Adam.

Dono had recently moved to New York, which made everything
worse. But my brother had never abandoned me and never would.
When I called to invite myself to visit him, he said, "Of course!
Gwyneth and I are headed to Cabo this weekend. You guys should
come!"

Vacationing with Dono and his intimidating new girlfriend (yes,
that Gwyneth) did not exactly sound relaxing, but anything was more

relaxing than living in fear of the next earthquake. I convinced Adam to take a few days off, and we booked our tickets.

Dono had chosen one of those all-inclusive, super-manicured beach-side resorts hidden from a main road behind walls and security gates. It was supposedly the nicest one in touristy Cabo, but it looked like a Club Med to me.

The first thing we did at the resort was dive into the ocean. My skin tingled with the salt and sun, and the ever-present hum of my anxiety was fainter under the pounding of the waves. Feeling actually *calm* for the first time in months, I left Adam in the water and meandered back to change for dinner.

On the private patio between our adjoining rooms, Gwyneth lounged, reading a script and looking appealing and elegant in her white bikini. I wondered what the script was. Gwyneth was new to acting and had only been in one or two films in small roles—most recently *Mrs. Parker and the Vicious Circle.*

I plopped down on the chaise longue beside hers, watching Adam bob in the ocean. Poor Dono was sick in bed.

Gwyneth closed the script and exhaled. "Well, that one didn't make sense," she said in her nasally Spence-girl accent.

I laughed, rolling on my side to face her. She was the kind of girl I'd always been cowed by—who wore her privilege unashamedly and seemed impossibly sure of herself and her choices. If Gwyneth had been at Immaculate Heart, the Aprils would have been the Gwyneths. I was two years older but would have wanted her approval.

"What was it about?" I asked, pointing to the rejected script.

Gwyneth shrugged her smooth, tawny shoulders. "Didn't get that far. I just want something really good and well written, you know?"

"I do," I said. Boy, did I.

Since I'd started acting eight years earlier, I'd had good, consistent work—twelve films and five TV shows, starring in most. But my career was officially in a fallow period. In a rash post-earthquake decision, I'd left my big agent at William Morris and signed with a young agent at a smaller agency where I wouldn't be lost in the crowd. Well, that's what I'd thought. My new agent didn't seem to know what to do with me. At least I still had Arlyne Rothberg as a manager, though I hadn't heard from her in a while either. I would call them both to check in the minute we returned to LA. I suddenly, desperately, wanted to work!

Gwyneth looked at her watch (a Cartier Panthère, slim and golden like her). "Shall we head to the lounge? I'd love a Sancerre."

Adam didn't drink and sadly we hadn't dared bring our weed. I liked to have fun with Gwyneth. At a recent party Adam and I had thrown at our still-empty new house, we'd all taken mushrooms and she'd curled up in Julius's dog bed, transforming the furry nest into an elegant divan. We'd played truth or dare that night and Vincent Gallo (who showed up everywhere, ready for fun) had dared Gwyneth: "Scoot your bum along the floor like a dog." Vinnie had the persuasion of a cult leader, but Gwyneth of course demurred. You could see even then that she, and only she, would create her reality. And if reality didn't cooperate with Gwyneth, she simply rejected it. Like the time my brother took her to the movies and the trailers had already started so she insisted they turn around and leave, explaining that the movie would be ruined if she couldn't have the entire experience.

Gwyneth went inside to get ready. Through the screened patio door I heard the rip of curtains, then my brother's groggy rasp: "*Hiiiii.* What time is it?"

"Half past four, darling," Gwyneth said, warmly yet crisply.

"God," said Dono. "I've slept the day away. I'm sorry, I'm sorry."

"If you say sorry one more time . . . ," Gwyneth huffed.

She reappeared on the patio in a black tank dress, short hair slicked back, sleek as a cat. "Ready?"

I shook my head. "I'm going to shower. See you in a bit." It was true my brother kowtowed to her too much. He was acting like a muff, as Karis and her Bedales friends would have said. Still, I didn't like it when Gwyneth talked to him like that. At breakfast, Dono had distractedly tipped his water glass (he was one of the world's most distracted people). A few drops had splashed Gwyneth and she'd snapped, "Idiot." With a laugh, but still.

When Gwyneth had gone to the lounge, I peeked in on Dono. My brother was slumped in bed, weakened by Montezuma's Revenge. He must have been the palest person in Mexico, but his lank, waifish look was killing it in New York. He'd just been named one of Ford's "New Faces for 1994."

I sat on the farthest edge of Dono's bed. "Is Gwyneth always mean to you like that?"

Dono laughed. "Only sometimes," he said. "But I'm annoying. I don't mind!"

My brother was smitten. He was twenty-seven and looking toward the future, to marriage and kids. Gwyneth was only twenty-one and wasn't ready for anything too serious. Well, at least not yet. Six months later, she'd get a part in *Seven* and fly to Reno to meet Brad Pitt—and we all know how that turned out.

"Shower and meet in ten?" I said.

"Twenty," said Dono. "I need some time to take care of . . ." He hitched his thumb toward the bathroom.

As I turned to leave, my gaze stopped on a stack of scripts next to the coffee table. A stack so tall it could have *been* a coffee table.

I looked at Dono, crestfallen. "Are those all hers?"

"Yeah," Dono said. "She's trying to get through them this week. Hey, you should take the ones she turns down!"

It was a sweet thought, but we both knew Hollywood didn't work like that.

———

Alice was gone when I returned to LA. She'd moved to New York to be with her big love, the model Rachel Williams. I felt relieved and vowed to myself, daily, *I will be better. I will be good.* Not that Mexico had made me whole and normal and fine again.

"Oh, hell, look at you," said Amelia, appearing from the guest-house one afternoon. Adam was at the recording studio and I was lying in the backyard, staring up at the trees and taking slow, deep breaths.

Amelia stood over me with her endless legs and her white-blond hair riffling in the breeze. She looked like an angel, reaching her hand toward me. She was my storybook friend. When we were together, even the most ordinary moments felt heightened and romantic. I reached up and gave her my hand and we stayed that way for a while, just holding hands and looking at each other. I ran my thumb over Amelia's ruby ring, a gift from Stevie Nicks that she treasured and I coveted. She wore a string bikini top and an Indian sari for a skirt—the one with two moth holes that George Harrison had given her mom, Jenny Boyd. I had one of George's Indian wraps too. He'd given it to Mom, a souvenir from visiting the Maharishi. It wasn't quite as good as if Donovan had brought it back for Mom, but the fact that George Harrison had touched it and Amelia had its twin made the threadbare sari one of my most prized possessions.

Maybe it was nothing magical or mystical that Amelia, Karis, and I had found one another. Our moms were close, after all. But I'd always felt it was more than circumstance that had brought my two best friends into my life. They understood me like nobody else could. Even their dads, the two Micks, had a certain way of making me feel seen. Karis and Amelia seemed to get this.

"Come on," said Amelia, pulling me from the grass. "No more *Fawlty Towers* for you. We're going to see Mum and Dad."

Mick Fleetwood and Jenny Boyd had a fascinating history. They'd married, had children, divorced, and then remarried. Now they were separated again but still friends, hanging out at Mick's rented spot in Malibu.

It was lunchtime when Amelia and I arrived, but Mick was still sleeping. Jenny made us lunch and we sat around the kitchen table, talking and waiting for Mick. I'd always liked Amelia's mom and her musical British accent. She looked almost the same as in her modeling days, with straight blond bangs, that tiny cute nose, and those famous dimples. Years of living in the shadow of her famous husband and flashier sister, Pattie, might have made her a bit deferential, but like all the rock star wives in Mom's circle, she was a powerhouse and trailblazer in her own right. When Amelia went for a swim and the two of us were alone in the kitchen, Jenny touched my arm across the table.

"I thought you should know, your father and I never had a romantic liaison."

"Oh," I said, not sure how to respond. "I think I knew that, but thanks." It was always a little strange being around people who knew my father better than I did.

Jenny seemed equally grateful for the interruption when in walked Amelia and Mick Fleetwood, who was tall and swashbuckling, with smoke-gray hair and sparkly, mischievous eyes. He wore only a tiny pair of running shorts and a contraption strapped to his bare stomach that made a loud *wee-wah, wee-wah* sound.

"This is helping my tummy!" he pronounced in his kingly accent.

Wee-wah, wee-wah went the machine as Mick poured himself a cup of tea and Amelia and I doubled over with laughter. Then, with a loud *kkkkrrrrrissshhh*, he ripped off the machine's Velcro straps and sauntered outside to lie in the sun.

The three of us women watched him through the window. *Fascinating*, I thought. I liked this funny, relatable side of Mick, so different from the Fleetwood Mac version who dressed to the nines in tailored velvet suits and fancy boots with spats.

"Like a lizard in the sun," said Amelia, giggling.

She and Jenny obviously adored Mick, wild and difficult as he could be. Why couldn't Mom and Donovan have stayed friends and co-parented me like this? They had gotten along famously once and surely could have learned to again. If only they'd tried, we could have made up our own version of a family. We could have been contenders.

18

Audience with the Queen
1994-1996

By the fall of that terrible Northridge Earthquake year, I'd mostly shaken the mean reds and was back on my feet with a fun role in *Four Rooms*, an anthology comedy with four separate storylines and four directors: Allison Anders, Alexandre Rockwell, Robert Rodriguez, and Quentin Tarantino. I was working with Allison Anders, who'd also directed me in *Gas Food Lodging*, in the storyline about three witches—me, Lili Taylor, and Madonna—attempting to reverse a spell cast on Diana, goddess of the hunt. It was a fun shoot. I did a sex scene in a cauldron and met Quentin Tarantino, who was very jolly and needled me about my film snobbery when I tried to impress him with all the great directors I loved. "You'd be surprised how much you can learn from B movies too," he told me.

But the real highlight of my *Four Rooms* experience was working with Madonna. That she appeared in my life at the very moment I was starting to push the boundaries of my gender and sexuality felt like a blessing.

As expected, Madonna wasn't warm and fuzzy or as interested in getting to know her castmates as we were her. All the actors shared a makeup trailer, but Madonna was soon moved to a private space because we couldn't stop staring at her.

I mean, it was Madonna. I'd only seen her in the flesh once before, from the audience at her Blond Ambition concert in LA in 1990. Adam had scored prime seats because the Beastie Boys' first tour had been opening for Madonna. He and I were secret fans. Commercial pop was uncool to us, so we were acting like, *Oh, isn't it ironic that we're here at this mainstream pop show?* But from the minute the Queen strutted onstage in her Jean Paul Gaultier bondage gear, all our judgment went out the window.

Madonna was fun and nice and a little bit of a mean girl too. She loved taking the piss out of Tim Roth, who played the bellboy in all four stories. My old friend Paul Starr was Madonna's makeup artist. Near the end of one long day of filming, when he swooped over for a last touch-up, she playfully smacked his hand and snapped, "If you put any more makeup on my face it will crack!" Paul just laughed and went on doing his thing. He kept telling me how guilty he felt about not doing my makeup too because he and I were such old friends, which was sweet, but I told him not to worry about it. I knew it was best to go with the flow and use the makeup artist who worked on the rest of us actors. I always prided myself on being easy to work with and had never once put up a fuss on a production.

I didn't expect to become best friends with Madonna, but it seemed necessary for my evolution that I at least talk to her. I played it cool, making myself available to her, but not too available. Waiting for her to make the first move.

We were shooting the spell-casting scene the day it happened. Madonna was resting between takes on the big white bed in what was supposed to be the Chateau Marmont. I was perched in a window nook, looking out at the hills to avoid staring at her.

"Take a load off, hon," said Madonna, patting the bed.

I'd been summoned! Cinching my terry cloth bathrobe, I lay down next to Madonna. Her eyes were still closed, so I closed mine and we lay quietly, side by side on our backs, as the lighting and production crews moved around us like busy ants. Turning my head ever so slightly, I opened one eye to look at her. She was almost otherworldly, with her feathery black lashes and fantastic bone structure. I had the urge to wrap her in a maternal embrace but didn't dare. Madonna took care of herself. She was a survivor.

Her eyes flicked open and she turned, catching me before I could look away. "What?" she said.

I said the first thing that popped into my mind: "My brother has the same birthday as you, August sixteenth."

"Oh yeah?" she said in her articulated, not-quite-placeable accent. "Who's your brother?"

"Donovan Leitch."

"Donovan's your brother?" she said. "I can't stand that guy."

Wow. I used to get that in high school—people loved Dono or they hated him—but adults were usually more polite. Maybe she didn't like my brother because they were so alike—two performative, hustling Leos.

Madonna might not have been a fan of my brother, but she took a small shine to me. When *Four Rooms* wrapped, just before Christmas, I was invited to a holiday dinner party at Castillo del Lago, her Mediterranean-style estate perched above Lake Hollywood. A few decades before Madonna, another bigwig, the mobster Bugsy Siegel, had lived there. It was magnificent, the whole exterior painted in ocher stripes inspired by a church in Portofino. The view from the grand dining room, with its honeycombed Moorish ceilings, stretched from Lake Hollywood to the ocean. Best of all, a Frida Kahlo painting, *Self-Portrait with Monkey*, hung over a small table in the foyer, a vase of peonies set below it like an offering. Kahlo and Balthus were my biggest inspirations to start painting in oil. Before the dinner, I slipped away with my cocktail to study the small, powerful painting. The artist stared defiantly back, her thick monobrow slightly arched. Frida was bisexual and a bit androgynous. She'd painted herself with a noticeable mustache and a feminine red ribbon snaking round and round her neck as if it might choke her.

It was a small group that night. Debbie Harry was there, with a spiky new haircut, dyed jet black. I worshipped Debbie as a teen, and still worshipped her, but my attention was mainly focused on Madonna's ex-lover and best friend, Ingrid Casares.

The earthquake may have shaken Alice's hold on me, but it hadn't cured me of my cheating problem. Adam had been away for months, touring the world for *Ill Communication*, and my work hadn't allowed me to follow him around like I used to. Without his calming presence by my side I'd get anxious and lonely and, a bit like a junkie looking for a fix, set out in search of a new conquest—or at least a good flirtation—to comfort myself. I didn't think of myself as a love or sex addict, but I did seek solace through love and sex. And I did get a high from winning a girl over. At this point in my life, my drug was women.

I'd been sleeping with Ingrid since we met through M (she let me call her that now, a big honor) at the beginning of filming *Four Rooms*. She was a Cuban American rich kid, a beautiful, out-of-the-closet tomboy who dated models and ran a Miami nightclub. At thirty—six years younger than Madonna and six older than me—Ingrid was younger at heart than both of us, almost childish at times. She had a devilish smile; sparkly, come-hither eyes; a fetching Jean Seberg pixie cut; and the most beautiful, dewy olive skin all over her delicious Cuban body. She was a type A clean freak, physically fit, always immaculate in wrinkleless pantsuits and diamond earrings. She was hung up on a married model but we'd had several nice sleepovers where we went down on each other under her gleaming white sheets while listening to her favorite song, William Orbit's "Water from a Vine Leaf," on repeat. It was nice to be with an adult who felt comfortable being gay. It would have been a perfectly healthy experience except I was of course married and racked with guilt.

Ingrid had not told Madonna about us. Their romance of over a year had only ended recently, and I sensed they still had some feelings to work through. Earlier that evening, as Ingrid and I returned from a walk around the estate, I'd sensed our hostess was not entirely pleased. Had she seen me take Ingrid's hand in the olive grove? It did not feel like an accident that I'd been seated at the opposite end of the table from Ingrid and Madonna. Chastened, I kept my eyes on my Versace plate for most of the dinner.

When Madonna left the table to take a call, her cute young boy toy asked us in a whisper, *"What on earth do I get her for Christmas? She has everything!"*

"Don't worry," someone said, "you won't be around by Christmas."

The boy toy laughed but I watched his face fall when he thought no one was looking.

M had reappeared. "I like your red stockings," she said to me, gliding back to her seat. I sat up straighter, like a teacher-pleasing kindergartner. I still lived for an honorable mention from someone I admired.

Now that Madonna had me in her sights, she began peppering me with questions about Adam and me and our wedding, which had been two years ago but seemed like another lifetime.

"A white wedding?" asked Madonna, her blue-green eyes glittering with interest.

"Yes," I said, carefully placing my fork, tines down, on my plate. *Why is she so interested in my wedding?* Was she trying to put me in my place or genuinely curious?

"Let me guess . . ." Madonna cocked her head, studying me. We were all quiet, waiting for whatever she was guessing at. Ingrid gave me a little shrug as Madonna continued: "I don't see you in a traditional gown. Vintage, I bet you wore vintage."

"Yes!" I said. She was *good*. "Victorian, with cap sleeves." I told her about the Santa Ynez estate and how it reminded me of Katharine Hepburn's house in *The Philadelphia Story*.

"I suppose a wedding is just a performance when it comes down to it," M mused. "Everyone playing a role."

I frowned, then corrected myself with a little laugh. "Maybe," I said. I didn't want to seem defensive, though I felt it. Madonna and Sean Penn's famously tempestuous four-year marriage had begun on a cliff with helicopters circling overhead. The photos had been everywhere: Madonna's classic strapless gown and long veil irreverently accessorized with a black bowler hat.

Maybe you played a role at your wedding, I wanted to say, *but Adam and I were real.*

We were real, weren't we? I never felt I was acting with Adam. My love for him was the most genuine love I'd ever felt. When we *were* together, we had good, sweet, lovely sex, and went out to restaurants and played basketball and watched old movies and did all the things happy, bonded couples did.

Still, Madonna's comment stuck with me. Now I kept thinking of Zoe, the day before the wedding, asking, *You know this is real life, right?*

Since the earthquake, what "real life" was had become even more elusive to me.

My time with Jenny Shimizu most definitely felt like a dream.

It was early 1995. Ingrid had moved on from me and I had moved on to Jenny, another of Madonna's exes. We got close when Sofia Coppola, our producer friend Andrew Durham, and I codirected a short film I wrote called *Bed, Bath and Beyond*. It was very silly and (I hoped) John Waters–esque—bursting with big houses, bad shoes, bulimic husbands, and waxers with whips! Roman Coppola and Spike Jonze did the cinematography. Jenny Shimizu played the hero.

Jenny was on the cusp of being an icon. She had modeled for Versace and Gaultier and would be the first Asian American model to walk the catwalk for Prada. Jenny had just posed with Kate Moss (and Dono!) in that famous black-and-white Calvin Klein CK One fragrance campaign that pans across a long line of models to end on her gorgeous face. Jenny not only rode motorcycles—in chaps and white tank tops—but she knew how to fix them. Jenny was a mechanic, how fab was that?

Jenny, Jenny, Jenny. To be wanted by such an exceptional person would always be my favorite drug.

She was a masterful lover, sometimes a dominant one. She didn't use whips or handcuff me to the bed, she just held this vibe. One day she took me to a dungeon where her friend worked, just to look around. I thought it was funny I was there at all and couldn't wait to tell Amelia about it. It wasn't tacky, gross, or cheap looking like I thought a dungeon would be. It was run by women and stylishly decorated. One room looked like a classroom; one was textbook dungeon, with handcuffs and studded leather benches; one room was like a hospital. I had never actually done S/M, but reading the bizarro sex scenes in *The Painted Bird* during my impressionable teenage years had planted a kinkiness deep within me that I hoped Jenny would unearth.

We didn't speak on the drive back to Jenny's place. The air was hot and thick with the sex we were going to have. I'd already decided I would let it go as far as she wanted, within reason. My safe word would be "London."

In her spare, elegant bedroom, Jenny pulled back the sheets and pushed me down.

"Where don't you want me to hurt you?" she said with a wry smile. Jenny had a genius, dry sense of humor, and God, she was beautiful. That skin! Those boobs!

I didn't know how to answer the question so I started to kiss her, but Jenny pushed me away. "Well?" she said, pinning my hands over my head.

"My face?" I offered, my heart beating faster than a heart should safely beat.

But Jenny didn't hit me, not once. Instead, she went to her dresser and pulled out a strap-on.

How to describe strap-on sex with Jenny? It made me needy and devoted. I wanted to be her girlfriend—no, her dog, like in that Stooges song "I Wanna Be Your Dog," which made sense for the first time:

> *And now I'm ready to feel your hand*
> *And lose my heart in the burning sands*

But Jenny didn't want me to be her dog. She left shortly thereafter for a modeling job and never came back to me, except as a good friend.

I would get over Jenny but not the feeling she'd given me. A few years in the future, when Howard Stern asked me about our romance on his show, I'd say she was my true initiation into the lesbian nation. I felt genuinely connected to my lesbian side now, and I wanted to dig into that.

I'd already chopped off my hair for a photo shoot, to my agent's dismay. My long, wavy, feminine hair had always been part of my look. Short hair was in vogue at the time, which helped, but it didn't suit me as well as it did Winona Ryder, Angelina Jolie, and Linda Evangelista, whose cropped coif, "the Linda," had ignited the trend. I couldn't tell for sure what Adam thought of my pixie cut. Being nontoxic and noncontrolling, he always said I was beautiful, no matter what. And had we been in a better place, he probably would have cheered me on for bucking the ingenue stereotype that had followed me throughout my career. But I think my new boyish look was confusing to Adam—another sign of my restlessness. He wasn't the only one who was confused. When I looked in the mirror, I didn't see an empowered young woman claiming her identity; I saw a stranger.

Continuing to dismantle my femme girl identity, I dabbled in old-fashioned pipe smoking and doubled down on wearing Adam's clothes, which I'd always liked to do. His closet was there for the plundering, as he lived out of a suitcase, always on the road. With my curves, I didn't pull off menswear any better than I did "the Linda." With their model bodies, Jenny and Alice had made androgyny look so effortlessly sexy that I'd thought I would too. What a disappointment. Still, for a while, it felt super-duper pretending to be Gary Cooper. I rented a pickup truck and dragged Karis with me to the Michigan Womyn's Music Festival (the gayest thing I'd ever do). Back in LA, I hung around at lesbian coffee shops like Little Frida's and the Abbey until I was adopted by the same group of young gay women who would later inspire the TV show *The L Word*. They took me to female-friendly strip clubs like Jumbo's and Cheetahs in Silver Lake and to the Garage, a gay dance club on Santa Monica Boulevard.

I met Mai Lei at the Garage.

I couldn't stop watching her on the dance floor. She was Chinese American, a skater girl with rambunctious energy, a very fit body, a bandana tied across her forehead, and long shining hair. Her handsome-beautiful face had symmetry and a little bit of mystery, like a well-designed room. But it was her dancing that really drew me—she was loose, fluid, and unselfconscious, like I wished I could be, with a comedic sensibility to her moves.

She looked bemused as I led her off the dance floor to a booth. Within minutes, I could tell we'd get together, and it would be different with her. Alice and Jenny had felt dangerous and unreal, but Mai Lei felt solid and down-to-earth. She was an all-American girl, in her own way. I learned that she loved dirt bike riding, cigarettes, and her foster cats; her nickname was BamBam because she was clumsy and broke things; she worked at the Abbey and played in a band; and she had the most infectious good energy. We instinctively held hands across the table, weaving our thumbs as we bantered.

"One, two, three, four, I declare a thumb war!" I said.

"If I win, will you come home with me?" she said.

I looked at her boyish hands, clearly stronger than mine, and nodded, signaling the true beginning of the end of my marriage.

Within days of meeting, Mai Lei and I felt like a real couple. I saw her several times a week, but I wouldn't see her unless I'd connected with Adam first, to secure my safety net. Compartmentalizing took major effort now that I was juggling two serious relationships. Once I'd called Adam wherever he was on tour and made sure we were okay, I'd get the dogs and cats all tucked in, then drive over to Mai Lei's grungy little bachelor pad in the flats and spend the night. I was always cleaning the place but I didn't mind. After all the high-flying, movie-money views I'd looked out on from hotels across Europe and Asia and my own special house, there was something grounding about Mai Lei's Hollywood vista of rooftops and telephone wires. The thud of helicopters chasing down outlaws was even oddly calming, bringing back faint memories of the very first LA apartment Mom, Dono, and I lived in, before Carl. I'd leave early in the morning and drive home, a pit in my stomach, to feed the animals and call Adam.

If you've never cheated, I admire you, but I really don't expect you to understand why I would do what I was doing to the love of my life. I still don't truly understand it myself. Back when I was with a pathological cheater (Anthony), I thought he was just being greedy—wanting to have his cake and eat it too. But surely it went deeper than that. I know it did for me. According to the shrink who tried to help me during this low point in my marriage, I was attempting to disrupt my intimacy with Adam, to keep him at a distance so that I wouldn't be destroyed if he abandoned me. Those old abandonment issues again. And of course, there were other layers to it: I was exploring my gay side; I was insecure and needed reassuring any time Adam wasn't in town or was busy; I was addicted to intrigue; I loved the validation I got from attracting a new partner . . . The layers went on and on.

Over the next year, 1995, I made two indie films—*Dream for an Insomniac* (with Jennifer Aniston, who was pre-*Friends* and, for one last moment, less famous than me) and *The Size of Watermelons* (with Paul Rudd and Donal Logue). I was the female lead in both and, as always, worked hard and went deep. But the shame I'd accumulated over my many affairs and the constant effort of keeping Mai Lei a secret from everyone but Amelia and Lala—the only two who'd understand—had worn me down. My glow was gone.

I was so distracted and worried by my newest infidelity that my only significant memory of making *The Size of Watermelons* is of the day Donal Logue and I snuck off to a Venice Beach tattoo parlor on our lunch break.

"I want ADAM, right here in kelly green," I told the tattoo artist, pointing right above my elbow.

The guy warned me it was a mistake, even bad luck, to get a tattoo of the name of your husband or wife, but I shrugged him off. Adam already had a small IONE on his ankle. Maybe if we *both* got them, that would cement the marriage?

Clearly, Adam and I were in trouble. He sent funny faxes from every port on his never-ending tour, and we kept it light and sweet when we talked on the phone or he came home for short visits between tour legs. I didn't tell him I felt abandoned by his protracted absences, because what would be the point? I was married to a rap star. He was doing his thing! And if we could just keep our heads buried in the sand for however long it took for me to do mine, maybe things would sort themselves out. That was my ongoing hope, and I think his too.

Meanwhile, I grew closer to Mai Lei, soaking up my new secret relationship for all it was worth. Though I wasn't loyal to her (there were other girls too), and she rightly didn't trust me, I loved her, thought her smile lit up the world. From the inside, I liked the life-within-a-life I had with her. The relationship felt so easy and natural, I started getting sloppy, having her over to the Case Study house, my home with Adam.

One cold January day in 1996, I heated the pool and Mai Lei and I spent several decadent hours splashing and playing, floating and talking. Steam rose off the water and the tall eucalyptus shook and rustled around us.

Mai Lei swam to me in the shallow end and I took her in my arms, holding her like a bride—the way Adam had held me in the pool at Le Parc the night he asked me to move in with him. Then I saw a figure in the house. The water went cold. Adam. Wasn't he coming back from New York tomorrow? What day was it, again?

He stood just inside the glass doors that opened from our bedroom to the back patio and the pool. Mai Lei hadn't seen him yet. She was still prone in my arms, black hair fanned in the water, talking in the fast, excited voice of a twenty-three-year-old girl telling a good story. I waved to Adam. He didn't wave back, just turned and walked into the next room. I felt like throwing up in the pool.

"Was that Adam? Oh my God, was that Adam?" Mai Lei leapt from my arms like a giant coppery fish, splashed up the steps, and grabbed her clothes. "Ione! Was that him?"

I couldn't speak. I felt as if I'd just witnessed a car crash, and Adam had been in the car. As if the world were ending. I was so, so afraid.

"I'm leaving," said Mai Lei, the garden gate slamming behind her.

When I finally got the courage to go inside, Adam said nothing, just held me as I sobbed and dripped onto his shoulder. "I'm sorry, I'm sorry," I said over and over. What else was there to say, if I couldn't say it would never happen again? Now that he'd seen it, it was real. There was no more speaking in code, so we didn't speak at all, just retreated to different sides of the house, each of us processing, mourning. I'd finally broken us.

If only we'd had it out that day, gotten to the bottom of things, maybe we would've had a chance. But that wasn't our way. Adam and I had never once fought in our entire seven-year relationship. I'd always thought that was our strength, but in fact it was our greatest weakness.

The next morning, after a long night on opposite sides of the bed, it was my turn to stand by the glass doors and have my heart shattered. It was cruelly sunny and bright out. The pool was gentle and still, light dappling the surface. I was reading a letter that had been sent to Adam, handwritten. It had been waiting for him on the kitchen counter the past few days. He must have opened it last night. Just now, he'd handed it to me, without a word. It meant something. I scanned the lines, trying to understand what.

It was from Kathleen Hanna, the lead singer of Bikini Kill. They'd met at the Summersault music festival in Australia. They were only friends, Adam said. The letter was not overtly flirtatious or inappropriate. She knew he was married and was trying, at least, to be respectful. But I could tell she wanted to leave an impression by the way she wrote—cool and smart and witty. And he must have liked her too, or why else would he have shown it to me?

I handed it back to him, my hand shaking.

"Should I write back?" Adam asked, his voice soft.

He wasn't asking me for permission to write her back, I understood; he was asking me to give him one good reason, the only reason that mattered, not to. But I couldn't give him that reason. I couldn't, in good conscience, promise to be faithful.

Through my shock, I tried to think. If my husband was going to like someone else ("like" was as far as I could let my imagination go), at least Kathleen was a good person. I admired her punk feminist mission and loved her songs, especially "Rebel Girl." She was not undeserving of him. I was the one who didn't deserve Adam.

"I guess you should," I finally said, not quite believing my ears. Was that really me, *my* voice, sending Adam away, condemning myself? Yes, but what else could I do? Adam had tried. He'd given me nearly three years to mess about within our marriage, but it hadn't been enough. I was almost happy for him, after all I'd put him through.

19

The Long Goodbye
1997

I moved to New York, supposedly to be near my brother but really because I couldn't bear to be far from Adam. We'd separated—I prayed not forever. Adam lived in our old West Village apartment (I tried not think of Kathleen there with him). I lived in a redbrick Chelsea town house, one floor above Zoe Cassavetes and around the corner from Dono and his incredible catch of a fiancée, Kirsty Hume. I named my apartment the Sanctuary because it looked out on an old seminary and also because—believe me—sanctuary was what I needed.

I was trying to be good to myself, to forgive myself. I kept flowers on the kitchen table and hung wind chimes in the branches of the apple tree outside my window. I painted while playing new (to me) records that didn't remind me of Adam—especially Van Morrison's *Astral Weeks* and anything by Thelonious Monk. In the Sanctuary, I felt more at peace than I had in years—like my old kid self, alone in my room, being creative and free. I had Tarot Sundays with Zoe and Sofia Coppola and always pulled the heart with three swords through it, which signified a lost relationship or accidental death. I went to clubs with Dono and Kirsty and their supermodel crowd. I tried but failed to make a cool and beguiling twenty-year-old DJ named Samantha Ronson my girlfriend. I filmed a made-for-TV movie in Canada and a Mike Figgis film, *One Night Stand*. I walked around the city alone. I biked to Chelsea Piers and swam as many laps as my age—twenty-six, then twenty-seven—crying tears I could barely feel under the water. I was mostly okay because I still had Adam in my life. Until I didn't.

For a whole year, Adam and I had managed to stay best friends, talking every other day and having dinners together. Kathleen was very cool and patient about this for a while. But I assumed she'd finally put her foot down the night I called Adam up to thank him for repairing my bike.

"Look, Ione," he said, cutting me off. "I live with Kathleen now. You can't call me at *ten thirty p.m.*"

The way he emphasized "*ten thirty p.m.*," like an exasperated parent—I felt like such a fool.

"I'm sorry!" I yelped, slamming down the phone.

Adam went quiet after that. Two weeks passed. And then came the letter.

I'd always thought *I felt the floor fall out from under me* was just an expression. But when I opened Adam's letter and read the words *I think it's time to get a divorce*, I actually had the sensation of the floor dropping from beneath my chair.

Steadying myself, I folded Adam's letter and placed it in my desk drawer. Then I called Arlyne Rothberg.

"Send me anything," I told her. "Something that films abroad would be great, but anything will do."

On set, you never had to be alone with your thoughts or make decisions about your real life. Someone was always there to tell you what to do, every minute of the day.

"Is everything all right, honey?" said Arlyne.

"Adam and I are getting a divorce," I told her, leaving my body as I said the words.

"Oh, honey, no!" said Arlyne into the frozen ear of the frozen young woman holding the phone at her desk. "But no one will ever love you as much as he does!"

Outside my window, the apple tree shook in the breeze, setting my wind chimes off. I wondered if they were too loud for the neighbors. I'd bought them with Adam on one of our road trips—Bob Dylan's *Desire* in the CD player, my hair wet from a cold river swim, the new-moon highway through the window . . .

"Ione?" said Arlyne.

"Hmmm?" I said, reeling inside. I knew she was right and hated her for it.

"Well, anyway, there's an Italian movie, but the script is terrible."

The script for *The Sands of Time*, an *Indiana Jones*–style epic adventure, was indeed terrible, thanks to a bad translation from Italian to English. But good actors were attached—Ben Cross from *Chariots of Fire* and Peter Weller, aka RoboCop. And it was a big-budget project, filming in Rome and Tunisia—suitably far away from the letter in my drawer.

I smiled so hard through my meeting with the Italian director, Alberto Negrin, I thought I'd explode. What fun this project would be, I told him. I loved period pieces! I loved travel! I loved Italy, and, wow, how great it would be to film in the Sahara, where *Star Wars* was filmed!

My enthusiasm won him over, and off to Rome and Tunisia I went.

We filmed mainly in Douz, the "gateway to the Sahara," in the south of Tunisia. Though I wasn't a confident horsewoman, the director put me on a fiery stallion and sent me galloping across the desert, chased by a caterwauling band of bad guys. On the third (unnecessary) take, the stallion threw me into a movie truck.

"I'm fine, I'm fine!" I insisted to the sweet-faced Tunisian carrying me to the emergency jeep. X-rays were taken, and thank God, I hadn't broken my leg.

Everyone on this project seemed to be going through some kind of transformation, and there was a unique sense of togetherness because of that. I didn't want to go back to New York and face the end of my marriage. I wanted to stay in Tunisia, riding surly camels, smoking Mars cigarettes, eating bread baked in ovens under the sand, and making out with hot Italian actors until the letter in my desk drawer disintegrated.

Maybe I can't stay away that long, but just a little longer won't hurt. When production wrapped, I moved in with a Roman crew member named Nicolo who was good in bed and always happy. When I asked why he was so happy, he said it was because his mama had died, and now the worst thing that could happen to him was over with, so he could enjoy life.

I was happy with Nicolo until he took me to the Amalfi Coast, where Adam and I had honeymooned. The first morning there, I awoke with heavy limbs and a throbbing headache, as if I'd had a whole bottle of lemon grappa the night before. But I'd had nothing to drink. This was a different kind of hangover, a different kind of regret. I slipped out of bed, careful not to wake Nicolo, and slowly walked to the church on the hill, Santa Sofia. There was a service under way, sparsely attended by a few old women in black dresses and head coverings, like in a Fellini movie, except in color. I sat in the back row, head bowed and pounding, as the priest spoke words I couldn't understand.

If only I could understand what this was all about—my life situation, I mean. How had it gone so wrong with Adam? Was I a bad person? Would no one ever love me as much as he had? It felt as if Arlyne Rothberg had cursed me by saying so. I wouldn't be able to forgive her for that. Maybe I didn't need her anymore, if that was her idea of supporting me. I made a mental note to fire her, and a few weeks later, I did.

When the ladies in black rose to their feet to take communion, I found myself following them to the altar. I'd never taken communion at our services at Immaculate Heart because you were supposed to be baptized to do it and everyone knew I wasn't. Maybe here was my fresh start? But the wafer on my tongue tasted like Styrofoam and the priest eyed me with suspicion—at least I imagined so.

"I have to get back to my life," I told Nicolo, back at the hotel.

We returned to his Rome apartment, where I showered and packed my suitcase for good. At the train station, I kissed him good-bye, dusting sand from his cheek. I lifted my hand to the breeze, felt more sand.

"What's this?" I asked Nicolo.

He said sand sometimes blew in from the desert, all the way from Tunisia and Morocco.

I thought that was quite poetic. As if the Sahara were following me, saying, *Goodbye, don't forget me.*

A month after I returned from Rome, I still hadn't seen Adam or responded to his request for a divorce. New York felt empty without him. Was it time to go back to LA? I wrote out a list of reasons to live in New York versus reasons to live in LA, to help me decide:

REASONS TO LIVE IN NEW YORK

1. Zoe lives below me
2. The city is like a TV that's always on
3. Sara at the dry cleaner who always cheers me up
4. There's always the option of a quick trip to Europe, but sometimes why bother, you're already in NYC
5. The sculpture garden at MoMA

6. Bumping into fab people at Florent
7. Chilly scenes and winter vibes
8. Walking by St. Brigid's Church, from the Frank O'Hara poem
9. I feel less hard on myself when I'm slutty in New York
10. Readings at St. Mark's Bookshop
11. Bodegas
12. Puerto Rican food, cinnamon Cuban coffee
13. Seeing Dono perform at Don Hill's
14. The romance of fall that makes me want to write
15. The nighttime sounds outside my apartment

REASONS TO LIVE IN LA

1. Book Soup magazine stand
2. Room for animals
3. Lying in the sun by my pool
4. Better for my career
5. Owl noises
6. Doing errands in a car
7. My old friends
8. Driving to the 29 Palms Inn with friends and taking mushrooms at Joshua Tree Monument
9. Mexican food. Mexican people.
10. Aron's Records
11. The smell of nighttime blooming jasmine
12. Hiking. Nature.
13. Popping into Canyon Country Store to pick up British candy
14. The back room at Musso & Frank's

15. Still so many new neighborhoods to discover, e.g.,
    Frogtown, Bunker Hill
16. The hills are alive

And that settled it. *The hills are alive* tipped the list in favor of LA, so I gave up the Sanctuary and moved home.

Now I stood in a churchyard in Luss, Scotland, feeling chubby and out of sorts in my lilac velvet bridesmaid dress with my half-grown-out hair at an awkward here-nor-there length. It didn't help that half the guests were dazzling supermodels—Shalom, Stella, Amber, and Helena were just a few of the mononymous icons who'd convened for Kirsty and Dono's wedding.

The newlyweds were kissing on the church steps for the photographer. This was none other than Patrick Demarchelier, who'd shot Kirsty's first magazine cover. I'd never seen Dono so happy. He was dashing in his kilt and dark sunglasses. Kirsty looked like a Botticelli angel with her over-the-shoulder platinum braids, silver crown, and Renaissance-maiden dress.

Dono had arrived at the church forty minutes early for the ceremony, Kirsty thirty minutes late. Had my brother been a bridesmaid, not the groom, he would have gotten her there on time. Since they'd met two years earlier, Dono had thrown himself into managing Kirsty's schedule—packed with shoots for Chanel and Gucci and *Vogue* and *Elle*—on top of doing his own modeling and film producing, and performing with his band, Nancy Boy.

Kirsty brought out my protector-slash-bodyguard side too. She'd sadly lost her mother as a teen, which made my heart soft for her. When they first got together and I was still in my clubbing-with-the-supermodels phase, I always made sure Kirsty got home safe when she stayed out even later than Dono wanted to. I loved Kirsty and was excited to have a new sister. We were already birthday sisters, both born on September 4, though I was six years older. Kirsty was just twenty-one, my age when I'd married Adam. Dono was thirty.

As one of Dono's best friends, Adam was at the wedding. He'd come without Kathleen, sparing me the torture of seeing them together. I'd seen him in the church but then he'd vanished. There was a ferry shuttling guests across Loch Lomond to the Cameron House hotel. Maybe he'd gone over already. But just in case, I told the other bridesmaids to go ahead without me and stood at the dock, hoping Adam would magically appear and we could ride the next, last boat together.

Not speaking to him these past few months had been torture for me. I wanted to look into his eyes and see if it had been torture for him too. But the boat was approaching and so was my father, tramping across the grass with Linda.

"Ah, it's good to be back in the old country!" said Donovan in greeting.

We hugged politely, then made small talk about how nice the ceremony had been, how lovely the weather, as the ferry captain helped us aboard.

I hadn't talked to my father since before I married Adam. Did he even know I'd married? I'd been nervous to see Donovan. Not butterflies-nervous, like I was to see Adam, but slightly trepidatious. A few months earlier I'd remarked in a magazine interview that I preferred Bob Dylan's music to my dad's—the one time I'd tried to hurt my father's feelings with a public jab. According to Astrella, I'd succeeded. Donovan had felt slighted by that. If he'd also been hurt that I hadn't invited him to my wedding, Astrella didn't mention it.

To my relief, Donovan seemed perfectly happy now. Up on the ferry deck, he took in the silvery lochs and rugged Highlands beyond, moved almost to tears to be in Scotland. "It's good to be here," he said again, this time quietly, to himself. He looked just as I used to imagine him when I was a kid—black velvet slacks and waistcoat, purple jacket, dark curls, like mine, wild in the mist.

I joined my father at the railing. "I think Dono and the boys are true," I said, using the Scottish term for "going commando." "No kilt for you?"

"Thought enough pairs of hairy legs would be here already!" he joked.

I laughed. *What should I say?* Part of me wanted to impress him, to tell my father that my paintings had been in a group art show in Tokyo, with work by Sofia Coppola and Kim Gordon. But he hadn't asked what I'd been up to, and my pride won out over my need for his approval, so I didn't say anything, just stood beside him, looking out at the mountains. Somewhere beyond them, about two hundred miles northwest, was my namesake, the Isle of Skye. I wondered if by any chance Donovan was thinking of the time he'd spent there with Mom, and if that made him think of me. It was funny to be nostalgic for a place I'd never been.

At the reception dinner, Adam sat two tables away and I couldn't catch his eye, which filled me with dread. I gave a nervous speech, and then it was my father's turn. I wondered what he'd say. Would he talk about a fresh start, how proud he was of the man Dono had become? The room hushed as Donovan pushed back his chair, pulled his guitar from under his table, and carried it to the mic. "Music is the best way I know how to communicate," he told us in his charming soft brogue, beginning to strum. *That's it?* I thought. I knew by now that my father was shy and undemonstrative—for sure most comfortable behind a guitar—but could he not have prepared a few personal words for Dono? Then Donovan broke into the most beautiful song, an old Scottish standard, and I forgot to be annoyed. It was incredible. Kirsty and her Scottish family all welled up. He brought the house down.

After the applause, the room hushed again, everyone watching with a collected breath as Donovan walked past his empty seat next to Linda and straight toward Enid, who was on display at the head of the family table. They hadn't yet spoken that night—nor in all the years since my father had called her at our little Hampstead flat to say he thought it would be best for my distraught mom if we didn't stay in England. "Take the children home," he'd said. "You should be with family."

"Nice to see you, Enid," Donovan said now with a shy nod.

Mom's true gangster elegance came out in that moment. She was like Don Corleone—head held high, surrounded by the family she'd created, a room full of people who adored her, would probably kill for her if she asked. She gave Donovan nothing, not even a nod, and the standoff stretched on until finally, the DJ broke the silence with "Starfish and Coffee," and my father sheepishly returned to his seat. At that moment, Adam appeared at the table, looking more than ever like an old-time movie idol in his sharp black suit. I always loved him in a suit. I loved him in all his clothes.

The classic first dance was opening up to the part where other couples joined in. "Dance?" I asked cautiously.

We hardly danced, just held each other, swaying in place. My head on his shoulder, our hearts pressed together, I ached for him to take me back to his room—to take me back. I knew the words I needed to say: *"I know what I want now. I'll give up affairs, forever. We'll start fresh. I'll be healthy. I'll go to counseling. I will be good. I will be faithful. I will do anything to make this work."*

But as much as I wanted those words to be true, I *still* didn't know if I could trust myself to make them so. Instead, I said into Adam's neck: "Everyone else feels like an imposter."

Adam said nothing. Maybe that was a good sign? My heart rose.

Now it was the second dance, the father-daughter dance. Dono surrendered Kirsty to her father, Shalom twirled with the bride's brother in his wheelchair, and Adam and I just kept swaying in place. Was this it, the rom-com wedding moment where we realized that against all odds and personality defects (mine), we should be together?

At the edge of the dance floor, I saw a commotion. Astrella, my half sister, was pushing our father toward me. *Oh no, no, no.* Sweet Astrella; she wanted us to have our father-daughter moment. But it was like watching a dog being led to a bath, my father literally digging his heels into the wood floor as she pushed him toward me. I tried to catch Astrella's eye, shaking my head, but in the atmospheric lighting, she didn't notice. With a last great push, she sent Donovan stumbling into Adam and me.

My father smoothed his velvet coat, looking embarrassed. "I, uh, may I?" he said.

I clamped my arms tighter around Adam's neck, like a child in a swimming pool, but he shook me off and walked away.

"*Och*, sorry!" said Donovan, watching him go. "Is he mad, then?"

"I don't know," I said tersely. Adam had found a door and disappeared through it.

"Oh no, oh dear," said my father, clearly more concerned about putting Adam out than any father-daughter-bonding business. I almost expected him to run after Adam to apologize, but, looking pained, he offered me his hand. I took it, and we shuffled awkwardly till the song ended. Then I turned and ran from the ballroom, looking for Adam.

He was walking down a long hallway, away from the wedding. I ran to him, calling him. He stopped under a glinting chandelier, crossing his arms as he turned to face me.

"Well, that was awful," I said.

"Damn, I hate your dad," said Adam. "I hate what he did to you."

"I know," I said, my hope flickering on again, ever so lightly. Adam had never criticized my father so overtly. Neither of us had. It struck me that it was about time and also that Adam must still love me, or why would he be so angry? Maybe there was still time for our happy ending, for Adam to drop his shoulders and take my hands and say, *"I love you. Let's not do this divorce. Let's get back together."*

But he just stood there, shaking his head. I could see it happening before my eyes—the truth of the matter finally sinking in: I would always be an abandoned daughter, always searching for proof of love. No matter how much proof Adam gave me, it would never be enough.

I'd only been back from the wedding a week when I came home from grocery shopping to find a strange man—perfectly ordinary, about forty—standing in my driveway.

"Ione Leitch?" he said.

I left the groceries in the trunk and hurried up the front walk, away from him. Who was this stranger? He didn't look like a fan or a stalker, but you never knew.

He asked again. "Are you Ione Skye Leitch?"

My hands shook as I fumbled with the front door lock. "Um, yeah," I said, not looking up.

The man tried to give me a manila envelope, but I instinctively kept my hands at my sides. I sensed what this was: divorce papers.

The man tried again, and I jumped away as if the envelope were on fire.

He retreated, placing his delivery on my car hood.

"You've been served," he said.

20

The Role of a Lifetime

1999–2001

In the first years after my divorce, I was crushed and wide open at the same time. I wanted solace. I wanted expansion. I was receptive to anything, a sponge. I'd always found New Agey stuff embarrassing but suddenly was drawn to lotus flowers and sunsets. I ripped off the corny dust jackets of *You Can Heal Your Life*, *Women Who Love Too Much*, and my old favorite, *Codependent No More*, and read them in my downtime on film sets. When self-help books didn't help, I tried my hand at group therapy, analyzed my dreams with a Jungian therapist, got a tutor to prepare for the GED test I'd never take, took acting lessons, tried out AA and Al-Anon meetings, spent weekends at the Omega Institute doing tai chi, did Tibetan meditations on dying, painted endlessly for my second art show, and tried out kundalini yoga.

The kundalini classes were at a culty Sikhism-based studio called the Healthy, Happy, Holy Organization (3HO). I might have gotten a little carried away with those.

Practicing kundalini at 3HO was almost like being back in Catholic school. It gave me structure, order, and at least some answers. I also loved the altered state yoga put me in. Gurmukh, our elegant, sinewy teacher, was a strong, charismatic, and caring mother figure. Dressed in her uniform of a white turban (pinned with a blingy jewel), white tunic, and white leggings, she would walk among us as we held "curative" positions for ages, took dizzying "breaths of fire," shook, chanted, and supposedly expanded our astro-magnetic fields. With all the music and incense and beautiful Indian fabrics and paintings of the gurus with their swords and halos and the pretty LA people feeling good together, it was easy to get swept up. Twice, I even traveled with Gurmukh to Amritsar, India, to sing and pray in the Golden Temple.

But the Sikh lifestyle and teachings felt off to me at times and couldn't provide all the answers I was looking for, so I never fully committed. I lived the practice the way I lived my work and romantic lives: in intense fits and starts. I wasn't willing to go all in and cut myself off from the other big experiences I wanted to have. Especially romantic ones.

Robert Downey Jr. was my first major guy crush after Adam. We'd first met through Dono, back in the late eighties, when Robert had just made *Less Than Zero* and I'd just made *Say Anything*. Robert had a great mind, and his humor was on another level. He was the kind of brave I wanted to be as an actor. No one threw caution to the wind like Robert. Back then, he was just starting out. He and Dono inspired me to get involved with Jane Fonda's campaign to save the oceans and we went up and down California, visiting college campuses. This was before Robert's big drug phase.

Then Robert got heavily into drugs and went to jail and got out of jail and we all reunited in 1997 on the set of *One Night Stand*, in which Robert starred and Dono and I had small roles. (I'm the girl in a skintight black vinyl dress who seduces Wesley Snipes on a balcony.) Anyway, the next time I saw Robert was in 1999, when he was in a state prison in the Central Valley for missing a mandated drug test. Robert was not yet mind-blowingly rich-and-famous and was struggling with legal bills; he'd even lost his house in Malibu. Dono and I thought he could use some cheering up, so we went for a visit.

I'd never been to visit anyone in jail before. They made me go to the restroom and cut the underwire out of my bra because you can't have wire or a braless woman inside a prison.

We met Robert in a big room with round tables where the prisoners could sit across from visitors. We asked how it was going and Robert said, "It's not so bad," though it was obviously a very bad place to be. He said he was maintaining his carb-free diet, which we thought was hilarious because this was not the kind of prison where they served special meals. As we talked, I kept thinking of the *Twilight Zone* episode "Shadow Play," where Dennis Weaver plays a man trapped in an eternal recurring nightmare that he's on death row. He keeps trying and failing to convince the other characters they're part of his nightmare, so if he dies, they'll die with him.

"Is it hard to stay sane in here?" I asked.

"I have some tricks up my sleeve," said Robert. Then he told us a story that made me fall in love with him. He said he had a ritual for laundry days. He would shower, smooth his sheets, lie down in his fresh-out-of-the-dryer prison uniform, close his eyes, and visualize himself in some wonderful, luxurious place.

After a few moments, his cellmate would ask, "Where are you now, Robert?" And he would usually answer, "Shutters" (a fancy hotel on the beach in Santa Monica). Then he'd walk his cellmate through the whole Shutters experience and they would both relax and feel better.

I thought it was so funny and eighties-bougie that Shutters was Robert's happy place. But also, what a trouper! The self-help appreciator in me was impressed with his positivity and mind-over-matter outlook. I joked (half-joked, really) that he should reserve us the conjugal visit room the next time I came.

Robert's jaw dropped. "Let's do it!" he flirted back.

This must have struck a chord because about six months after that visit, Robert called me up.

"I got out of jail yesterday!" he said. "Would you wanna go to a movie or something?"

I met him at his temporary place in Marina del Rey, which was almost entirely taken up by a brand-new red baby grand piano. He asked me if I'd keep it for him when he moved and I said yes, though I had no place for a red baby grand piano. I don't remember what movie we saw, just that on the way out, while the credits rolled, he pulled me in for a kiss against the dark back wall of the theater. He had a really great hard-on and it was very sexy, but then he drove me home. I was bummed that he didn't take me back to his place but didn't let it dampen my hopes. He'd just gotten out of jail! The guy probably needed to sleep, *then* to fuck. And we did have a second movie date. A Hollywood bigwig screened *Wonder Boys* for us in the private theater at his old-school-tycoon house. Robert had made the movie right before he went to prison the second time and hadn't gotten to see it yet. He was so good, I fell even harder for him. I went home and made him a great big charcoal drawing on nice paper stock of me in a retro bikini, my hair in two braids, with my old black dog by my side and the word "stay" written across it (wink, wink). Robert seemed genuinely into the drawing, and me, when I brought it to him. But he didn't take the bait, and I never did get that red piano. I may have been too unsettled for him; we were too alike. Or perhaps Robert could hear my ticking clock?

Though I'd always been baby-crazy, I'd never felt ready before. But in 2000, as I approached my thirtieth birthday, I felt a calm, clear certainty that I wanted a child. This was not like my girlhood fantasy of adopting a doorstep baby. This was real.

I'm not sure what flipped the switch for me. Maybe I was looking for unconditional love. Maybe it was my age. Maybe the fun of chasing tail was finally wearing off, replaced by the fun of chasing little kids in games of tag. I had a little brother and a godson now! Mom and Richard had a five-year-old named Jack who was born via surrogate when Mom was fifty. Amelia was the mom of a six-year-old boy named Wolfie.

Amelia was the first person I told about my baby urge. I had to share the news in person, so I drove to her house in Silver Lake. Wolfie was at school and Amelia was napping with her neurotic rat terrier, Ratty. I crawled into bed with them and poked Amelia.

"I want a baby," I whispered as she stretched awake.

"Really?" she said, sitting up.

"Yes!" I said.

"With who?" said Amelia.

I shrugged. Adam popped into my brain, but I shook the thought of him away. My last flicker of hope for us had long ago extinguished. I hadn't spoken to Adam since the divorce negotiations a couple years earlier. I'd gotten the Case Study house, which we'd purchased together, and a small lump sum, which I used to pay off the rest of the mortgage. To my lawyer's frustration, I refused to ask for a fractional percentage of royalties on the albums the Beastie Boys made when we were together. I couldn't take more from Adam after what I'd done to him.

"Maybe you should ask a friend to get you pregnant?" said Amelia.

I thought about that for a moment. It didn't feel right for me.

"I guess I want the whole shebang," I told her. "A baby *and* a husband." It was true. Even considering the mess I'd made of my first marriage and the fact that my attraction to women wasn't going anywhere, my sexual orientation was tilting more straight than gay.

"I want a husband too," said Amelia. (It had not worked out with Wolfie's father, the British musician and future member of Nine Inch

Nails, Atticus Ross.) Pulling some paper from the piles of books and journals spilling off her bedside table, Amelia suggested we write down what kind of men we wanted.

My list basically described Adam: *kind, funny, brilliant, handsome, highly creative, musical*, etc. This depressed me and I started to crumple it up, but Amelia snatched the paper away, smoothing it out.

"There are loads more fish in the sea," she said, "no matter how rough the sea."

And what do you know? A few days later, our dear, darling, eccentric, and hilarious mutual friend Tatiana von Fürstenberg called me to say she had a close old friend who was the perfect man for me. She wanted to set us up. Maybe there was something to this witchy manifesting stuff after all?

My match was a New Yorker named David Netto. Aside from "musical," he checked almost all the boxes on my list—and was rich to boot (I hadn't listed that, I swear). Tats seemed to think I would check his most important boxes too. "He'll find your movie-star life fun," she said. "And he really goes for earthy, zaftig, sexy women."

I hadn't known that "earthy and zaftig" was how I presented, but okay.

"David's from the Upper East Side. His grandfather practically invented the Band-Aid," said Tatiana, who didn't care about this kind of thing but knew lots of "good" families. She herself was an actual princess, the daughter of Prince Egon and Diane von Fürstenberg. "We used to take David along on our holidays," Tats continued, "because ours were fun and his were quite staid—summers at the Maidstone and all that."

The old *Preppy Handbook* scholar in me perked up at "Maidstone." It was an elite country club in the Hamptons that was rumored not to let Jews like me in, which had always intrigued me. The therapist I was seeing at the time suggested that I craved access to exclusive places and acceptance from hard-to-please people because Donovan hadn't let me in. A valid theory.

Tatiana could not stop singing David Netto's praises.

"He was the only boy I was allowed to go clubbing with because my parents trusted him completely. He was quite preppy but when we went out he'd style himself like Duran Duran with eyeliner and a white powdered face and big eighties hair," said Tats.

I trusted Tatiana and liked eccentrics, so I decided to give this David character a shot.

A week later, he was in Los Angeles and Tats brought him to my second annual wig party at the Heartbreak Hotel. That's what my friends and I now called my Case Study house. No surprise, I didn't like to be alone and welcomed any newly single, blue, or lonely friend who wanted to stay. I loved coming home to find people swimming half-naked in the pool, reading books by the living room fire, or making art in my studio. It was almost like being back at Wilton Place, only I was the matriarch now. The only things missing were a child and a partner.

The party was soigné and a little unhinged, thanks to the wigs and their accompanying personas. I had a B-52's bouffant. David unapologetically wore no wig. He was tall and handsome with a vaguely transatlantic, Vincent Price–like accent that I could have listened to all night, though we didn't get to have an actual conversation till the very end of the party. Finally, he approached me, carrying himself with the elegance of an older person, or at least a person from an old world. His fine wool blazer and pale blue silk scarf were very Savile Row.

"This wine tastes like owl piss," he said, carefully placing his glass on a coaster (the only guest who'd bothered).

I laughed. I'd soon learn that David was extremely funny, as long as you weren't on the receiving end of his thorned wit. Our conversation was brief, then he abruptly left. *Well, that was that*, I thought, disappointed.

But a day later, he called from New York. Hearing his voice, I immediately got that strange feeling I'd had when I first met Anthony and then Adam, like Something Big was going to happen.

"I had fun at your party," he said, sounding surprised by this.

"Good, that makes me happy," I said.

"I want a child and a wife," he said.

Whoa. This might have been the most straight-to-the-point person I'd ever met, and I kind of liked it.

"I want that too," I said. "I mean a child and all that."

We hit some banter back and forth like a nice light game of tennis, then he said, "I'm leaving tomorrow for a short vacation. My friend Patsy and I are going to Rockhouse to see if it's going to work or not between us."

"Oh, that's . . . nice!" I said, with all the airiness I could muster. "Where is that?" It was too soon to feel let down, of course. I had no claim on him.

"Negril. I may call you when I'm back," said David, matter-of-factly. "Goodbye."

I hung up, equally baffled and intrigued.

A few weeks after that, David called again to tell me the trip had proved he and Patsy were just great as friends and nothing more. He said he'd also "tested the waters" with another friend of his to the same result. It was a shame, he said, because both women were terrific, came from "good" families, and lived in New York.

"Sorry it didn't work out," I mumbled, not knowing what else to say. And that was it. We hung up without making plans. *What is happening here?* I thought. *Why did he call to tell me all this?*

While David seemed ambivalent about testing the waters with me, our friends in common were intent on bringing us together. Blair Kohan, a literary agent who lived up in Bel Air, had gone to Sarah

Lawrence with David. She'd heard I was in the running for the part of his wife and called out of the blue to invite me along on a New York business trip. "I have a room at the Mercer," she said. "Come stay with me and have a real date with him."

The idea of chasing after this odd, prickly man was unnerving, but then again, he intrigued me. I didn't meet many men my age who were so keen on settling down.

I booked a seat on Blair's flight and booked a date with David, and the next thing I knew he and his driver were collecting me from the Mercer Hotel.

"I don't normally have a driver," David said as I got in the car. "This is just for tonight."

I took it as a good sign that he wanted to impress me but also understood the fine line between rich and douchey-rich.

We sat at the bar at Blue Ribbon Brasserie on Sullivan and had Paella Royale and some sides, then a Chocolate Bruno for dessert. David was bright, funny, and maybe a bit nervous, which I liked. I was curious what might come of this.

"Would you like to come up?" I asked in the Mercer lobby. "I'm sure Blair would like to see you."

David said yes, he'd like to come up, then briskly turned to the reception desk. "May I have a room for tonight and tomorrow night, please?"

Oh, I thought.

We got right to the sex, which was perfunctory and clean and straightforward, like him. There was no talk of birth control. I was trusting the process. I wanted a baby and a husband and this felt crazy and fast, but here he was inside me—a highly endorsed catch! We *were* on the same page, right? If we weren't, then I'd get to be a single mom with Amelia. How could I lose? Oh, right: Like me, the baby wouldn't have a father in the picture. I went a little cold as this hit me. But then, in the thick of it . . .

"*I hope we have a baby*," David whispered.

The next day was too cold to run around seeing old friends, so I stayed at the hotel, like a kept woman. David went off to do some work. He'd just left his job at an architecture firm to start his own interior design business, which would no doubt be a huge success given his impeccable style and social connections.

On the second morning of our Mercer Hotel speed date, we woke early and walked through Washington Square Park to the apartment David was renovating for himself. It was small but beautiful, the gutted rooms looking out on the Washington Square arch. David said he'd donated to the project that was restoring it. I'd never known a philanthropist before. I'd never known anyone like him: educated and rich but not a boring Wall Street type. Like Mom, I liked a good provider but would never stand for boring, and David was anything but. He could have stepped out of one of my favorite old movies. It was like dating Vincent Price, David Niven, and Gene Wilder all rolled into one! I liked his weirdness. His creativity. His obscure references that I only got half the time. Boy, was he smart.

Looking out on the grand arch that David practically owned a piece of, I saw my fantasy life unfolding before me. David's structured, elegant world could be my fortress. I had my own money and my own privilege, but David's money and privilege were on a whole different level. He had some sour grapes about the fact that his uncle had inherited most of his grandfather's massive fortune and then donated much of it to the Metropolitan Museum of Art. But still, David was not hurting in any way.

Big deal, so you're not in love, I thought, breathing in the fresh, chalky Sheetrock smell of my possible future home. It was early days. That would come.

David stood behind me at the window and I leaned into him, expecting his embrace. It didn't come. I could have been leaning against the wall.

"You should probably get back to LA," he said coolly.

Pop! went my crazy fantasy bubble. I straightened up, embarrassed. I had not booked a flight home. I was unfocused and ungrounded, and David could tell. He wanted solid-earthy, not messy-earthy. I'd made him uncomfortable.

"Of course," I said. "I got swept up. I miss New York. It's just hard for me to leave sometimes!"

David left me in his suddenly chilly living room and went to stand by the front door, waiting for me to collect my bag, coat, and self.

"I'm not interested in stopping our plan," he said. "I still want a wife and child. I just think you should touch base at home."

I flew home with a heavy heart. Who was this cold, austere man I was hitching myself to? I really didn't know, but I wanted to. I would get to him, thaw him, and find out. I considered it a point of pride, my ability to soften prickly hearts. I'd done it with Anthony, hadn't I? Never mind how that turned out. This could be different, I told myself. I was a pro now.

We emailed a bit over the next two weeks but didn't talk. I felt chastened for being too big, too much, and kept my responses polite and formal. Then he called, inviting me back. Despite my nagging feeling that more hurt was in store for me, I accepted the invitation. I didn't want to look too hard at whether we were the right two people for each other, and I don't think David did either. For all our differences, we did have one important trait in common: Once we set our eyes on a prize, we were tenacious about winning it. For David, it seemed the prize was not me, necessarily, but what he thought I could give him: a chic marriage, beautiful children, a fun social life, a warm extended family to make up for his lonely childhood, a well-run home. I also wanted those things and even more. I wanted David's whole world. I already understood that winning this prize would be all about roles and appearances—with

some love in there too, I hoped. I was auditioning for the role of a
lifetime, bigger than anything I'd ever auditioned for: the role of
David Netto's zaftig, earthy, sexy, indie-movie-star wife.

I flew back to New York, and for our second date, we went upstate
to stay with his friend Gil Schafer. David picked me up from the airport, this time channeling a country-weekend-casual James Bond, with
white leather driving gloves snapped at the wrists and a tweed jacket. I
started to play the Crosby, Stills, Nash & Young CD I'd been listening
to on my Discman but David said he loathed all that "depressing sixties
music" and popped in Avril Lavigne. *Hmm, this could be a problem.*

Middlefield was a colonnaded Greek Revival manor overlooking
the rolling green pastures and fairy woodlands of Dutchess County.
For most of the car ride there, David had filled me in on the property and how Gil had designed every inch of it. I was nervous about
spending an entire weekend with two exacting architects, but Gil, in
his wool sweater and corduroys, was immediately welcoming—like
a warm hug after the brisk car ride with David. Leaving the two of
them to chat by the fire, I went to freshen up in the guest bedroom.
The room was lovely, with blue walls and a canopy bed draped in an
Indian print like the textiles I'd fawned over in Amritsar. I hung up
my clothes in the antique armoire, then lay down for a few minutes,
staring out at the manicured meadow and reassuring myself that, yes,
this world of weekend homes and fine linens and hedgerow follies was
for me. Wasn't this the Jonathan Club life I'd always wanted—since
before I wanted movie sets and rock stars and girls and nightclubs
and drugs and kundalini awakenings? *Yes, yes*, I reassured myself
some more. With David, I could have babies and glamour and order
and still get my feet dirty when I wanted to. The old-money set was
mad for gardening.

I took my toiletry bag into the gorgeous bathroom, unpacked the
pregnancy test I'd bought on the way to LAX, and peed on the stick.

It was positive, as I knew it would be. I'd been feeling hormonal ever since the Mercer Hotel weekend. Now it was more than a feeling. Now it was *real*. Shaking with excitement, I freshened my hair and makeup and went downstairs to tell David the news.

David was over the moon about the pregnancy and immediately invited me to live with him. I got a house sitter for my home and animals in LA and moved to New York, where David proposed. I was in shock and a little numb, but I do remember that David put on Liz Phair—an artist we both liked—before getting down on one knee. The ring was big and blingy because David had a flashy side too. That was another thing I liked about him. I said yes.

His Washington Square apartment was done now. We moved in together and posed for *Vogue* magazine beside a Louis XV desk that cost as much as a house in some parts of the country.

As the photographer and his assistant packed up, I overheard them talking.

"The kiss of death," said the photographer.

"What's that?" said the assistant.

"These couples and their interior shoots," the photographer said. "They all break up after. Some don't even last till publication."

Great, I thought. I was quite the collector of bad marriage omens.

While David chatted with the photo editor, I retreated to our *Vogue*-approved bedroom, shut the door, and with great effort, peeled and pried off my Galliano dress with the wine-colored flowers and flowing train. It was a splurge, bought in Rome for a wedding we'd been to just the weekend before. I hadn't wanted David to pay for it. I'd wanted to show him that his fiancée could buy her own Galliano. I'd worn it again for the shoot because I liked how it accentuated my bump. Also because it was sleeveless and showed off the tattoo on my triceps. As a divorce present to myself, I'd had ADAM turned into MADAME.

I loved my MADAME tattoo, which wasn't meant as the French equivalent to "Mrs." but quite the opposite. It said I was my own woman. I was grown up, glamorous, and in charge. I called my own shots and followed my heart without shame or apology. A madame didn't need a man to define her, she defined herself.

It was something to strive for, anyway.

In the meantime, I was behaving more like a mademoiselle—disappearing into David's world just as I'd disappeared into Adam's and Anthony's before that. Though I missed the Heartbreak Hotel and Amelia and Wolfie and Mom and everyone in my LA life, I didn't miss my kundalini world. I got all the structure I needed from living with David.

And why shouldn't I play by David's rules? I often asked myself. My fiancé was dashing, witty, generous, responsible, and fun. And he came with the most wonderful group of friends. They were as rich and blue-blooded as they come but genuinely interesting, creative, and accomplished in their own rights.

I even got to know and love Patsy, the old friend of David's with whom he'd tested the waters before diving in with me. We went to stay in her villa in the Côte d'Azur, which was spectacular, one of the grandest homes on the Riviera, I was told. David and I happened to visit Patsy at the villa at the same time the Red Hot Chili Peppers were staying nearby at the Hôtel du Cap. One day, I was sunbathing by the pool and two men popped out of the sea below and climbed onto the rocks on Patsy's property. It was Flea and John Frusciante! They'd come to see me. "I'm afraid Patsy doesn't like this," David whispered. "Can you take them somewhere else?" But the house staff was freaking out with excitement, so our hostess relented and invited John and Flea for lunch.

"So . . . you two are different," Flea said, referring to David.

"We are not!" I said defensively.

It wasn't the first time I'd heard this—more like the twentieth. David's friends were always saying it. They never said *how* we were different, so I assumed they meant: David was organized and I was a mess; he had money and I didn't (relatively speaking); he was smart and together and I had no direction; his career was on the rise and mine was up and down—or in the toilet, even.

It didn't occur to me that what they might have meant was: *David doesn't mince words and you speak carefully; he's harsh and you're gentle. Take care of yourself.*

David's handsome, mannered parents may have been the only interested parties who never so much as hinted at our incompatibility. Nor did they seem to mind my lack of a pedigree. I had Tatiana's stamp of approval, after all.

David's mother, Kate, was a demure woman in her midseventies. She was a real lady and didn't show her cards readily. The only time I saw her lose her composure was when I told her, over lunch at the Colony Club on Park Avenue, that I was pregnant.

Kate gasped, grabbing my hands over our plates of broiled trout with parsley butter. A fork tumbled to the floor. "How far along?" she asked as a waiter swooped up the fork.

"A few months," I said.

She beamed. "Out of the woods," she said. "This is wonderful, just wonderful." I was so relieved. If she thought I wasn't good enough to carry on her lineage, well, then the lady could act.

Just weeks later, Kate had a stroke and fell into a coma.

David filled his mother's hospital room with white roses and we stayed by her side around the clock. I styled her hair but didn't talk to her as much as I felt I should. I didn't know her well enough to know what to say. I *wanted* to say, "*Please hold on to meet your granddaughter,*" but that seemed irrational, unfair.

She passed away not long after that.

"We'll name the baby Kate," David said.

"Of course," I said. We already knew we were having a girl. Now it seemed fated.

I told myself it was the shock of losing his mother that made David increasingly difficult to please. I tried to be on my best behavior, to wear my best clothes, to be nice and easygoing. But he always found something to criticize about me.

I was disorganized. I was a flake. I was always distracted. Could I just listen to his feedback and not get defensive?

One night we went to Balthazar with a lovely couple I'd never met before. Both were fans of *Say Anything* and for a small portion of the evening—from the appetizers till the mains arrived, that's all—we talked about the film and what John Cusack was like. I told them we'd had a sweet friendship and I'd always admired him and he'd never felt at home in LA so had recently moved back to Chicago. (I did *not* mention that I'd slept with Johnny after my divorce because I'd needed to get him out of my system and it had worked—now I knew we were meant to be in love only in the movies.)

On the taxi ride home, David was quiet, brooding. Something was coming. I gripped the quilted padding on my Chanel bag, waiting for it.

"You are not the star I thought you were," said David, quite archly.

"What?" I said, my heart slamming. I'd heard him but I was stalling, like someone caught in a horrible lie.

"*Say Anything* was a long time ago," he said.

I couldn't speak. So this is what he really thought of me? What all his friends thought of me? *What's wrong with her? Why couldn't she keep it going?* I was like the star quarterback fifteen years later at the bar, rehashing his high school glory days. I followed David into the apartment, hanging my head in shame.

Looking back, I think, *Why was I so quick to disown myself? What did I have to be ashamed of? Not being famous forever? Growing older in an industry that eats its young?* So I wasn't a movie star anymore, I was a working actress. I made a living being creative and doing what I loved. How few people get to do that? Most recently I'd been in a run of independent films—*Went to Coney Island on a Mission from God . . . Be Back by Five, Mascara, Jump, Moonglow, The Good Doctor, Men Make Women Crazy Theory*, and my favorite, with Natasha Lyonne, *But I'm a Cheerleader*. There was some TV thrown in there too. A few of the projects were quite fabulous and others less so, but they all interested me. I didn't feel I was selling my soul, though I did sometimes feel tired. And I did want more for myself, including better roles.

The morning after David called me a has-been, I woke feeling particularly anxious and alarmed.

"Good morning," I said brightly, but not so brightly as to annoy him, pouring a coffee. "Is everything okay?"

David did not look up from the *Times*. "Can we wake up one morning without it being like Anne Frank's house?"

"Ha-ha," I said. But in a tiny, twisted way, he had a point. *Not* that I am comparing myself to Anne Frank, but he could surely see I was in survival mode. Why? Was it the hormones? Was it that we'd rushed it all? I'd only known David for seven months.

I will not run from this, I will not run from this.

"I think I need some time," I heard myself say.

David put down the paper. "For what?"

"I just need to take a moment and not plan a wedding yet," I said, bowed over my coffee cup.

David was astonished. "Why? What are you saying?"

"I'm sure it's just the hormones," I said. "But I feel overwhelmed. Not by you! I want to be with you. It's just the whole planning-a-wedding thing . . ." I may have used air quotes around "planning a wedding."

Now he looked devastated. "But we're not even planning it yet. We don't even have a date. We'll wait till Kate's one, if you want."

"Let's just see," I said.

David gaped at me. "But we jumped out of a plane together!" he cried, always one for sweeping metaphors. "We were doing this together!"

I wouldn't look at him. Setting a date was as good as a promise. I needed to be careful here. I needed to stand my ground. To have some time to think. Not just about my compatibility with David, but about monogamy. This was not a forgiving man. There would be no room in our marriage for imperfection, let alone indiscretion. One lapse in judgment and I'd be dead to him.

"I'm not saying no," I said. "I just need time."

David sent me to his shrink.

"Is it David or marriage that you're having resistance to?" the analyst asked me.

I closed my eyes, took a literal and figurative pregnant pause. "I don't know," I said.

I really couldn't tell what was up with me. It felt like every cell in my body was screaming, "RUN!" But what did I have to run from? My gorgeous, witty, stylish, brilliant fiancé? My Washington Square Park view? Summers in Maine and weekend trips to Rome?

"I think this baby is like a time bomb," said the analyst, letting me off the hook. "It puts too much pressure on the marriage question. I think you're wise to wait."

Now David was mad at me *and* his analyst. He did not think I was wise.

"We will stay together under one roof for now. I will be a dutiful father and take care of you both," he said. "But I will never recover from this."

"From me putting off the wedding?!" I said.

"Yes. From all of this. Us."

And he was done.

At the time, all I could think was, *Shit! What have I done?* But I can see now that it was something brave. I'd followed my instincts, listened to my screaming cells, learned from my past mistakes, protected myself from jumping into marriage too fast, too soon, with a man whom I felt deep affection for but who had a way of making me feel small and insignificant.

But I was too scared to admit those things and felt I'd made a terrible mistake by postponing the wedding. Kate could have had a mother and a father together under one roof for the rest of her life. How many stepfathers would I give her instead?

I spent the rest of my pregnancy living civilly with David in the flawless cursed-by-*Vogue* apartment. He was decorating it so beautifully, bringing home an original Cy Twombly drawing one week, a blue Yves Klein coffee table the next, a David Hockney after that. I stood inside my high-society fantasy life, watching from afar.

One day, at seven months pregnant, I wept so violently in the shower that I worried I might hurt the baby. But I couldn't stop. Hearing my rough sobs, the echo of water splattering tile, I felt a rush of déjà vu. What was this? What was I remembering? Then I understood. It wasn't my past I was repeating, it was Mom's. *I* was the echo. I was Enid all over again: a new life inside me, a dream life behind me.

21

Song of the Single Mom

2001-2006

"That's it, then," said David, staring down at newborn Kate, with her black shock of Elizabeth Taylor hair. "If anything happens to her, we'll just have to kill ourselves." He was such a drama queen, but I knew what he meant. Nothing else mattered anymore. We hadn't made it as a couple, but from that day forward, we were bonded by this child and our shared biological imperative to keep her alive.

David had been with me throughout the labor—from the moment my water broke in the shoe department of Barneys in Beverly Hills, through the hours I labored at home in the bathtub with the Sikh doula, to the final countdown at Cedars-Sinai. He'd stroked my hair, taken calls from our friends, played Miles Davis's *Kind of Blue*, and even brought me his mother's quilted silk bed jacket and some of her jewels to put on after giving birth, like a real old-school dame. I'd eventually gotten an epidural and felt so good, I told David to invite anyone who called to the hospital. By the end, I was surrounded by thirteen people, including Mom, Dono, Kirsty, Amelia, and my godmother, Cynthia. Even David's personal trainer showed up.

David turned out to be the dutiful father he'd promised to be, and more. Though we were now strictly platonic, he lived with Kate and me in Laurel Canyon for the first months of her life and spoiled me with help. I had a night nurse; a house cleaner (the sheets, pillowcases, and duvet covers were always fresh and ironed, nothing better); an occasional cook; and fresh flower deliveries every two weeks. It was a lot, but I liked it. And aside from a few waves of postpartum depression, I loved being a mom.

There was something bittersweet about starting this new chapter of my life at the Case Study house, where I'd imagined Adam and me raising kids. I didn't think of my home as the Heartbreak Hotel anymore, but I could feel Adam's shadow there. It was a soft, gentle shadow, but a shadow nonetheless. When I started swimming again, to get back in shape, I sometimes thought I saw Adam through the French doors to my bedroom, and my heart would catch. But it was just an illusion. I hated remembering the day he'd found me with Mai Lei but couldn't stop. To remember was to punish myself, which I felt I deserved.

With Mom just around the corner, I never felt alone or unsupported. Enid's caregiving style was perfectly loose and seventies—not bending over backward to entertain and placate the way my generation did. She would put some pots and pans on the kitchen floor while she cooked, and Kate would bang happily away. Watching them together, I realized that Mom had given us her whole life. She had been my sole parent, and aside from some rocky years with Carl and Billy and her brief depression after her restaurant closed, she had been consistent and stable, never missing a family meal at the table. I was realizing more and more how lucky I was to have Enid for a mom.

"Let her be," Mom would calmly say when I swooped in to help Kate roll over. "A little struggle builds self-esteem." But I could not bear to see my child uncomfortable or upset in any way and always came to her "rescue." I was a real Gen X parent, romanticizing my free-roaming past while doing everything in my power to keep Kate safe. David was satisfied that I was doing a good job, and he was my toughest critic, so maybe I was.

We were good together as co-parents, though we could drive each other crazy and living together under one roof was not ideal. So he could be a regular presence in Kate's life, David bought a divine little Richard Neutra house in Silver Lake and divided his time between that home, his Washington Square Park apartment, and his beach house in the Hamptons.

I hated being apart from Kate, but I wanted her to be close and bonded with her dad, so we agreed from the beginning that they would have regular time together at the Neutra house, and every July at David's place in Amagansett. So I could be near her too, I'd rent a beach house close by. It was a little awkward the first summer, hovering around the edges of David's Maidstone–and–Devon Yacht Club world. I sometimes felt like Billy Flynn, the hard-up dad played by Jon Voight in my favorite childhood tearjerker, *The Champ*. David was Faye Dunaway, the rich ex-wife.

Kate was eight months old when I hired Grace, an angel in disguise as a nanny, and went back to work. Already feeling a bit lost and wobbly as a new mom, I figured why not embrace where I was at and said yes to a role in an off-Broadway play called *Evolution*. I don't know if I hit it out of the park, but I got a huge buzz from performing live and loved the actors and writers and the circus of it all. For the duration of the production, Kate and I lived with David in his New York apartment. I was never entirely comfortable, but David made an effort, and was happy to have the cast and our mutual friends over for cocktails several nights a week. We'd all sit around that blue Yves Klein coffee table, the actors talking in our loud theater voices, the women clamoring for the attention of the star in the room and the play's star, Peter Dinklage. Peter loved it when Kate and her nanny met us at our rehearsals downtown. I remember him walking us home, pushing her stroller and saying, "I can't *wait* to be a dad." It was obvious he was going to be the best father.

When *Evolution* wrapped, I returned to LA and did some so-so TV work with some great actors. I got to work with Anthony Michael Hall on a TV series called *The Dead Zone*, and then with Blythe Danner, Peter Fonda, and (the real) Faye Dunaway on *Back When We Were Grownups*.

But my career didn't quite fulfill me again until I got the recurring part of Mrs. Veal, a horny pastor's wife, in a buzzy new comedy series, *Arrested Development*. I was new to comedy and found it to be pure joy. I especially loved it when the show's creator, Mitchell Hurwitz, was struck with last-minute ideas that we actors got to improvise together on the spot. I had layers now, and I wasn't afraid to take up space—like Joan Cusack! (I'd aspired to be brave like Joan since *Say Anything*.) *Just try again*, I thought if a take fell flat. *You can always try again*. It felt life-changing to let my inner comedian finally come out to play. Like Moon Zappa said, all those years ago: "Ione, you're funny!"

By the time I worked with Drew Barrymore and Jimmy Fallon on the Farrelly Brothers' film *Fever Pitch* in 2004, I was finding my stride again as an actor and a mom. And for the first time in the three years since Kate was born, I felt ready to take on a relationship. *Maybe Jimmy Fallon will be my next big thing*, I thought. He was so exuberant and of course famous from *Saturday Night Live*, and I had my eye on him. But when I told Drew I thought he was cute, her body language visibly stiffened. I didn't have a clue why, but I took the hint and cooled my jets on pursuing Jimmy, thankfully. It turned out he was in a new relationship, on the down-low, with his future wife and Drew's business partner in Flower Films, Nancy Juvonen. When I figured out they were together, I got a bit downcast. Robert Downey Jr. had just announced his engagement to the film producer Susan Levin. How could I compete with these power women who blew out their hair and ran movie sets and kept their famous men's lives running smoothly too? I couldn't even "run a house," according to David.

After *Fever Pitch* I jumped into another great film with a polar-opposite vibe, the thriller *Zodiac*. Working with David Fincher was such a high. Like all great directors, he was technically masterful but also a wizard at creating atmosphere and mood. My character was a mentally unstable addict, and I was concerned at first about how to portray her in a layered way. But the world David Fincher had created washed over and through me, and I was able to inhabit that woman in the car at night with the serial killer, clutching her newborn. I'm often told it was one of the most haunting moments in the film.

It seemed almost miraculous. I was back, at thirty-five, to living the dream: working with artists I admired, supporting myself, and growing creatively.

At the same time, I'd managed to co-create a pretty successful modern family. David had recently married a wonderful woman, Liz. She was the most loving, patient stepmom to Kate I could have asked for. And Kate had a new half sister, Liz and David's adorable baby, Madelyn, whom I loved as genuinely as Liz loved Kate. It had taken some effort to finesse our co-parenting arrangement, but it was all about the kids, and we somehow made it fun. "How are you all so friendly?" people would ask. I thought maybe it was because David and I were together so briefly. We were just becoming friends when we broke up and were *still* becoming friends.

Each night, when I tucked Kate into bed (our loyal Pekingese, Pop Up, curled up by her pillow), I'd tell her the abbreviated story of her day, backward. Like: *You had a bath, we had dinner, our neighbor stopped by with cupcakes, you stepped in Pop Up's spilled food and got grossed out, we put a Band-Aid on your knee, I met you and Grace at the playground, you fell off the swing and skinned your knee*, and so on, all the way to back to *you woke up*. I couldn't know everything that had happened in her time at preschool or with Grace, so Kate would delightedly fill in any missing bits she could remember. We could have gone through the day chronologically, but going backward was the fun part. It was more than a game, though. It was a way to honor the day—the good feelings, the painful ones, the achievements, the stresses, the hurts, the big deals, and the little details alike. Most of all, I did this so my daughter could get into the habit of processing her days instead of floating through them, outside herself, like I had as a girl.

I had a lot to be thankful for, but something was still missing: love. I'd only manifested half of my dream family—a child, but not a partner. It was definitely a husband I was looking for, and I felt a bit guilty about that, as if I were somehow letting down the queer community. But what can I say, I wanted a man in my life.

So, when Matthew Perry called me out of the blue, inviting me over for a "a sober drink," I only had to think about it for approximately fifteen seconds. I hadn't talked to Matthew since we made *A Night in the Life of Jimmy Reardon* almost twenty years earlier, and I normally didn't accept booty calls, which I assumed this was . . . but it was Matthew Perry! I was curious, and he was adorable and handsome and rich and presumably sober, so I said yes. We made a date to meet at his place the next Thursday afternoon, when Kate would be with her nanny.

I dressed for our daytime date in a pinstriped pencil skirt and heels, imagining I was Doris Day heading out to meet Rock Hudson for a fifties Technicolor affair. I still loved to frame my life as a movie or a novel; whether that was to separate myself from it or to put it into context, I wasn't sure. The Matthew who met me at the door of his penthouse apartment overlooking Sunset Plaza was taller than I remembered, and quite dashing. He still had a great head of hair, a playful twist to his smile, and laughing blue eyes—lined with crows'-feet now. Somehow I didn't see Chandler from *Friends*, I saw the boy I knew when we were sixteen and seventeen.

In his sparse, gleaming kitchen, he offered me bubbly water and a Marlboro Light, which I accepted. I hadn't smoked pot since Kate was conceived, but cigarettes were an easy way to bond, and I sometimes indulged for that reason, now that Kate was getting older. As we leaned against the counters, smoking and catching up, I started to relax. Matthew was as funny as ever, with such perfect tone and timing. I could remember us in 1986 so clearly, two kids lying on twin beds in an old Chicago hotel, talking and laughing. I'd played him the new Joan Armatrading, which he didn't like. She was too heavy for him. He was lighter then, less guarded.

"Want to watch a movie?" he said, stubbing out his cigarette.

I followed him into his clean, anonymous bedroom, decorated in tans and creams, with few personal effects. The TV was on, the news playing with no sound.

"What do you want to watch?" he asked.

"Let's just get under the covers," I said, wanting to skip to the good part. Standing on opposite sides of the bed, we neatly stripped down and got in. He had a long, lumpy scar on his shoulder. I gasped when I saw it, and he joked, "Don't worry, you didn't do it."

The sex was perfectly pleasant, though the silent talking heads on the flat-screen distracted me and Matthew seemed faraway. Neither of us gave it our all.

"This was fun," he said, after lighting another cigarette. "We should do it again sometime."

"Same time next week?" I said, stepping into my heels. It hadn't actually been *that* fun, but the ingenue in me still believed every no-strings fling had the potential to become a great romance. I was the same way with acting projects. My agent would send me a script that I couldn't connect with and I'd twist myself into pretzels trying to make it work for me, instead of realizing, *If I have to try this hard to fix it, something's not right.*

I came back to Matthew's the next week and it went exactly the same: a single cigarette in the kitchen; banter and bubbly water; "Watch a movie?"; emotionally distant sex; another cigarette.

As I got dressed, the second time around, it occurred to me that letting Matthew in on my retro Rock-and-Doris fantasy might turn up the heat. "We could make this a standing Thursday appointment," I suggested, putting on some lipstick. "Like in the fifties, when men had little black books, you know?"

But Matthew just took a drag on his Marlboro and looked at me quizzically.

That was the last time I ever saw him, though for years he'd text to say hi every so often. Even through his distance, he was always endearing and sincere. The last time I'd hear from Matthew was on October 16, 2023, about a week before his death. He wrote:

Hi! I hope all is well. I was meditating (I meditate now) and "In Your Eyes" started playing. And I instantly thought of you and how beautiful you are . . . I hope you are healthy and happy.

I was healthy and happy, and in a completely different place in my life by then. No longer looking for a tryst whenever I felt restless or lonely. So I didn't flirt back. I do wish I'd called him, to properly catch up, but no one talked on the phone anymore. So, after a brief, sweet text exchange, we signed off as friends.

22

Begin
2006

I'm thinking about how I just want to open up
And give and give and give
And it's okay for you to care
Cause I can feel you in the air
And while you wonder, How's this gonna end?
I only want it to begin
—Ben Lee, "Begin"

It was the big premiere of *Marie Antionette*, Sofia Coppola's movie starring her cousin Jason Schwartzman as Louis XIV and Kirsten Dunst as Marie Antionette. The film was a knockout—brave, romantic, funny, touching, and innovative. I ate up every millisecond of it. The whole audience did. I loved Sofia and it was thrilling to watch her produce another great film.

I was exhausted from a long week of mothering a four-year-old but wouldn't have missed the after-party for the world. I wore cherry-red lipstick and my favorite back crepe dress with cutouts like leaves.

I'd had a sort-of first date with Jason the night before, at his place. We'd been eyeing each other at parties for years. He was insanely cute and talented, and I never could resist a short, ambitious dynamo of a man. Anthony and Adam had both been "short kings," as they say.

I was super motivated to find a partner, so I'd finally called Jason up. He'd invited me over but had seemed more lit up about showing me his art books and rare vinyl than about making out, which we did, but not for long. After a few minutes, Jason jumped up to "change the record" but didn't change the record. I took that as my cue to leave.

But I hadn't yet read that early-aughts self-help blockbuster *He's Just Not That Into You* and had come to the party hoping Jason might see me all glammed up and fall for me, or at least decide to put some effort into me.

He understandably was focused elsewhere, bopping around, talking to Will Ferrell and Anjelica Huston and Kirsten Dunst. I got it, it was his movie premiere, but I wished I was on his arm, making the rounds. Toward the end of the night, I found my sexy, lovely (and sadly for me, gay) photographer friend Thomas Whiteside, and we sat on a bench in the outdoor courtyard, people-watching.

That's when I saw Ben Lee. I waved him over and introduced him to Thomas.

Ben was an old friend of Adam's. I'd always thought of him as the Australian Wonder Boy, emphasis on "boy." At fourteen, he'd started a three-piece band called Noise Addict. The group was quickly signed to Thurston Moore's record label, then to the Beastie Boys' Grand Royal.

I'd loved Ben's music for years by the time we first met. I was twenty-six then and he was eighteen, about to enter into a long-term relationship with the actress Claire Danes. When Adam and I were first separated and living in New York, we'd gone together as friends to Claire and Ben's SoHo loft for dinner a few times. Maybe that sounds odd since Adam was with Kathleen then, but it didn't seem unnatural. Being with Adam had never stopped feeling natural.

I still hadn't made sense of our breakup and why I'd caused it when I loved that man so much. I *still* loved him, a decade later.

The Aussie Wonder Boy was twenty-eight now, fit and lean and very cute, with curly russet hair and piercing blue eyes. He was about my height. Definitely a short king.

He came toward us with a sunbeamy smile. "Can I join you guys?" He gestured to the bench.

"*Please*," said Thomas, clearly intrigued.

The three of us sat and talked till the party wound down and I had to get home to relieve the sitter. Well, mostly Ben talked. He had a commanding, charismatic, almost mesmerizing presence.

The next day, I called Thomas to rehash the night.

"I'm sad Jason didn't pan out," I sighed.

"But what about Ben?" he asked.

"Hmm . . . ," I mused. "He's just a friend."

I had never thought of Ben as more than that. He was eight years younger than me, and I still pictured him in my head as eighteen. And he didn't seem to have a bad-boy bone in his body, so I'd be going against type. But then again, he had confidence in spades, and I liked that. One time he and Claire and Adam and I had gone out dancing in New York. The nineties–New York It Girl Bijou Phillips was dancing with us and kept lifting her short skirt, which was attracting *a lot* of eyeballs, and Ben very sweetly suggested she should put it down. Normally I hated it when men told women what to do, but Ben wasn't being controlling or condescending, he was clearly trying to protect Bijou. It struck me as very *together* of him to look out for her when the rest of us just laughed. It was a small thing, but I'd remembered it, kept it tucked into a little pocket in my mind.

A few days after the *Marie Antoniette* premiere, Ben called and asked me on a date. I said yes, partly thinking, *What am I doing? He's the Wonder Boy! He's a kid!*

We went to the ArcLight in Hollywood to see a John Lennon and Yoko Ono documentary. Just a suggestion: Don't see a movie about an intense, enmeshed marriage on a first date. It was awkward. But afterward? Less awkward. In the parking lot stairwell, Ben leaned in and we had a long, sultry pash (the Aussie term for "passionate kissing")—so long and sultry that I heard my grandpa Benny's voice in my head, reminding me to be a lady in public.

Ben came over to my house one night when Kate was at her dad's. We sat on my sofa and fooled around. It was nice, but no fireworks. "That was pleasant," I said after. "Kind of like a day at a lake."

Ben laughed. I liked that he could take a joke. After he went home, I felt a little sad that there hadn't been fireworks, then reminded myself to keep an open mind.

For our next date, he took me out for a minimalist macrobiotic meal at Inaka, then back to his temporary rental apartment across from the Grove. He'd moved from New York on a trial basis and had decided to stay.

"I *reeeally, reeeally, reeeally* didn't like LA at first," he told me in his cute Australian accent. We were standing in his small, mostly empty living room because there was only one chair. "But then I started meeting people who grew up here"—he pulled me toward him—"people like you"—he sultry-pashed me—and now I *reeeally* like LA."

Ben confidently led me to the bedroom and unbuttoned my shirt, then his.

Our chemistry was unreal. It was the best sex I'd had since Jenny—sensual, connected, lusty, and playful. It was obvious he respected me and my body. There was no question about a condom, he just took care of it. And me.

After, I lounged about topless and Ben put on his red-striped boxers and asked if he could read me "The Balloon" by Donald Barthelme.

I said sure and tried to follow along, but Ben's golden skin and tennis legs and the obvious thing under those boxers distracted me. The more he read, the lustier I got.

"'What was admired about the balloon,'" Ben read, "'was finally this: that it was not limited, or—'"

"Have you been lifting weights?" I interrupted.

Ben looked down at his skinny six-pack, embarrassed but proud. "*Yeeeah*, a bit," he said as I pounced.

Our second round was gonzo, even better than the first. That day-at-the-lake feeling was over and done with. Now it was fireworks over the lake.

"Wow," I said after. "What got into *you* tonight?"

Ben looked bashful again. "It's kind of a funny story . . ." he said.

Apparently, he'd been as tripped out about dating a thirty-six-year-old divorcee and mother as I'd been about dating someone I met when he was just a teen. To ease his nerves before our date, he'd stopped by the Sunset Marquis bar for a drink. And who was sitting at the bar? Adam Levine from Maroon 5. They knew each other a little through the music scene and Ben ended up telling Adam that he was on his way to meet an older, sophisticated woman and was feeling unsure and intimidated.

"Nonsense, brother," said Adam Levine. He ordered two shots and gave Ben a five-star rock star pep talk. By the time Ben met me at the restaurant, he was ready to go.

It *was* a funny story. One of those "only in LA" stories. And lucky

Ben, getting advice from slick Adam Levine at just the moment he needed it.

I went home around midnight to relieve the sitter, slept for six hours, got Kate off to preschool, and then texted Ben: *How about some morning sex?*

I was still high from the night before. Our romp had activated something in me. I wanted more and felt confident I could bag this kid again, easy-peasy. I was hot and sexy and desirable, still in my prime. Why play games? Ben wasn't some stranger. God, what a relief. I could just be myself.

An hour passed. Weird; he hadn't texted back.

How about this afternoon? I wrote.

Another half hour passed.

How about later? I wrote.

No response.

Tonight?? I wrote.

I could not figure it out. Why wasn't he writing back?

I have your guitar, I wrote. He'd left it at my house, after our day at the lake.

Should I bring it by? I wrote.

Ok, sure, he wrote, finally.

I drove there as fast as I could. By the time I rang Ben's buzzer, it was already half past two. Kate had gone to Mom's after school. She was happy there but I was anxious to get her home and settled before dinner and bedtime. That only left an hour, max, for another round of whatever sex magic that had been last night. Ben answered his door in ripped jeans, a Sonic Youth T-shirt, and a long red Indian scarf. I handed him the guitar. He stood in the doorway, blocking my entrance.

"Can I come in?"

"Oh, I was just . . ."

I stared at him.

"Sure." He relented, stepping aside.

I followed him into the living room, navigating the suitcases and guitar pedals. I was curious about what had happened to the man who'd ravaged me and read to me and been so very into me just the night before.

"Is everything okay?" I asked him.

"*Yeeah*," said Ben. "It's just that you seem to be coming on a bit strong?"

What?!!! A bit strong??? I thought. "Really?" I said. "I thought we had fun."

"We did have fun. But texting me five times after is too much."

"Oh my God!" I said, insulted.

"Whatever you're feeling," he said, "I am not."

Ouch. Wow. Ouch. I did not know what to say to that, so I said, "Well, I'll be going now."

I called Tatiana and told her what happened.

After agreeing, as any good friend would, that Ben had a lot of nerve, Tats said: "Listen, here's what you do. Don't contact him for two weeks."

"*Two weeks?*" I said.

"Two weeks," said Tats. "Not a day less."

I thought this sounded bananas but I accepted the challenge because I had to try *something*. So I wouldn't be tempted to text or call him, I tried never to be in the same room as my phone and even left it at home when I went out, which felt a bit like walking around naked all the time, but it worked.

After about eight days, Ben called. "Hey, how's it going? I've been thinking about you," he said.

I guess he liked being the hunter too.

If I hadn't been so happy to hear from him, I would have been depressed that my hard-to-get routine had worked. Mom always used to tell me I should be less available to boys, and I'd tell her that was old-fashioned and fake and I'd just be myself, thanks very much.

But now Ben was at my front door with a grin on his face and an offering of farmers market kumquats.

We sat by the pool and had a long talk. "I like you *a lot*," he said. "I just like taking things slow, to see if it's real and we're not just chasing a high or something."

But I want to feel high, I thought. *Don't be a bore.*

Then I remembered I wanted to approach relationships differently, in a healthier way.

Maybe Ben's way—calm and steady—could be romantic too? It didn't sound all that romantic to me, until I thought of that moment in *Say Anything* when Lloyd asks Diane, "Are you here because you need someone or because you need me?"

Lloyd doesn't care about the answer in the movie. He'll just risk it and see. But Ben wanted it to be *him* I needed. And almost more than that, he wanted to know the real me, not the crazy romance monster who'd come out after our hot-sex date.

I pictured myself, white-knuckled on the 101, practically drag-racing to Ben's the last time. Was it Ben himself I'd been flying toward or another big experience, another escape?

The answer was pretty obvious. But that was then.

I looked at him now, leaning back on his elbows, face tilted up to the sun, patiently waiting for me to speak. There was something so bravely *present* about Ben. I'd never known anyone so genuinely interested in whatever the moment held. He seemed to be constantly in a state of unwrapping the world, examining and wondering about it. I imagined that for a person who lived like this, every experience was big.

"I'm up for taking it slow," I told him.

Ben turned his sparkly gaze toward me. "Yeah? Think you can do slow?" he said in a cheeky way that made me laugh.

I nodded vigorously. "I want to try!" I really did. Ever since I could remember, I'd been racing through life, reaching for the next gilded moment, and the next, and the next. I went for the big rush above all else, ignoring the scared child within me—my feral Topanga girl, as I used to think of her. I'd dropped that poor girl's hand so many times along the way to where I sat now, with Ben, it was a wonder she didn't hate me. But I could feel that she didn't. I could feel that she was happy, excited, and completely unafraid. Buzzing with anticipation but not itching to run. It felt like Christmas and I'd just received a curiously thrilling new book—a love story about two people who get to know each other, the real essence of each other, and stick it out. I didn't want to race ahead anymore. I wanted to savor every line, every page, every chapter. I couldn't wait to begin.

Epilogue

In the winter of 2008, Ben and I were married in an abbreviated Hindu wedding ceremony in a small rural town in southern India. (Cringe-worthy, I know. This was before the mainstream conversation about cultural appropriation.) I wore a green sari and henna on my hands and feet. Ben wore a traditional gold tunic suit. It was a feast of color and sound, and the brave friends and family who made the journey to this far-out destination wedding were given a taste of what our marriage was going to be like: unconventional, adventurous, and a little bit cosmic.

I was fearful about getting married again, as much as I wanted to. I still hated myself for blowing up my first marriage. What kind of person wrecks their own home? Could I be trusted not to do it again? Before saying yes to Ben's proposal, I'd given myself a firm but loving lecture, as if I were speaking to my best friend:

So what if you've never been faithful before? So what if you still carry heartache over Adam and maybe always will? So what if you're bisexual and that's not going away? It doesn't have to go away. You will figure it out, with Ben, who knows all of this about you and loves you anyway. People do this. They have relationships with nice people and they stay. If they can do it, you can do it.

Ben, who's as traditional as he is experimental, wanted to wait until we were officially married to try for a baby. I guess I couldn't wait a minute longer, because on our wedding night, I got pregnant.

The morning I gave birth to our daughter Goldie, with Ben and Kate at my bedside, I was struck by how different the experience was this time around. With Kate, I'd been cheered on by thirteen friends and family members. By the time Goldie was born, I was ready for a different type of life—quieter and more intimate.

Ben and I raised the girls together in the Case Study house, my own Wilton Place. Kate, of course, also spent time at her dad's. The house-shuttling wasn't always easy for her and I felt perpetually guilty about that, but what mattered most was that both her homes were loving and supportive. Ours was always full of vibrant, creative, and eccentric characters coming and going, and the girls benefited from their influence, much as I benefited from the lively creative scene my mom cultivated at Wilton Place. But instead of the anything-goes atmosphere that prevailed in my own childhood, I wanted my girls to have a more calm, secure upbringing.

About that, like most things, Ben and I are in alignment. Throughout the girls' childhoods, we lived a very un–rock 'n' roll lifestyle, going to bed early so we could wake up and make them breakfast before taking them to school. I surprised myself by becoming one of those super into-it moms—organizing bake sales, carpooling to dance recitals, and crying with pride at school plays (if you've never seen a group of hormone-jacked sixteen-year-old thespians do *The Crucible*, I can tell you it's almost life-changing). When Kate opted to go to boarding school, I visited often, always outstaying my welcome as I soaked in the New England prep school experience of my dropout dreams. It was wrenching to say goodbye, but I didn't worry about Kate being able to take care of herself. By then, Ben and I had been preaching about boundaries, consent, and self-care for a good decade. Having done heroic amounts of therapy in my thirties, I finally had the language to talk about emotions, not that I was always good at it. There have been plenty of moments when I've felt myself reverting back to my childhood conditioning and avoiding heavy conversations with the girls. But then I'll remember my tongue-tied younger self, unable to communicate my feelings to Anthony and Adam, and I'll push through the discomfort and knock on that closed bedroom door.

Goldie is now fifteen, Kate twenty-three. Goldie is an artist and a natural leader. Kate, who is attending college in Australia, is intellectual and curious. Both have grown into strong, confident young women.

Meanwhile, Ben and I have been married for sixteen (faithful!) years. Is it a coincidence that the three major relationships in my life have been with musicians? Maybe not. I grew up wishing my father's songs had expressed love for me. Now my partner sings achingly beautiful, romantic songs about me, and silly, sweet ones for our daughters to make them laugh. His love, devotion, and camaraderie make the world feel limitless, yet safe, for all of us. And nothing has helped me make peace with my fatherless past more than seeing Ben father my daughters.

Along the way I've learned that yes, there is such a thing as true intimacy, the kind that isn't about escape or safety but about staying openhearted, even when things get tough (which is a far greater test than staying faithful—who knew?). A deep relationship is a labor of love, and sometimes the work is not just hard but really fucking scary. There have been times when my marriage downright terrified me. But that's a story for another book. My point is, intimacy can't be willed into being with magical thinking. It's not a prize you win, like Cinderella, for being the prettiest girl with the daintiest foot. I know that now but no longer blame myself for not knowing it when I was very young.

As for my relationship with acting, I've found peace there too. I accepted years ago that I might not be made of the right stuff to be a full-on Hollywood power player. At industry events, there are always some people who know who I am and some who don't. I don't take it personally anymore. We're all at various stages of the Hollywood game and for me, it's just fun to still be here.

Not caring obsessively about what people think has been so freeing. At fifty-four, I'm more playful and lighthearted than I ever was. I paint, direct short films and music videos, and happily let the work ebb and flow, as it always has. It thrills me when exciting like-minds seek me out—as when Lena Dunham and Jenni Konner offered me a role in their show *Camping*; Chloë Sevigny cast me in her directorial debut, *Kitty*; and Alexi Wasser thought of me for *her* directorial debut, *Messy*. These days, I'm getting more consistent offers to be in well-written, high-quality projects, which is all I ever really wanted from this career.

One of the upsides to not being a "bright young thing" anymore is I get to share what I've learned with today's young creative women who want to know what it was like when I came up and how to get through it all. These women aren't interested in me because I've had a predictable, traditional career arc, but probably specifically because I haven't. It's a cool seat to find myself in.

Creative community—being involved in lots of projects and scenes—has always been important to me. Through our production company, Weirder Together, Ben and I stay connected with vibrant artists across generations. It's pure fun to produce podcasts, release our friends' albums and EPs, and throw parties to turn people on to up-and-coming musicians. What strikes me the most about the younger artists I meet is their confidence. It's heartening to see a new generation of creative women acting as CEOs of their own destinies—developing their own material, building teams, and taking charge. I was never presented with that vision. Back when I started, younger women had to reach icon status before their perspectives were heard, let alone respected.

I'm grateful that Kate and Goldie get to come of age in the post-#MeToo era, empowered to trust their voices and instincts. It was great being a Gen X kid, but it's taken me half a lifetime and the example of my forthright daughters to stand up for myself and say everything in those times when it would be easier and more convenient not to. Even now, they're showing me how to do it.

Recently, Kate saw me typing away and said to me: "I hope you're not playing down how messed up it was with Anthony."

"You mean the drugs?" I said

"No, that he was *an adult* and you were only sixteen!"

"Oh, that," I said. "Well, times were different then."

"See," said Kate. "That's what you always say. But it wasn't okay, then or now. I think you need to be clear about that."

So, for Kate and Goldie, and me, too, I want to be clear about that. I don't think it was okay. My hackles rise just imagining Goldie in my sixteen-year-old shoes.

My daughters will have some questions for me if they've read this far, and I'm here to answer. I do hope they've taken something from my story, especially that there's no shame in searching, scrambling, and aching for more; it may feel like failing, but it's just part of being alive. The secret, as the girls have heard me say before, is to learn to love and struggle and fail without abandoning yourself. And if you do abandon yourself—like I did once or twice—well, you can always get reacquainted.

Five years ago, Ben, Goldie, and I went to visit Donovan in County Cork, Ireland. I had no idea what to expect, so this time, I expected nothing. On the flight there, I prepared myself by imagining I was on my way to visit some quirky old family friends instead of the man I still wished would be a good old-fashioned father.

Met from this fresh angle, Donovan and Linda did not disappoint.

Goldie was ten, and it was her first time meeting her grandfather that she could remember. She was tickled.

"I didn't know my grandparents were wizards!" she said the first night I tucked her into bed, upstairs in Don and Linda's pink Georgian-era mansion. I laughed, keeping it to myself that they were really just old hippies. Although their candlelit, tapestry-strewn home *was* straight out of *Harry Potter*, with logs crackling in the fireplace, tarot cards on the kitchen table, and views of wild ponies grazing on acres of green. And there *was* something wizardlike about how well Don and Linda had maintained their hippiness. It was as if they'd been frozen on a wintry mountain for fifty years and had woken up and defrosted themselves and here they were, exactly as they'd been in 1969.

It turned out to be a glorious five-day visit. We took rambling country walks to medieval churches and sparkling storybook lakes as Donovan lectured us on the grand Irish traditions of music, theater, poetry, and radical thought, and said lovely, funny things like "I do believe in fairies, I do, I do."

On our final morning together, my father and I took one last walk on the moors. At the old stone circle on the hill, Donovan called for my great-great-grandmother, Ma Kelly, to be with us in spirit as he sang into the wind. We never did have our big breakthrough conversation, but there we were together: two wounded poets who'd both struggled with responsibility, intimacy, and commitment. Our eyes met in recognition of the comedy and the beauty of this wonderful moment. I laughed, and he laughed. And finally, that was enough.

Writing this memoir felt like a natural extension of how I'd lived my entire life—as if from inside the pages of a book. Each romance, each job, each heartbreak was catalogued in real time as a "story" that I told myself. To be the heroine (sometimes the anti-heroine) of my own imagined tale was a survival mechanism, making life's challenges—like the heightened, stressful day I first met my father—seem more manageable, safe, comprehensible. By creating this distance from my most difficult experiences, I protected myself from feeling the true sting of their pain.

As a lifelong bookworm, educated through novels more than traditional schooling, maybe it's no surprise that my inner narrator was always at work. I'm grateful to her for helping me process my sometimes overwhelming life. But the stories I told myself could also weigh me down, keeping me from giving fully of myself in the now.

Mom and I carry such similar stories, it's a little eerie. Both of us have found caring, wonderful partners who make living here, in the present, far more beautiful than living in the past. But neither of us has ever fully recovered from our first great heartbreak, in our twenties. I believe a part of Mom still clings to her sixties daydream with Donovan, just as a part of me still mourns my nineties daydream with Adam.

But I'm beginning to feel that grief shifting, lifting.

For years, I had a recurring dream, the same every time: I'd be at a swank afternoon party, on the Amalfi Coast—a mosaic of dappled sunlight, golden bodies, white tablecloths. I'd slip away, scanning the cliffs for Adam, for closure.

I'd find him on the edge of town, sitting on a limestone wall.

"Can you ever forgive me?" I'd ask.

But he'd just stare out at the waves, as if he couldn't hear me.

Then, the night I finished the last chapter of this book, I had a new dream. It started the same, with the party on the cliffs. Only this time I wandered away not looking for anyone, just taking a walk.

At some point, I realized I was walking with Adam.

"Hey, it's good to see you," he said.

"Hey, it's good to see you too," I said.

We hugged and said good luck and goodbye. And that was it. I didn't need answers. There was no desperate charge in the air. Just the tinge of sorrow that comes with saying so long to an old friend.

I woke smiling with relief, knowing exactly what the dream had meant. Writing this book has been my way of surrendering my past, as well as an act of self-forgiveness. Finally, with love and a little fanfare, I'm letting my stories go.

Acknowledgments

Firstly, a special thank-you to Genevieve Field, my collaborator and comrade. Thank you for a beautiful, metamorphic experience.

Thank you to my lovely agent, Erin Hosier, at Dunow, Carlson & Lerner. Your inspiring, passionate, and eloquent notes on every draft have elevated this book.

I'm grateful to my genius editor, Pamela Cannon, and the team at Gallery Books—especially Jennifer Bergstrom, Aimée Bell, Hanna Preston, Jamie Selzer, Sally Marvin, Jennifer Robinson, and Sophie Normil—for their guidance and encouragement.

Thank you, Oren Segal, my manager and friend, who believed in this project and elegantly led me to all the right people to make this book really happen.

Thank you to my agent, Julia Buchwald, and team. And to Catherine Poulton, my manager in Australia.

To Mom, for being a genius of maternal love, for making Dono and me your main focus, for passing on your love of the underdogs in the world, and for growing every year into an even better version of yourself.

To Ben, the love of my life. You are my biggest supporter. I still get excited every time you walk into the room. Thanks for your songs and your talent for making life fun and deep. The way you father the girls has practically healed me.

To Kate: You have always been a marvel to me. You dazzle me with your mind, wonderful singing voice, charismatic presence, style, and adventurous choices. Your calming presence comforts everyone near.

To Goldie: You soften me with your love and amaze me with your talents, humor, art, and sophisticated mind. You are good to your friends and true to yourself.

Thank you, Goldie and Kate. We have so many laughs together. You both give my life meaning. I love you.

Thank you to my big brother, Donovan; I've always been your biggest fan. You entertained me with dance, music, and much-needed fun from the moment I was born. Thank you for starting my career.

To my little brother Jack, whose Italian nickname, Albicocca, didn't stick but who is still just as sweet and good as an apricot.

To Grandpa Benny and Grandma Tillie, whose cockamamie New York–ness was such a hoot. We couldn't have loved one another more. You thought the world of me, which helped give me a feeling of security and confidence.

My father, Donovan. Despite the rocky road we traveled and the time it took to get to know each other, I am proud to be your daughter and I thank you for connecting. I have your artistic and poetic streak in me.

And to Linda for believing it was possible for our family to heal.

To my childhood neighbor Eve Babitz, and her mom, Mae, for being a part of my artistic bohemian childhood.

To the *Gnomes* book and the Z Channel, for influencing my psyche in the best way.

To the albums I listened to on repeat as a kid: *Really Rosie*, *Rubber Soul*, and *The Point!*

To literature, art, fashion, buildings, nature, and dance.

To my godmother, Cynthia Webb, for mothering me then and now. And to my godfather, Klaus Voormann, for your art, which inspired me to become a painter.

To Mom's friends who made my childhood great: Marsha, Johnny, Nurit, Peter, Tony, Vicky, Ken, Amy, Bobby, Bradley, David, and Paul Fortune.

To all my daughters' friends, who made my house so full and fun.

To Grace for helping me with Goldie and Kate.

To all my teachers at Cheremoya Avenue Elementary School.

To my childhood and teen friends who loved and got me: Rob, Mike, Jason, River, Halle, Zoe, Moon, Lala, Maya, Russell, Samantha, Elexa, Vanessa, Noah, Sofia, Kelly, Frankie, Ritchie, Tatiana, and Alexia.

To my biological sisters, Astrella, who has done the most to bring the family together, and sweet Oriole.

And to my chosen sisters: Amelia Fleetwood, Karis Jagger, and Daphne Javitch.

To David Netto for taking a leap with me, loving me, and for our wonderful shared experience in raising Kate together.

To Adam and the Horovitzes, my old family.

To more family: Ilona, Richard, Liz, Madelyn, Kirsty, Violet, D3, Libby, Coco, Sebastian, Jules, and all my cousins, uncles, and aunts.

To all the dogs and cats in my life. You were all better than me.

To the directors who created worlds and atmospheres for me to work and play in.

To actors: Many say we are annoying, shallow, and self-involved (and we are), but I love actors so completely and find our craft very noble.

To my life-changing acting teachers Harry Mastrogeorge and Greta Seacat.

To the wonderful ones who are gone but never forgotten.

Thank you to everyone who is in these stories. It is profound to have felt so much affection, admiration, and love for you. I know I told some secrets and shared some personal moments; I hope I did them justice.

Photo Credits

1. Phillip Jackson/ANL/Shutterstock
2. Courtesy of the author's personal collection
3. Courtesy of the author's personal collection
4. Demetrius Demetropolis
5. Demetrius Demetropolis
6. Courtesy of the author's personal collection
7. Courtesy of the author's personal collection
8. Enid Graddis
9. Courtesy of the author's personal collection
10. Courtesy of the author's personal collection
11. Enid Graddis
12. Courtesy of the author's personal collection
13. Johnny Rozsa
14. Amy Etra
15. Johnny Rozsa
16. Courtesy of the author's personal collection
17. Courtesy of the author's personal collection
18. Amy Etra
19. Gail Zappa
20. Courtesy of the author's personal collection
21. Courtesy of the author's personal collection
22. Enid Graddis
23. Amy Etra

24. Archive Photos via Getty Images

25. Courtesy of the author's personal collection

26. Archive Photos via Getty Images

27. Courtesy of the author's personal collection

28. Gemma La Mana

29. Pictorial Press Ltd/Alamy Stock Photo

30. Gemma La Mana

31. United Archives GmbH/Alamy Stock Photo

32. Enid Graddis

33. Entertainment Pictures/Alamy Stock Photo

34. Courtesy of the author's personal collection

35. Courtesy of the author's personal collection

36. Courtesy of the author's personal collection

37. Courtesy of the author's personal collection

38. Courtesy of the author's personal collection

39. Amy Etra

40. Courtesy of the author's personal collection

41. Courtesy of the author's personal collection

42. Courtesy of the author's personal collection

43. Steve Eichner/WWD/Penske Media via Getty Images

44. Courtesy of the author's personal collection

45. Robert Montalbono

46. Ione Skye

47. Jean-Paul Aussenard/Getty Images

48. MediaPunch Inc./Alamy Stock Photo

49. Courtesy of the author's personal collection

50. Donovan Leitch Jr.

51. Linda Leitch

52. Ben Lee

53. Linda Leitch

54. Courtesy of the author's personal collection

55. Enid Graddis
56. David Netto
57. Courtesy of the author's personal collection
58. Johnny Rozsa
59. Ione Skye
60. Diane Gaeta
61. Ione Skye
62. Ione Skye

About the Author

Ione Skye made her film debut opposite Keanu Reeves in *River's Edge*, followed by her iconic role as Diane Court in *Say Anything*. Skye has appeared in other notable film and television projects, including *Zodiac*, *Wayne's World*, *Fever Pitch*, *Arrested Development*, *Camping*, *Good Girls*, *Beef*, and many more. Skye is also a painter who has exhibited and sold her work for twenty-five years. She is the author of the children's book *My Yiddish Vacation* and cohost of the weekly podcast *Weirder Together*. Ione is the mother of two daughters and lives in Los Angeles with her husband and collaborator, the musician Ben Lee.